URBAN LEGENDS OF CHURCH HISTORY

"In this book John Adair and Michael J. Svigel have gone on a church history myth-busting rampage like a bull in a China shop. Whether it is secular conspiracy theories or pious prejudices, they expose the fake news about church history. The whole book is one big, 'Well, actually, no, that ain't true, what really happened was . . .' This book is a great cure for a whole lot of stupid. Mandatory reading for anyone beginning church history!"

—Michael F. Bird, academic dean, lecturer in theology, Ridley College, Melbourne, Australia

"Busting myths and misinformation with wit, wisdom, and goodwill, Adair and Svigel have done a great service to the church with their *Urban Legends of Church History*. From their extensive knowledge and with helpful illustrations, the authors deliver a clear explanation of key moments and topics throughout church history. The authors' goals are not merely to expose legends, but to apply history's lessons today for the sake of Christian unity and the health of the church. Every pastor and teacher should have this book on their shelf."

—Lynn H. Cohick, provost and dean, professor of New Testament, Denver Seminary

"As an orthodox, Protestant, evangelical Christian, I believe there has never been a more important time to know church history than right now. In *Urban Legends of Church History*, John Adair and Michael Svigel offer gentle and straightforward responses to some of the most important misconceptions, half-truths, and fallacies throughout the history of the church. For too long, these urban legends have shaped our Christian culture."

—Kyle D. DiRoberts, associate professor of biblical and theological studies, Arizona Christian University

"This volume bears witness to the fact that, if things are repeated long enough, if they are found in copious footnotes in worthy publications, and if they were written by trustworthy spokespersons, they will make it into the world of repeatable 'truths.' Such is the point of this well-written, well-documented book. Myths make for more exciting stories, we suppose, but they do little service in accurately representing reality. I highly recommend this work, written by two competent scholars, who believed the unvarnished story of our Lord's church is far more beautiful than fabrications. The examples employed to demonstrate what we have all experienced when we found what we thought was, yet was not, are extremely instructive and revealing. It deserves a serious read by anyone concerned with re-presenting the past so as to understand our present and live in hope for our tomorrows."

—John D. Hannah, research professor of theological studies and distinguished professor of historical theology, Dallas Theological Seminary

"Adair and Svigel have ventured forth upon a quest—to slay the dragon of popular misconception. This is no fool's errand. Armed with sharp and incisive acumen, they jab at fallacies and slice through fabrications. They summon readers to face evidences and to feel the force of arguments. Those who do so bravely are sure to learn from the adventure."

—Paul A. Hartog, professor of theology, Faith Baptist Theological Seminary

"Urban legends can frequently entertain or amuse, but when they involve the church's history and doctrine, they can have quite serious consequences that negatively impact the church. Adair and Svigel's handy and accessible volume identifies and confronts some enduring misapprehensions in the church. With a winsome and engaging tone, they bring theological expertise and historical knowledge to these issues, presenting and examining claims even-handedly, undergirding their explanations with abundant primary source evidence. This book will benefit any Christians interested in a faith based on facts rather than myths. For directly addressing and expertly answering these urban legends, Adair and Svigel are to be profusely thanked."

—Stefana Laing, assistant professor of divinity, Beeson Divinity School

"Urban legends are not benign. They distort our understanding of the historic Christian faith. The authors invite readers to evaluate each legend in light of the historical evidence. The relevance is made clear through helpful applications at the end of each chapter. One may not agree with every interpretation, but the treasure of church history is furthered in this work."

—Bruce Rosdahl, professor of Bible and theology, department chair for Bible and theology, Southwestern Assemblies of God University

"Adair and Svigel have done the church a great service in this book. Despite the efforts of church historians to set the record straight, many pastors, teachers, and bloggers are perpetuating distortions of some pretty important aspects of the history of our faith. Such leaders need to consult the handy treatments in these pages of the things they're getting wrong. The witness of their people is at stake."

—Douglas A. Sweeney, dean and professor of divinity, Beeson Divinity School

"As long as there are popular authors like Dan Brown and Bart Ehrman, there will be a need for a book like this. Adair and Svigel have searched out dozens of legends and myths in church history and offer corrections for many strange ideas about events in the last two thousand years. This book is valuable because it addresses issues that we have to deal with almost every day. Reading it is like having a church history professor constantly at your elbow."

—William Varner, professor of Bible and Greek, The Master's University

URBAN LEGENDS OF CHURCH HISTORY

40 Common Misconceptions

MICHAEL SVIGEL AND JOHN ADAIR

B&H
ACADEMIC
NASHVILLE, TENNESSEE

Contents

What's an Urban Legend?

We hear pastors preaching them from their pulpits. Teachers spout them in their classrooms. The internet promotes them as unquestioned truth. Books, films, and TV shows retell them with intriguing plots. And well-meaning but ill-informed people believe them. In fact, almost all of us stand guilty of receiving or repeating half-truths, exaggerations, misconceptions, or outright fallacies about the history of Christianity.

In the following pages, we capture and cage some of the most repeated fabrications, exaggerations, half-truths, and inaccuracies wandering wild in popular and Christian culture. Did Emperor Constantine really ruin Christianity? Did a council of bishops vote on which books belong in the Bible? Did the one true church go underground during the Dark Ages? Was America founded as a Christian nation? From the fable of a paganized church to the myth that the early church worshipped on the Sabbath, these historical errors have impacted the health of the church at large and the faith of individual believers.

Chapter Structure

The title of each chapter is a brief summary of the urban legend itself—not the assertion of an actual historical truth. Then, in each chapter, we expand on the urban legend under the first heading, "The Legendary Story." This section, typically a paragraph or two, sums up the gist of the legend as if coming from the lips of a proponent of the myth. Sometimes those opening paragraphs may sound like "straw men," designed to be easily defeated. Believe us when we say we've heard each of these myths in almost these very words and often with the same tone. In the body of the chapter, we'll express more nuanced forms of the urban legend.

The second section, "Unraveling the Legend," briefly previews our response to the urban legend, either correcting an error, moderating an exaggeration, or softening an extreme. This is our gentle and straightforward assertion of the facts, not a complete exploration of the ins and outs of the issue. Following that brief introduction, we delve into more detail, giving examples of people responsible for keeping the legend alive and citing primary and secondary sources from church history that help dispel the myth. Finally, each chapter has a brief "Application" section that highlights some implications for us today. We also provide a handful of resources for deeper study and reflection on facts related to the topic in each chapter. Along the way, look for sidebars that serve up "mini myths" dealt with in a single paragraph.

Correcting the Legends

This book covers four periods: the early church (50–500), the medieval period (500–1500), the Protestant era (1500–1700), and the modern age (1700–present). Each period has ten chapters that address some of the most important myths of church history related to that period.

As we address the urban legends, we do our best to distinguish between outright fabrications that bear almost no resemblance to historical facts, and events that are based on the truth. Much of the time, the problem is one of exaggeration. The urban legend is based on some historical fact(s), but like a game of "telephone," the tale has gotten taller and taller with the telling.

It is worth making one more comment to express the point of view presented in this book. As much as we would like to claim we're stating "just the facts," the truth is that all history is perspectival and subject to interpretation. We are writing from a certain vantage point as orthodox, Protestant, evangelical Christians. We strive to be fair with the evidence, even when it doesn't exactly support our own theological and practical preferences. But we can't pretend to be purely objective, dispassionate, or disinterested observers.

A Comment on Notes and Citations

Unless otherwise noted, Scripture quotations come from the Christian Standard Bible (CSB). Quotations from the Apostolic Fathers are from *The Apostolic Fathers: Greek Texts and English Translations*, ed. and trans. Michael

W. Holmes, 3rd ed. (Grand Rapids: Baker Academic, 2007), cited throughout as "Holmes" followed by the page number.

Most excerpts or quotations from the patristic period come from the Ante-Nicene Fathers (ANF) or the Nicene and Post-Nicene Fathers (NPNF), both of which are available online. When citing a classic source, we have tried to keep the nonexpert in mind, using the author's full name and a full English title of the work. The parenthetical citation after an early Christian writing points to the volume and page number in the Ante-Nicene Fathers or Nicene and Post-Nicene Fathers series. For example, ANF 3:34 refers to volume 3, page 34 of the Ante-Nicene Fathers. The Nicene and Post-Nicene Fathers span two separate series. For these we indicate the series in the first number (1 or 2), then the volume within the series, followed by the page within that volume. For example, NPNF 1.3:34 refers to the first series, volume 3, page 34. For quotations of writings that are not part of the ANF or NPNF series, we typically use standard bibliographic form.

Acknowledgments and Dedication

We want to thank a few people who helped us and encouraged us along the way. First, we thank David A. Croteau, author of *Urban Legends of the New Testament* and coauthor of *Urban Legends of the Old Testament*, for inviting us into this project. We also want to thank the editors at B&H Academic for their tireless work, as well as our agent, Steve Laube, for his assistance throughout the project. We got some research assistance from interns at Dallas Theological Seminary: Christopher Crane, Sean Davidson, Kevin Gottlieb, Joshua Hankins, Park Lukich, and Torey Teer. Thanks for contributing.

We next want to express our thanks to our wives and families for putting up with the long hours in front of the computer and out of sight while we completed this project. We love you and appreciate your part in our ministry.

Finally, we acknowledge the work of two men who inspired and encouraged us in our study of historical theology and church history, who have been our teachers, colleagues, and friends over the years: Dr. D. Jeffrey Bingham and Dr. John D. Hannah. We dedicate this volume to them with gratitude.

John Adair
Michael J. Svigel

PART I

—

Urban Legends
of the Early Church
(50–500)

Early Church Time Line
(Some of the dates below are approximate.)

35–95: Age of the Apostles

35–99: Clement of Rome

35–110: Ignatius of Antioch

40–95: New Testament written

50–70: *Didache* written

53–117: Emperor Trajan

56–120: Tacitus

64: Roman fire under Nero

66–73: First Jewish Revolt and destruction of the temple

69–155: Polycarp of Smyrna

75–134: Aristides of Athens

75–135: *Epistle of Barnabas* written

90–140: *Shepherd of Hermas* written

100–165: Justin Martyr

110–180: Melito of Sardis

120–180: Celsus

120–185: Theophilus of Antioch

120–200: Irenaeus of Lyons

132–135: Jewish Bar Kokhba Revolt

133–190: Athenagoras of Athens

150–200: Solidifying the New Testament canon

150–215: Clement of Alexandria

160–225: Tertullian of Carthage

170–240: Hippolytus of Rome

184–253: Origen of Alexandria

200–258: Cyprian of Carthage

200–268: Dionysius of Rome

200–300: Further clarifying of the New Testament canon

213–270: Gregory the Wonderworker

234–304: Porphyry of Tyre

244–311: Emperor Diocletian

250: The Decian Persecution

250–325: Lactantius

260–336: Arius of Alexandria

263–339: Eusebius of Caesarea

272–337: Emperor Constantine

290–374: Athanasius of Alexandria

303–304: Great Diocletian persecution

313: Edict of Milan

313–386: Cyril of Jerusalem

325: Council of Nicaea

330–390: Gregory of Nazianzus

335–396: Gregory of Nyssa

339–397: Ambrose of Milan

349–407: John Chrysostom

379–395: Theodosius I

380: Edict of Thessalonica

381: Council of Constantinople

300–400: Settling of the New Testament canon

347–420: Jerome

354–430: Augustine of Hippo

360–418: Pelagius

360–435: John Cassian

400–461: Leo I (the Great)

418: Council of Carthage

431: Council of Ephesus

451: Council of Chalcedon

529: Second Council (Synod) of Orange

529: Founding of Benedictine Order

540–604: Pope Gregory I (the Great)

553: Council of Constantinople II

—

CHAPTER 1

The Earliest Christians Worshipped on Saturday

The Legendary Story

Exodus 20:8 says, "Remember the Sabbath day, to keep it holy." This command isn't a random ordinance tucked away in the ceremonial law of the Levites. This is one of the BIG TEN! No wonder the early church gathered for worship on Saturday, the Sabbath. But by the time of Emperor Constantine (272–337), the day of worship for Christians had changed from the biblical Sabbath (Saturday) to Sunday to make life easier for the mob of pagans suddenly flooding the churches. Accustomed to worshipping the *sun* god on *Sun*day, church authorities changed the day of worship to accommodate the masses. Since that time, Christian observers of the Sabbath have been picked on, put down, or even persecuted for staying true to the Christian Sabbath as Jesus, the disciples, and the earliest Jewish Christians had observed in obedience to the Ten Commandments.

Introduction: Unraveling the Legend

The actual historical evidence shows that even the earliest Jewish disciples of Jesus in the first century commemorated Christ's resurrection every Sunday. Though many Jewish Christians may have also continued to observe the Sabbath as part of their Jewish heritage, culture, and tradition, the first day of the week (Sunday) was the normal day of gathering for corporate worship because that was the day of the Lord's resurrection. In fact, evidences that the original followers of Jesus worshipped on Sunday—*not Saturday*—are "numerous, unanimous, and unambiguous."[1] Why, then, do some people claim the early church observed the Jewish Sabbath?

The Sabbath-to-Sunday Myth

Over the years we've encountered several sects that gather for worship on Saturday (the Jewish Sabbath) rather than Sunday.[2] When asked why they do this, the responses vary. Some believe the regulation in the Ten Commandments still requires Christians to observe the Sabbath day on Saturday.[3] Others claim this was the day the New Testament believers and the ancient church assembled for worship, and they want to return to that original practice.[4] Obviously, if the earliest Jewish followers of Jesus worshipped on Saturday, somewhere along the way somebody changed the day of Christian worship.

In 2003 the urban legend of the original Christians' worshipping on Saturday went mainstream. In his best-selling novel *The Da Vinci Code*, Dan Brown put the myth of Sabbath-keeping Christians on the lips of the undeterred protagonist, Robert Langdon: "Originally . . . Christianity honored the Jewish Sabbath of Saturday, but Constantine shifted it to coincide with the pagans' veneration day of the sun. . . . To this day, most churchgoers attend services on Sunday morning with no idea that they are there on account of the pagan sun god's weekly tribute—*Sun*day."[5] Like several cults, sects, and hack historians before him, Dan Brown laid the charge of the switch from Saturday to Sunday at the feet of Emperor Constantine, motivated by the popularizing and thus paganizing of Christianity.

Putting the Sabbath to Rest

Several years ago, I (Mike) attended a series of scholarly presentations on the role of Emperor Constantine in the history of the early church.[6] One of the

---

[1]   See Everett Ferguson, *Early Christians Speak: Faith and Life in the First Three Centuries* (Abilene, TX: Abilene Christian University Press, 1999), 1:69.

[2]   Samuele Bacchiocchi, *From Sabbath to Sunday: A Historical Investigation of the Rise of Sunday Observance in Early Christianity* (Rome: Pontifical Gregorian University Press, 1977).

[3]   See, e.g., John C. Williams, *Ten Commandments: The Christian Code of Conduct* (Ringgold, GA: TEACH Services, 2013).

[4]   David C. Pack, *Saturday or Sunday: Which Is the Sabbath?* (Bloomington, IN: iUniverse, 2009). Pack is a teacher of the Restored Church of God, a sect that claims to be the heirs of Herbert Armstrong's Worldwide Church of God.

[5]   Dan Brown, *The Da Vinci Code* (New York: Anchor Books, 2003), 305, italics in original.

[6]   These were subsequently published in Edward L. Smither, ed., *Rethinking Constantine: History, Theology, and Legacy* (Eugene, OR: Wipf and Stock, 2014).

presentations directly addressed the issue of Sabbath keeping and Sunday worship.[7] As I listened to fellow patristic scholar Paul Hartog carefully walk through the actual historical facts, I got the feeling some of us in the room were a little embarrassed about having to address this issue in a scholarly venue. There were just no good historical evidences and arguments to support the myth that original Sabbath worship was replaced by Sunday worship centuries later.

The earliest Christians gathered on "the Lord's Day."[8] By AD 95, the phrase "the Lord's Day" (Gk. *kyriakē hēmera*) had apparently become a common term for the day of Christian corporate worship centered on preaching and the Lord's Supper (called the "Eucharist" or "thanksgiving"). The apostle John so used it in Rev 1:10, assuming his readers in western Asia Minor would know immediately what he meant by "the Lord's Day."[9]

Before that, the apostles referred to Sunday as "the first day of the week," on which Christ rose from the dead (Matt 28:1; Mark 16:2, 9; Luke 24:1; John 20:1). Already in the earliest days of the church, the apostles and their disciples gathered together for worship on the "first day of the week," that is, Sunday, in commemoration of the resurrection of the Lord Jesus Christ. Acts 20:7 says, "On the first day of the week, we assembled to break bread. Paul spoke to them, and since he was about to depart the next day, he kept on talking until midnight." The practice of "breaking bread" is probably a reference to the corporate worship of the believers, centered on the Lord's Supper and fellowship around the preaching of the Word (see chapter 4). We also see Paul addressing the collection of money for the churches in 1 Cor 16:1–2, instructing the Corinthians to make the collection "on the first day of the week" (16:2). Because this was a collection from among members of the church, it indicates this was the day they regularly gathered as a corporate body.[10]

---

[7]   See Paul A. Hartog, "Constantine, Sabbath-Keeping, and Sunday Observance," in Smither, 105–29.

[8]   See R. J. Bauckham, "Sabbath and Sunday in the Post-Apostolic Church" in D. A. Carson, ed., *From Sabbath to Lord's Day: A Biblical, Historical, and Theological Investigation* (Grand Rapids: Zondervan, 1982), chap. 9.

[9]   See discussions in G. K. Beale, *The Book of Revelation: A Commentary on the Greek Text*, The New International Greek Testament Commentary, ed. I Howard Marshall and Donald A. Hagner (Grand Rapids: Eerdmans, 1999), 203; J. Ramsey Michaels, *Revelation*, The IVP New Testament Commentary Series, ed. Grant R. Osborne (Downers Grove, IL: InterVarsity Press, 1997), 58–59; Grant R. Osborne, *Revelation*, Baker Exegetical Commentary on the New Testament, ed. Moisés Silva (Grand Rapids: Baker Academic, 2002), 83–84.

[10]   Paul could have simply meant that believers were to make their giving a priority, setting aside money for the Lord at the start of each workweek. Craig S. Keener, *1–2 Corinthians*, The New Cambridge Bible Commentary, ed. Ben Witherington III (Cambridge: Cambridge University Press, 2005), 136. However, considering the constellation of evidences for early worship on Sunday, this gathering of financial support is best read as occurring during the regular meeting of the church on the first day of the week.

Now, we do know that on the Sabbath the apostles would go to the Jewish synagogues to preach about Christ to the Jews and God-fearing Gentiles (Acts 13:14; 13:42; 13:44; 16:33). But this *evangelism* was not the same as gathering together for the apostles' teaching, the breaking of bread, and prayer—characteristics of early Christian worship (Acts 2:42). It also seems likely that the very first Jewish believers continued to observe many aspects of the law, including the Saturday Sabbath rest,[11] but this did not interfere with the very early adoption of a Sunday-morning observance as well.[12]

So, from the New Testament we see an early emphasis on Sunday, the "Lord's Day," the day the Lord rose from the dead, also called the "first of the week." When we move forward in church history to the very next generation of Christians—to people who actually sat under the teaching of the apostles and their disciples—the picture becomes even clearer.[13]

In the *Didache*, a church manual that, according to an emerging consensus of specialists, was probably written around Antioch between AD 50 and 70, the instruction is simple: "On the Lord's own day [*kata kyriakēn de kyriou*] gather together and break bread and give thanks."[14] The "Lord's own day" parallels the term used in Rev 1:10.

At about the same time (around AD 80 or so), an anonymous but highly respected writing (later attributed to "Barnabas") makes it clear that Christians intentionally worshipped not on the "seventh day" (the Sabbath), but on the "eighth day," Sunday, as a memorial of the resurrection: "We spend the eighth day in celebration, the day on which Jesus both arose from the dead and, after appearing again, ascended into heaven."[15]

Around AD 110, Ignatius, leader of the church of Antioch, wrote a letter to the church in Magnesia of Asia Minor while on his way to execution in Rome. In that letter he addressed the problem of Judaizers' infecting the church with divisions and false doctrine. He found himself having to explain the Christian practice of worshipping on Sunday rather than on the Sabbath, which was the practice of Judaizers rather than orthodox Christians. He stated that even Jews who had once kept the Sabbath as part of the old covenant, once they "came to the newness of hope," were "no longer keeping the sabbath but

---

[11]   Paul F. Bradshaw, *The Search for the Origins of Christian Worship: Sources and Methods for the Study of Early Liturgy* (New York: Oxford University Press, 1992), 192.

[12]   See Arthur G. Patzia, *The Emergence of the Church: Context, Growth, Leadership, and Worship* (Downers Grove, IL: InterVarsity Press, 2001), 212–13.

[13]   James F. White, *A Brief History of Christian Worship* (Nashville: Abingdon, 1993), 30–31.

[14]   *Didache* 14.1 (Holmes 356).

[15]   *Barnabas* 15.9 (Holmes 429).

living in accordance with the Lord's day [*kata kyriakēn*], on which our life also arose through him and his death."[16] Note that Ignatius was not pushing for a new day of worship, nor was he defending a recent change from Saturday to Sunday. Rather, he simply explained why the original Jewish disciples of Jesus switched from keeping the Sabbath to worshipping on Sunday, the Lord's Day, the day of his resurrection.[17] This historical evidence shows that even first-generation Jewish believers in Jesus didn't insist on Sabbath observance. They worshipped on Sunday too.

Before we dismiss this evidence as "outside the Bible" and a later corruption by the church fathers, remember that Ignatius was not some reclusive monk from an isolated corner of the Dark Ages. He was already an old man by AD 110, which means he was middle-aged when the apostles themselves still lived and ministered. And as pastor in the significant missionary-sending city of Antioch, Ignatius would surely have known some of the apostles and their disciples. Further, we know that he was a close friend of Polycarp, pastor of Smyrna, who was himself appointed as a leader in the church by the apostle John. So, the teaching about Sunday worship by Ignatius almost certainly came from the apostles and their disciples, whom Ignatius would have known personally.

But what about Emperor Constantine in the fourth century? Didn't he change the official day of worship from Saturday to Sunday? Obviously not. Already in Ignatius, around AD 110, we see that Jewish and Gentile Christians worshipped on Sunday. That was 200 years before Constantine's alleged hostile takeover of the ancient faith (see more in chapters 6 and 8). By the time of Constantine, then, the church had already been worshipping on Sunday for at least two centuries. However, Constantine did play a fairly significant role in allowing Christians to legally worship on Sunday by granting Christianity the status of a legal religion (see chapter 9). Simply put, Constantine did not change Saturday worship to Sunday worship.[18]

Application

The observance of Sunday worship makes a difference for Christians today, just as it did for the early church. Sunday worship was itself a confession of faith. It was the day God began his work of creation (Gen 1:1–3) and the day Adam

---

[16] Ignatius, *Magnesians* 9.1 (Holmes 209).

[17] See William R. Schoedel, *Ignatius of Antioch,* Hermeneia (Philadelphia: Fortress, 1985), 123–24.

[18] See Hartog, "Constantine, Sabbath-Keeping, and Sunday Observance," 105–29.

and Eve were to commence their service and obedience to their Creator (Gen 1:28–31). Christ was raised on Sunday (Matt 28:1), and he taught Scripture and broke bread with two of his disciples on Sunday (Luke 24:13–35). The baptism of the Holy Spirit and establishment of the church occurred on Pentecost, which was always on a Sunday, during which the believers were gathered for prayer (Acts 2). When we as Christians gather weekly on Sunday for worship, we're doing so as an ongoing testimony to key elements of our faith that occurred on that day. Observance of Sunday (rather than Saturday) is also a tangible mark that we are people of the new covenant, which was intended to be different from the old (Jer 31:31–32). In this way we confess that Christ is the fulfillment of the law (Rom 10:4) and that we are created in him as part of a new creation (Gal 6:15), in which old things have passed away and new things have come (2 Cor 5:17).

Resources

Hartog, Paul A. "Constantine, Sabbath-Keeping, and Sunday Observance." In *Rethinking Constantine: History, Theology, and Legacy*, edited by Edward L. Smither. Eugene, OR: Wipf and Stock, 2014.

Patzia, Arthur G. *The Emergence of the Church: Context, Growth, Leadership, and Worship*. Downers Grove, IL: InterVarsity Press, 2001.

—

CHAPTER 2

The Church Apostatized Shortly after the Apostles

The Legendary Story

The apostle Paul warned, "After my departure savage wolves will come in among you, not sparing the flock" (Acts 20:29). So, almost immediately after the first century, the churches experienced a tragic departure from the truth. Poisonous false teachings corrupted the purity of the faith "delivered to the saints once for all" (Jude 3). A hierarchy of bishops and priests replaced the simple gathered church community of caring, sharing believers. In short, apostolic Christianity went off the rails. It took a great restoration movement centuries later to restore the purity of the gospel and the true representation of Christianity on the earth.

Introduction: Unraveling the Legend

Though Christianity certainly developed and changed over the centuries, the process was actually slow and gradual. The true story isn't one of a sudden plummet over a cliff or even a uniform decline into error. Rather, Christianity experienced ups and downs in the first several centuries with regard to doctrinal fidelity, spiritual vitality, and moral integrity. Though some parts of the church did apostatize and different ages saw greater corruption and doctrinal infidelity than others, pockets of light and a remnant of faith and obedience have always persisted throughout the history of the church.

Slip-Sliding Away?

As we read the documents of the early church and examine the twenty-first-century expression of Christianity, things have obviously changed. In fact, if we pick up writings of theologians from the fifth century or tenth century or fifteenth century, we'll see the same thing. But how severe were these changes? Were these developments positive, negative, or neutral? Did they completely obscure the original teachings of the apostles, essentially wiping out the authentic proclamation of the saving message of the gospel found in the New Testament period?

Some Christians as well as many false Christian cults and sects believe the true church apostatized immediately after the apostles. This view is often called "primitivism" or "restorationism" because such groups believe their own doctrines and practices are a restoration of the original, primitive purity of the one true church. Everything between the age of the apostles and their own movement, therefore, would be regarded as apostate, corrupt, or at least imperfect and impure.

For example, to explain the absence of their form of charismatic experiences from most of the history of the church, some Pentecostal and charismatic Christians have argued that the church apostatized after the apostles. With this apostasy went many of the miraculous sign gifts, which some claim could only be found in a tiny, struggling remnant of persecuted Christians outside the apostate churches.[1] Pentecostal theologian Kenneth Archer notes, "Pentecostals knew that past church history lacked a consistent attestation of the supernatural gifts operating throughout Christianity. Rather than dissuading them, it reinforced the veracity of their claim. Pentecostals were convinced that they were simply returning to primitive Christianity and that they had restored the Full Gospel."[2] In other words, some Pentecostal preachers viewed their doctrines and practices not as novelties but as a restoration of the primitive church that had fallen into apostasy.

Similarly, since the nineteenth century a group of Baptist teachers has alleged a great apostasy occurred in the early church that all but quenched the

---

[1]   See Bradley Truman Noel, *Penetecostal and Postmodern Hermeneutics; Comparisons and Contemporary Impact* (Eugene, OR: Wipf and Stock, 2010), 64–65; Harlyn Graydon Purdy, *A Distinct Twenty-First Century Pentecostal Hermeneutic* (Eugene, OR: Wipf and Stock, 2015), 24.

[2]   Kenneth J. Archer, *The Gospel Revisited: Towards a Pentecostal Theology of Worship and Witness* (Eugene, OR: Pickwick, 2011), 32.

light of the authentic, visible churches during the Dark Ages.[3] One proponent of this view, James Robinson Graves (1820–1893), noted, "All the churches of Christ, before the 'apostasy,' which took place in the third and fourth centuries, and gave rise to the Greek and Latin Catholic hierarchies, were what are now called Baptist churches."[4]

This same story line is also found among sects and cults. For instance, the Church of Jesus Christ of Latter-Day Saints (the Mormons), claims, "Fewer than 400 years after the death of the Savior, the Church as Jesus organized it was nowhere to be found in the whole world. This began the period known as the Great Apostasy. The New Testament Apostles and Book of Mormon disciples were gone."[5] This "great apostasy" perspective on church history is also the view of such heretical sects as Jehovah's Witnesses.[6]

Points of Continuity

The truth is that a great degree of continuity prevailed in doctrines and practices between the first-century apostolic churches and the next several generations—especially in the most crucial theological and practical matters. In fact, on several central issues, most churches continued to speak with one voice.

During the period of the church fathers (c. 100–500), the confession of Jesus as the God-man who was born of a virgin, lived a sinless life, died as an atonement for sin, rose from the dead bodily, and ascended into heaven, remained at the core of the church's preaching and teaching (see chapters 5 and 8). Thus, Ignatius of Antioch around AD 110 wrote, "There is only one physician, who is both flesh and spirit, born and unborn, God in man, true life in death, both from Mary and from God, first subject to suffering and then beyond it, Jesus Christ our Lord."[7]

The consistent confession of Christian truth carried Christianity forward for centuries. In fact, we can see the basic contours of orthodox theology throughout the history of the church, as certain beliefs never changed:

---

[3]   This view does not represent that of all—or even most—Baptists today. For a fair description and critique of Landmarkism by Baptist historians, see Anthony L. Chute, Nathan A. Finn, and Michael A. G. Haykin, *The Baptist Story: From English Sect to Global Movement* (Nashville: B&H Academic, 2015), 169–74.

[4]   James Robinson Graves, *Old Landmarkism: What Is It?* (Memphis: Baptist Book House, 1880), 167.

[5]   Shanna Butler, "What Happened to Christ's Church?" *New Era* 35, no. 2 (February 2005): 8.

[6]   M. James Penton, *Apocalypse Delayed: The Story of Jehovah's Witnesses,* 3rd ed. (Toronto: University of Toronto Press, 2015), 258.

[7]   Ignatius, *Ephesians* 7.2 (Holmes 189).

the triune God as creator and redeemer; the fall and resulting depravity of humanity; the saving person and work of Christ; salvation by grace through faith; the inspiration and authority of Scripture; incorporation of the redeemed into Christ's body, the church; and the hope of humanity's resurrection and the restoration of creation.[8]

Similarly, Christians maintained continuity from generation to generation through certain shared practices. They continued to confess the trinitarian faith centered on the person and work of Christ through the practice of baptism and observance of the Lord's Supper. They worshipped through prayer, praise, and preaching on Sunday mornings in commemoration of the resurrection of Christ. And they sought to live godly lives by the power of the Spirit, shunning wickedness and striving for righteousness.

Far from immediately falling into apostasy, the first several generations after the apostles carried the torch of the Christian faith forward in the midst of great adversity and persecution. It's telling that in the sixteenth century, when Protestants sought to reform the church of the late Middle Ages, they looked to the first five centuries of the church as a model for doctrinal and practical fidelity (see chapter 23). Despite their human faults and failings, the Protestant Reformers viewed early Christians such as Polycarp, Ignatius, Irenaeus, Athanasius, Gregory of Nazianzus, John Chrysostom, Augustine of Hippo, and Gregory the Great as torchbearers, not flame quenchers.

Points of Diversity

While unity and continuity prevailed in central doctrines and practices from one generation to another, the far-flung churches throughout the world did have many points of diversity and differences of opinion. Church historian J. N. D. Kelly notes, "Looked at from the outside, primitive Christianity has the appearance of a vast diffusion of local congregations, each leading its separate life with its own constitutional structure and officers and each called a 'church.' In a deeper sense, however, all these communities are conscious of being parts of one universal Church."[9]

Some areas of diversity included eschatology (end-times doctrine), perspectives on the role of free will and God's sovereignty in salvation, methods of administering baptism and the Lord's Supper, and certain culture-specific

---

[8]   See Michael J. Svigel, *RetroChristianity: Reclaiming the Forgotten Faith* (Wheaton, IL: Crossway, 2012), 104–5.

[9]   J. N. D. Kelly, *Early Christian Doctrines*, 5th rev. ed. (New York: HarperOne, 1978), 189.

forms of liturgy.[10] Yet diversity doesn't necessarily mean disunity; nor does it necessarily imply deterioration. The early churches recognized that differences of opinion on noncentral doctrines and practices were acceptable and appropriate in the global body of Christ united in the fundamental doctrines of the faith.

Yet this early Christian unity in the essentials and diversity in the non-essentials did eventually give way to a deterioration of doctrine and practice in the Middle Ages that threatened the unity and purity of the churches.

The Gradual Decline

Though deterioration is a historical fact, doctrinal and practical corruption came gradually, not suddenly. So slow were the changes in Christian theology that they were barely noticeable from generation to generation. While the church's vital teaching concerning the Trinity and Christ remained unchanged, differences developed in other matters. Diversity of opinion developed over the role of human will and good works in salvation as well as the extent of humanity's depraved nature after the fall. Along with this, differences in the doctrine of salvation began to appear—with some emphasizing the need to willingly cooperate with God's means of grace offered through the church.[11] Soteriology (the doctrine of salvation) saw the most significant departure from the patristic period.[12]

Other novelties, such as the seven sacraments, the papacy, purgatory, the intercession of Mary and the saints, and the devotional use of icons, also crept in over centuries—not decades—and were accepted by many Christians by the early medieval period (c. 500–1000). During the late Middle Ages (1000–1500), noticeable decline in doctrine and practice led many discerning pastors and theologians to call for reform, indicating that at no point had the entire body of Christ completely apostatized. For example, figures such as John Wycliffe (c. 1325–1384) and John Huss (c. 1369–1415) pointed out significant deviations from the original teachings of the apostles and prophets in Scripture as well as from the teachings of the early church.

So, decline in the purity of doctrines and practices did occur, but the drift

---

[10] See Svigel, *RetroChristianity*, 108–12.
[11] For a thorough treatment of the history of justification, see Alister E. McGrath, *Iustitia Dei: A History of the Christian Doctrine of Justification*, 3rd ed. (Cambridge: Cambridge University Press, 2005).
[12] John D. Hannah, *Our Legacy: The History of Christian Doctrine* (Colorado Springs: NavPress, 2001), 216–26; Jaroslav Pelikan, *The Christian Tradition: A History of the Development of Doctrine*, vol. 3, *The Growth of Medieval Theology* (Chicago: University of Chicago Press, 1978), 50–214.

from essential unity to deterioration, corruption, and conflict was mostly felt in the later patristic and medieval periods. And even in the midst of discernible decline, various pockets of the church throughout the world continued to preserve relatively sound doctrine and practice (see chapters 11, 13, 14). The church of the patristic period certainly had its highs and lows, but the idea that it radically apostatized immediately after the apostles is a myth.

Application

Just as the corruption of Christianity was a slow, barely perceivable process that occurred over centuries, our own corruption of character both individually and corporately happens through a slow process of neglect. Unless we are vigilant, errors of doctrine and distortion of practices will inevitably creep in without our even being aware of it. We must constantly look back to Scripture and the earliest Christian generations as standards of our own faithfulness and make constant course corrections. Also, we should be encouraged that even amid spiritual decline, God keeps his promise to never let the church succumb to the gates of Hades (Matt 16:18). He will not leave us as orphans (John 14:18), but he will be with us even to the end of the age (Matt 28:20). Yes, as a loving Father, God disciplines his children when they go astray, but he will never leave us or forsake us, even when we veer far from the right path (Heb 12:5–6; 13:5).

Resources

Kelly, J. N. D. *Early Christian Doctrines.* 5th rev. ed. New York: HarperOne, 1978.

Pelikan, Jaroslav. *The Christian Tradition: A History of the Development of Doctrine.* vol. 1: *The Emergence of the Catholic Tradition (100–600).* Chicago: University of Chicago Press, 1978.

Svigel, Michael J. *RetroChristianity: Reclaiming the Forgotten Faith.* Wheaton, IL: Crossway, 2012.

CHAPTER 3

The Sands of the Colosseum Are Stained with the Martyrs' Blood

The Legendary Story

Since the first century, every generation of Christians has grieved over and honored martyrs, those who gave up everything—even their own lives—for the sake of Christ. In the first centuries of the church's history, with Rome at its zenith, pagan emperors and government officials routinely brought Christians into the Roman Colosseum for execution. The massive arena, filled with bloodthirsty crowds calling for the lives of those who refused pagan worship, bore witness to these deaths. Nearly 2,000 years later, the ruins of the Colosseum—her sands "stained" with the blood of true believers—stand as a striking reminder of pagan overreach and Christian martyrdom, a monument to the sacrificial call of Christ in a contemporary world deaf to the suffering of God's people. Christians should therefore treat the Colosseum as a sacred space, a memorial to lives well lived.

Introduction: Unraveling the Legend

Christians suffered martyrdom in the Roman Empire. Historians do not dispute this historical fact. However, Christians were not *routinely* executed for their faith in the Roman Empire. While public executions of Christians occurred in the Roman Empire generally and in Rome specifically, that was hardly the preferred method for dealing with this small religious group.

Furthermore, no evidence exists that Roman officials brought Christians to the Colosseum in Rome for execution.

Martyrdom in the Early Church

Jesus, Stephen (Acts 7), and James (Acts 12) set the biblical pattern for Christian martyrdom. Early Christians understood martyrdom to be the greatest expression of faithfulness available to the believer. As Herbert Workman has written, "Cross-bearing is the mark of every disciple of Jesus."[1]

Persecution of Christians in the early church was primarily an isolated and regional occurrence. Actual martyrdoms were less a result of imperial policy and more a result of overzealous local officials. To be sure, there were a few wider persecutions—after the Roman fire in AD 64 at the hands of Nero, under Decius in AD 250, and the Great Persecution under Diocletian in AD 303. The most conservative estimates number the deaths of Christians in the first three centuries after Christ at fewer than 1,000.[2] The actual number is probably greater than that but likely to seem small in comparison to twentieth-century mass killings, such as the Holocaust or the Rwandan genocide. Paul Hartog has argued, "The number probably totaled in the thousands (rather than hundreds), but likely would not have reached into multiple tens of thousands."[3] However, with a correspondingly low Christian population in these years, each death would have taken on great significance in the fledgling community. But did these martyrdoms occur in the Colosseum?

A Shaky Foundation

One story most prominently associated with martyrdom in the Colosseum is that of the third-century Persian martyrs Abdon and Sennen. As prisoners under the reign of the emperor Decius—one of the most significant persecutors of Christians in ancient Rome—these two men buried the bodies of Christian martyrs. When they wouldn't recant their own Christian faith,

---

[1]   Herbert B. Workman, *Persecution in the Early Church*, repr. ed. (Oxford: Oxford University Press, 1980), 3.

[2]   Rodney Stark, *The Rise of Christianity: How the Obscure, Marginal Jesus Movement Became the Dominant Religious Force in the Western World in a Few Centuries* (San Francisco: HarperCollins, 1997), 164.

[3]   Paul Hartog, "The Maltreatment of Early Christians: Refinement and Response," *Southern Baptist Journal of Theology* 18, no.1 (Spring 2014): 58.

officials sent them to the gladiators (the beasts wouldn't touch them), where they were killed.[4]

The prominence of the story likely reflects strong evidence to support it, right? However, scholars date the writing of this account quite late, up to 500 years after the alleged event. Scholars also argue that the account contains fictitious statements: for instance, suggesting it is much more likely that Abdon and Sennen were martyred under the reign of Diocletian in the early fourth century than under Decius about fifty years earlier.[5] Further, gladiators generally trained to fight other gladiators rather than virtually helpless Christians who eschewed violence in their day-to-day lives.

Despite the fact that modern scholars—and even the Roman Catholic Church[6]—doubt the reliability of details in this martyrdom account, the story was known to churchmen later in church history. When Pope Pius V (1504–1572) put together the Tridentine calendar in 1568, he included these two as martyrs to be remembered every July 30. That the pope knew and honored the martyrs of this story fits with a tradition that Pius V believed the sands of the Colosseum to be "impregnated" with the blood of Christian martyrs.[7] Later, in 1675, Pope Clement X (1590–1676) affixed an inscription to the Colosseum that made reference to the "countless martyrs" who died there.[8]

Indeed, P. J. Chandlery's *Pilgrim-Walks in Rome*, a devotional tour guide from the early twentieth century, takes these shreds of "evidence" and develops the legendary narrative with an emotive description that would grip any reader. The Colosseum martyrs, he says, were subject to private tortures, public scourging, wild beasts, and finally, if still alive, gladiatorial combat.[9] Such fantastical narratives have settled in the Christian imagination, such that in contemporary times, remembrance services for the martyrs of the world see

---

[4]   Virtually all information about Abdon and Sennen comes from their *Acts*, a brief recounting in Latin of their trials and torments. The written work likely was finished before the ninth century. Several times, the *Acts* refer to this martyrdom taking place in Rome at the "amphitheater," a clear reference to the Colosseum. For a summary in English, see Alban Butler, *Butler's Lives of the Saints*, repr. ed. (Westminster, MD: Christian Classics, 1981), 213. For the original Latin, see *Acta Sanctorum*, July 30, ed. Johannes Carnadet (Paris: Victor Palmé, 1868), 34:148–49.

[5]   Butler, *Butler's Lives*, 213.

[6]   Questions and sketchy details have even caused the Roman Catholic Church to downgrade Abdon and Sennen to the lowest class of remembrance for martyrs and saints.

[7]   Maurice M. Hassett, "Coliseum," in *The Catholic Encyclopedia*, vol. 4, *Cland–Diocesan*, ed. Charles George Herbermann (New York: Robert Appleton, 1908), 101–2.

[8]   P. J. Chandlery, *Pilgrim-Walks in Rome: A Guide to Its Holy Places* (New York: The Messenger, 1903), 203.

[9]   Chandlery, 204. The only source Chandlery cites for this detailed picture of martyrdom? A mid-nineteenth-century novel, *Fabiola*, penned by an English cardinal named Nicholas Wiseman.

the Colosseum bathed in red light to symbolize the blood that (supposedly) was spilled there.[10]

Going to the Circus

Early church writings by church fathers, historians, and those interested in sharing the stories of martyrs provide no direct evidence for executions at the Colosseum in Rome. As Kate Hopkins and Mary Beard have argued, "The fact is that there are no genuine records of any Christians being put to death in the Coliseum."[11] Yet one ancient writing mentions another place in Rome as the site of Christian martyrdom: the Circus of Nero and Gaius.

The Roman Circus took the form of a long, extended oval, much like a racetrack in modern times. Romans usually used circuses for horse or chariot races. The Circus of Nero and Gaius was located on Vatican Hill—the present location of the Vatican. In fact, St. Peter's Square before the great cathedral stands precisely on the spot where such martyrdoms took place.

Roman historian Tacitus (AD 56–120) wrote in the early second century of Nero capturing, convicting, and killing Christians. Of the martyrdoms of Christians, Tacitus recounted, "Derision accompanied their end: they were covered with wild beasts' skins and torn to death by dogs; or they were fastened on crosses, and, when daylight failed were burned to serve as lamps by night. Nero had offered his Gardens for the spectacle, and gave an exhibition in his Circus, mixing with the crowd in the habit of a charioteer, or mounted on his car."[12]

Could it be that Tacitus was not only reflecting the historical reality, but also his contemporary situation as well? Ignatius, bishop of the church at Antioch (c. 35–110), wrote letters to other churches while on his way to Roman martyrdom. In two of those letters, Ignatius spoke of being fed to the wild beasts, a practice Tacitus associated with Nero's Circus. Indeed, when Ignatius described how he imagined his upcoming martyrdom, he used terms eerily similar to those of Tacitus: "Fire and cross and battles with wild beasts, mutilations, mangling, wrenching of bones, the hacking of limbs, the crushing of my whole body, cruel tortures of the devil—let these come upon me,

---

[10]   Xavier Le Normand, "The Night the Colosseum Was Covered with the Blood of Martyrs," Aleteia, February 25, 2018, https://aleteia.org/2018/02/25/the-night-the-colosseum-was-covered-with-the-blood -of-martyrs/.

[11]   Keith Hopkins and Mary Beard, *The Coliseum* (London: Profile Books, 2005), 103.

[12]   Cornelius Tacitus, *The Annals of Tacitus* 15.44, bks. 13–16, vol. 5, trans. John Jackson, Loeb Classical Library 322 (Cambridge, MA: Harvard University Press, 1981), 285.

only let me reach Jesus Christ."[13] In another letter, Ignatius used similar language: "Why, moreover, have I surrendered myself to death, to fire, to sword, to beasts?"[14]

The similarity in description between these contemporaries, Tacitus and Ignatius—Tacitus about a historical period and Ignatius about their own day—suggests that executions of Christians in Rome were likely to take place in the circuses of Rome—Nero's Circus, possibly, but more likely by Ignatius's day, the primary circus in Rome, the Circus Maximus.[15] Indeed, it seems that people used Nero's Circus for tombs "as early as the second century."[16]

Other deaths for the faith occurred throughout the empire via torture, beheadings, feeding to wild animals, and burning at the stake. So, although periods of violence against Christians and martyrdoms did occur sporadically throughout the first several centuries of Christian history, no definitive evidence exists suggesting these deaths took place in the Colosseum.

Application

Christians were martyred in the early church. Of this we can be certain. And while the extent might at times get overstated in the church today, it's important to recognize and remember our brothers and sisters who offered everything they had for the sake of the gospel. Such stories inspire believers to persevere in the midst of their own trials.

Second, the way martyrs were honored in the early church reshapes the vision of the "ideal" Christian life. Oftentimes today, the ideal is depicted as victory over sin, yet in the context of a decidedly comfortable life that prizes self over service. The honoring of martyrs offers a new vision of victory: enduring in the midst of suffering, standing tall in the face of opposition, and giving away all that we are for the sake of Christ and neighbor.

---

[13] Ignatius, *Romans* 5.3 (Holmes, 231).

[14] Ignatius, *Smyrnaeans* 4.2 (Holmes, 251–53).

[15] In the imperial period of Rome (first century BC–AD third century), the only important circus in the city was the Circus Maximus. Nero's Circus had been built as a space to practice driving chariots. While it was likely the site of martyrdoms—especially in Nero's day—the Circus Maximus stands as the most likely location for such activity. See Peter Connolly and Hazel Dodge, *The Ancient City* (Oxford: Oxford University Press, 1998), 176.

[16] Lawrence Richardson, *A New Topographical Dictionary of Ancient Rome* (Baltimore: Johns Hopkins University Press, 1992), 84. This suggests public execution would have moved to the more popular Circus Maximus by Ignatius's day. A graveyard would not have been a likely site for a large public gathering, such as an execution.

Resources

Hartog, Paul. "The Maltreatment of Early Christians: Refinement and Response." *Southern Baptist Journal of Theology* 18, no. 1 (Spring 2014): 49–79.

Workman, Herbert B. *Persecution in the Early Church*. Repr. ed. Oxford: Oxford University Press, 1980.

___

The Lord's Supper Was Originally a "Love Feast" or "Community Meal"

The Legendary Story

The ordinance called the "Lord's Supper," as practiced in churches today, is a far cry from the simple fellowship meal observed in the early church.[1] The original Lord's Supper was also called the "love feast" and modeled after the annual Jewish Passover feast. However, within a few generations it became a weekly ritual with just a piece of bread and sip of wine. Today's ritual of the Eucharist deviates significantly from the early church's informal Communion fellowship meal.

Introduction: Unraveling the Legend

The earliest biblical and historical evidence of Lord's Supper observance points to weekly partaking of bread and wine as a commemoration of Christ's death, a recognition of his life-giving presence in the church, and a renewed consecration to the sanctified life. The love feast (or, better, "charity meal") in the early church was a separate, as-needed practice to provide for the hungry. Though early Christians celebrated "Pascha" (Passover) as an annual commemoration of the resurrection, this, too, was in addition to the weekly celebration of the Lord's Supper in church.

---

[1] Depending on one's church tradition, the "Lord's Supper" may also be called the "Eucharist," "Communion," or the "Lord's Table."

Anytime, Anywhere, with Anyone?

Some time ago, a young man contacted me (Mike) with concerns over his church's teaching on and practice of the Lord's Supper. The pastor taught that the biblical Lord's Supper was never intended to hold a special place in Sunday worship. Rather, the Lord's Supper, he alleged, was *any* meal that believers enjoy together. That pastor confidently asserted that the traditional in-church observance of the Lord's Supper was a gross misunderstanding of its original intent. He insisted that he partook of the *real* Lord's Supper three times a day—whenever he "broke bread" with fellow believers at breakfast, lunch, or dinner!

That pastor isn't alone in seeing the traditional partaking of bread and wine (or grape juice) in a worship service as a deviation from the original Supper. One author puts it this way: "It is plainly obvious that the way it is practiced in most churches has moved a long way from the meal which Jesus shared with his disciples. . . . The Lord's Supper should be a sit-down evening meal for small groups of Christian believers. It doesn't need a priest or a special minister to make it valid. It should be a joyous celebration time in homes or houses."[2]

In discussions with pastors, teachers, and students, I have discovered that equating Lord's Supper observance with any fellowship meal sometimes stems from confusion regarding the term "to break bread." Everett Ferguson clarifies: "The phrase, 'break bread,' referring to a general custom, could refer to beginning a meal or to the specific remembrance of the death of Jesus. The context must decide which is meant in each case."[3] Some read the term "to break bread" as if (a) it always means the Lord's Supper, (b) it always means any meal with others, or (c) it has both meanings, so the Lord's Supper is actually any fellowship meal with others. This latter error—of which the pastor mentioned earlier was guilty—is akin to the exegetical fallacy D. A. Carson calls "unwarranted adoption of an expanded semantic field."[4] In other words, just because a word or phrase means one thing in one context, it doesn't necessarily mean the same thing in every context.

---

[2]   Nigel Scotland, *The New Passover: Rethinking the Lord's Supper for Today* (Eugene, OR: Cascade, 2016), 184.

[3]   Everett Ferguson, "Lord's Supper and Love Feast," *Christian Studies* 21 (2005–6): 30.

[4]   D. A. Carson, *Exegetical Fallacies*, 2nd ed. (Grand Rapids: Baker, 1996), 60–61.

The context of each passage must determine the *kind* of "breaking bread" involved. The phrase may mean: (a) any normal daily meal (Luke 24:30—like our breakfast, lunch, or dinner); (b) a joyous fellowship or community meal with believers (Acts 2:46—like our potlucks or banquets); (c) a charity meal for the benefit of the poor (Matt 14:19—like our soup kitchens or charitable food banks); or (d) the memorial bread and wine of the Lord's Supper observed in church (1 Cor 10:16—the same as our Communion).

The Lord's Supper was meant to be observed in the context of the worshipping church during her Sunday morning gatherings (Acts 20:7). By confusing the various distinct uses of the phrase "to break bread" with its special use for the Lord's Supper, some scholars, pastors, and teachers have misinterpreted the observance of the Lord's Supper as any everyday meal or as a special potluck meal. This has led some churches to eject the Lord's Supper from their Sunday morning services altogether, to reduce its frequency to special (that is, "rare") occasions, or even to offer it to unbelievers.

The two most frequent myths that have diluted or destroyed the historical practice of the Lord's Supper in church have been conflating the Lord's Supper with the Passover meal and confusing the Lord's Supper with the "love feast."

Was the Lord's Supper a Full Meal, Like the Passover?

In 1 Corinthians Paul made the point that "after supper" Jesus took the cup (1 Cor 11:25). The Passover meal itself was over. What Jesus instituted came afterward. He distinguished it from the traditional Passover meal with words and actions not part of any traditional Passover seder. Ferguson writes of the institution of the Lord's Supper in the Gospels: "Mark and Matthew make nothing of the meal setting, except to mention it as the occasion when Jesus gave a special meaning to the bread and the cup. They focus attention on what was important for the continuing practice of the church."[5] The Passover meal was an annual hallmark of the old covenant, commemorating Israel's redemption from bondage in Egypt. In contrast, the weekly Lord's Supper was the church's ceremony marking the establishment of the new covenant, pointing to redemption through Christ's incarnation, death, and resurrection until he returns (1 Cor 11:26).

---

[5]   Ferguson, "Lord's Supper and Love Feast," 28.

The earliest historical records of the church's practice of the Lord's Supper or "Eucharist" (from Greek *eucharistia*, "thanksgiving") also focused on the bread and the cup. The early manual for churches, the *Didache* (c. 50–70), gives instructions concerning the prayer of blessing for "the cup" and the "broken bread."[6] These two elements—the cup and the bread—constitute what the *Didache* regarded as the "Eucharist." Further, the text instructed the church leaders, "But let no one eat or drink of your Eucharist except those who have been baptized into the name of the Lord."[7] This emphasized the fact that the Lord's Supper was a churchly practice, to be overseen by church leadership and centered on the participation in the bread and cup. The same text elaborates: "On the Lord's own day, gather together and break bread and give thanks, having first confessed your sins so that your sacrifice may be pure."[8] As a living sacrifice of praise and thanksgiving (Rom 12:1; Heb 13:10–16), the gathering for the Lord's Supper was a reminder of the church's unity and community centered on the person and work of Christ.

Another very early report on the Thanksgiving meal comes from Ignatius of Antioch around AD 110. Ignatius himself lived in a time and place that almost certainly overlapped with some of the apostles and their immediate disciples. To prevent false doctrines and practices from infecting the church, Ignatius urged the sister church in Smyrna, "Let no one do anything that has to do with the church without the bishop. Only that Eucharist which is under the authority of the bishop (or whomever he himself designates) is to be considered valid."[9]

Historically, observance of the Eucharist was regarded as part of the church's regular meeting, officiated by proper leadership, pointing to the body and blood of Christ as the basis of our salvation and unity as a church. It was not a Passover seder or any meal believers enjoyed with others outside the church gathering. Both the *Didache* (50–70) and Ignatius of Antioch (c. 110) were early enough witnesses that their words provide a window into the earliest perspective on the Lord's Supper.

---

[6]   *Didache* 9.1–4 (Holmes 357–59).
[7]   *Didache* 9.5 (Holmes 359).
[8]   *Didache* 14.1 (Holmes 365).
[9]   Ignatius, *Smyrnaeans* 8.1 (Holmes, 255). Also see Ignatius, *Philadelphians* 4.1 (Holmes, 239).

MINI MYTHS

"The Church Fathers Taught Transubstantiation"

Though the early church fathers had a very high view of the Lord's Supper (or "Eucharist") and it held a central place in corporate worship from the beginning, they did not teach "transubstantiation" per se. Jaroslav Pelikan notes that Pope Alexander III "was the first to speak of 'transubstantiation,' in a work prepared about 1140."[10] However, earlier Fathers did often closely associate the real presence of Christ with the bread and wine of the Eucharist, but not with dogmatic insistence that the invisible substance of the elements miraculously transformed into the actual body and blood of the God-man. Earlier Fathers were content simply calling the bread and wine the "body and blood" of Christ and leaving its power and profundity a mystery.

Was the Lord's Supper the Same as the "Love Feast"?

Besides viewing the Lord's Supper as a Passover meal, some have regarded it as equivalent to the "love feast" mentioned in Jude 12 and paralleled in 2 Pet 2:13 with reference to a "feast." Too often the love feast has been understood by modern readers as a "fellowship meal," like a church potluck, Sunday school picnic, or some other time of "food, fun, and fellowship." However, we believe equating the love feast with the Eucharist is a mistake. Rather, what is called the "love feast" was more likely a "charity meal" primarily held to provide sustenance for needy members of the congregation—widows, orphans, and the poor. In this understanding, its inspiration would not have come from the Last Supper, but perhaps from the Lord's miraculous feeding of the hungry in Matt 14:19 and the early church's practice of providing for the needy through the voluntary benevolence of the rich (Acts 4:34–35).

---

[10]   Jaroslav Pelikan, *The Christian Tradition: A History of the Development of Doctrine*, vol. 3, *The Growth of Medieval Theology* (Chicago: University of Chicago Press, 1978), 203.

In some places the charity meal was supplemented with (or supplanted by) a monetary or food offering intended to provide for the poor and needy. In contrast, the Lord's Supper involved partaking of ceremonial bread and wine as a memorial confession of Christ's person and work, a medium of spiritual fellowship with Christ himself, and a means of covenant renewal among the local church community. Everett Ferguson remarks, "The Lord's supper and the love feast were two distinct activities—the one a remembrance and proclamation of the death and resurrection of Jesus and the other an act of benevolence and fellowship. . . . The activities themselves had discreet meanings from the beginning."[11] Similarly, Marcel Metzger, an expert on the history of Christian worship, writes concerning the charity meals, "The community meals were at once a realization and an expression of charity and mutual support, another aspect of communion in one single body. In times of want and famine . . . the demands of mutual help led in all likelihood to the organization of daily meals for the benefit of the needy."[12]

Ignatius of Antioch distinguished the Eucharist from the love feast in the same passage we quoted earlier from his letter to the church in Smyrna. He first noted the necessity for duly appointed church leaders to oversee a valid Eucharist (*Smyrn.* 8.1), which he identified as bread and wine as a means of confession and consecration (*Phld.* 4.1). In *Smyrnaeans* 8, Ignatius mentioned three distinct practices of the gathered church: (1) the Eucharist (8.1), (2) baptism, and (3) the charity meal (8.2). All of these were to be conducted under the oversight of the church's leadership.

Simply put, the love feast *was not* the same as the Lord's Supper in the early church. Neither was the love feast simply a fellowship meal, like our modern potlucks, or any meal we have with other believers. Rather, when we read the Bible in its historical-theological context, it becomes evident that the "charity meal" was often observed in conjunction with the gathered community as a way for the well-off to provide for the needy. Thus, the modern equivalent of the "charity meal" in our churches is not the Lord's Supper, a potluck, or a church-wide picnic, but a benevolence offering for the poor.

---

[11]　Ferguson, "Lord's Supper and Love Feast," 35.

[12]　Marcel Metzger, *History of the Liturgy: Three Major Stages*, trans. Madeleine M. Beaumont (Collegeville, MN: Liturgical Press, 1997), 21–22.

Application

The contemporary desire to reimagine the Lord's Supper as an informal church potluck or any meal we enjoy with fellow believers seems to point to the fact that something is missing from our sometimes individualistic, ritualistic, formal, and seemingly lifeless observance with a tiny bite of cracker and sip of juice. Part of the problem may be a rampant misunderstanding of the function of the Lord's Supper in the local church. Originally, the Lord's Supper was meant to be the "altar call" in the church's weekly gathering—the physical means by which a person responded to the call to remember the person and work of Christ, recommit to the baptismal pledge, reconsecrate oneself to Christian service, reconcile with fellow believers, and repent of sin.

Rather than replacing the historical Lord's Supper with a potluck or Passover meal, churches and individuals can restore the important function of the observance by reemphasizing it as the point at which believers offer their bodies as a living sacrifice, holy and acceptable to God (Rom 12:1). Rather than a hasty tack-on at the end of a long service once every few weeks or months, the Lord's Supper can serve as a point of renewal in churches. Of course, churches also should not neglect the community-building function of common meals such as potlucks and picnics or ministry to the poor and hungry through charity meals or benevolence. However, confusing these with the ancient church's weekly observance of the Lord's Supper leads to a less historically authentic expression of the church's gathering.

Resources

Ferguson, Everett. "Lord's Supper and Love Feast." *Christian Studies Journal* 21 (2005–6): 27–38.

Skarsaune, Oskar. *In the Shadow of the Temple: Jewish Influences on Early Christianity*. Downers Grove, IL: IVP Academic, 399–422.

CHAPTER 5

The Earliest Church Didn't Know the Difference between Orthodoxy and Heresy

The Legendary Story

The church of the first few centuries had only a vague understanding of "orthodoxy" and its distinction from what would later be called "heresy." Though "proto-orthodoxy" existed in some places, most believers in the early church and many church fathers would not be regarded as "orthodox" by later standards. In fact, in some places what we call "heresy" today actually preceded orthodoxy as the common form of Christianity in that region. Only later did the so-called orthodox church take over and squash the competition.

Introduction: Unraveling the Legend

Christianity has always clearly and unambiguously held to certain central and foundational "orthodox" tenets summed up in early writings, hymns, confessions, and creeds. Though the earliest followers of Jesus tended to allow more diversity regarding noncentral issues than Christians in later church history, the earliest Christians had an uncompromising view of the boundary between truth and error—orthodoxy and heresy.

Would the Real Christianity Please Stand Up?

A perspective common in the public square today is that the on-the-ground reality throughout the Roman world was radical diversity and even rabid conflict among many groups, each group claiming to be the true form of Christianity. Some say it is more accurate to picture multiple "Christianities" rather than a single "Christianity." This picture has flooded airwaves, news-stands, bookshelves, websites, television screens, and movie theaters for sev-eral decades—from popular fiction (such as Dan Brown's *The Da Vinci Code*) to public television documentaries.

One popular supporter of this view, Bart Ehrman, alleges the ultimate victory of one Christianity over the others this way:

> One form of Christianity decided what was the "correct" Christian perspective; it decided who could exercise authority over Christian belief and practice; and it determined what forms of Christianity would be marginalized, set aside, destroyed. . . . And then, as a coup de grace, this victorious party rewrote the history of the controversy, making it appear that there had not been much of a conflict at all, claiming that its own views had always been those of the majority of Christians at all times.[1]

The Background of "the Bauer Thesis"

To understand this popular perspective today, we need to back up a couple of generations to the German New Testament scholar Walter Bauer (1877–1960), especially his 1934 work *Orthodoxy and Heresy in Earliest Christianity* (2nd ed., 1964), which served up scholarly sentiments that had been simmer-ing for more than a century.[2] Bauer presented the thesis that certain forms of Christianity later regarded as "heresies" were originally not designated as such by early followers of Jesus. Rather, in some cities or regions these diverse forms of Christianity were earlier and stronger than what later became "orthodoxy." The form of Christianity we call orthodox, therefore, was a later development. The resulting picture, of course, is that the earliest churches didn't really know the difference between "orthodoxy" and "heresy," because such clear categories developed later.

---

[1]   Bart D. Ehrman, *Lost Christianities: The Battles for Scripture and the Faiths We Never Knew* (Oxford: Oxford University Press, 2003), 4.

[2]   Walter Bauer, *Rechtgläubigkeit und Ketzerei im ältesten Christentum*, 2nd ed., ed. George Strecker, Beiträge zur historischen Theologie 10, ed. Gerhard Ebeling (Tübingen: Mohr/Siebeck, 1964). An English translation followed in 1971. Walter Bauer, *Orthodoxy and Heresy in Earliest Christianity*, trans. Philadelphia Seminar on Christian Origins, ed. Robert A. Kraft and Gerhard Krodel, The New Testament Library, ed. Alan Richardson et al. (London: SCM, 1971).

According to Bauer, the earliest Christianity was characterized by diversity and conflict. He argued that in the second and third centuries, the Roman church increasingly promoted and enforced its unique version of orthodoxy. This eventually became the majority view while other forms shrank to a minority or were weakened through debate and eventually extinguished by force. Bauer suggested that in the third and fourth centuries, official church historians concealed the reality of early diversity by replacing it with what became the official, "traditional view"—that Jesus Christ handed down an orthodox teaching to the apostles, who were then sent with authority to establish churches throughout the world. In other words, the later church rewrote the history of the early church to make it look like their form had been there all along!

Bauer's peers in European universities, steeped in historical-critical scholarship and liberal theology, mostly accepted the general contours of the Bauer thesis.[3] Though they did critique Bauer on several details of his evidence and arguments, they regarded his rejection of the "traditional view" as valid. They agreed that the traditional view of a single original orthodoxy was untenable and that early Christianity was characterized by sometimes "radical diversity."[4] Today, many critical scholars widely embrace the view that diversity and conflict characterized the early church and that "orthodoxy" was merely one of many developing and competing forms of Christianity.

In subsequent generations, critics of Christianity have repackaged the Bauer thesis for popular consumption. And storytellers peddling far-fetched fiction have exaggerated and embellished the thesis in fanciful ways. As the story often goes, in some places people viewed Jesus as a divine being sent from heaven. In other places, they portrayed him as merely a human teacher whose radical message got him killed. Some communities understood him as a holy man chosen by God to be a divine agent in judgment. Others thought God had raised him from the dead. There were also those who believed he lived on metaphorically through the memory of his teachings.

In this account of history, early Jesus followers constituted a hodgepodge of competing Christianities with only a vague sense of identity, each vying for converts to their own rendition of "Jesus." This history usually ends with the

---

3   See the helpful discussion in George Strecker and Robert A. Kraft, "Appendix 2: The Reception of the Book," in Bauer, *Orthodoxy and Heresy*, 286–316.

4   See Karen King, *What Is Gnosticism?* (Cambridge, MA: Harvard University Press, 2003), 114. Ehrman writes regarding Bauer's claims, "If anything, early Christianity was even less tidy and more diversified than he realized." Ehrman, *Lost Christianities*, 176.

Holy Catholic Church emerging from the smoke of religious conflict, forcing their narrow view of Jesus on everybody else, and enforcing a uniform brand of Christianity on the world. This quasi-tyrannical Christendom, then, continued to the modern era, when objective critical scholars finally swooped in, cleared the smoke screen, and proved that the earliest decades after Jesus were characterized by many Christs and many Christianities.

A Better View of Unity, Diversity, and Identity

The narrative just described has become fashionable in many academic circles, popular publications, and media outlets. It makes for an intriguing plotline in best-selling novels and blockbuster movies. But is it true?

The problem is, even the most nuanced versions of this history lead to misunderstandings at best and gross exaggerations at worst. Both the New Testament and the teachings of the early church demonstrate that even the earliest Christians had a pretty clear picture of what it meant to self-identify as "Christian." Repeatedly, early Jesus followers told the same basic story of who Jesus was and what he did. The preaching of the early church—including the written Gospels and epistles—centered on a basic message of the person and work of Christ in his first and second comings, including an "incarnational narrative" of the heavenly, divine Son of God becoming incarnate, living a perfect life, dying for sins on the cross, rising bodily from the dead, ascending into heaven, and waiting to one day return as judge and king. This basic story served as the center of Christian identity and unity in the first few generations of the church.

This original understanding of "orthodoxy" was summed up in baptismal confessions regarding the Father, the Son, and the Holy Spirit and by what early church fathers called the "canon of the truth" or the "Rule of Faith" (often referred to by its Latin equivalent, *Regula Fidei*). This summary of the Christian faith could be described as the trinitarian creation-fall-redemption narrative centered on the person and work of Christ in his first and second comings. The second-century church father Irenaeus of Lyons (c. 120–200), himself a disciple of Polycarp of Smyrna (c. 69–155), who was a disciple of the apostle John, expressed the *Regula Fidei* this way:

> This, then, is the order of the rule of our faith, and the foundation of
> the building, and the stability of our conversation. God, the Father,
> not made, not material, invisible; one God, the Creator of all things:

this is the first point of our faith. The second point is: the Word of God, Son of God, Christ Jesus our Lord, who was manifested to the prophets according to the form of their prophesying and according to the method of the dispensation of the Father: through whom all things were made; who also at the end of the times, to complete and gather up all things, was made man among men, visible and tangible, in order to abolish death and show forth life and produce a community of union between God and man. And the third point is: the Holy Spirit, through whom the prophets prophesied, and the fathers learned the things of God, and the righteous were led forth into the way of righteousness; and who in the end of the times was poured out in a new way upon mankind in all the earth, renewing man unto God.[5]

This basic trinitarian narrative of the truth centered on Christ's redemptive work constituted the "faith" into which all Christians had been baptized. As the only correct view of the story of creation and redemption, any deviation from this trinitarian/incarnational narrative would have been regarded as heresy. The earliest Christians therefore had a clear understanding of orthodoxy and heresy from the very beginning.

The Real Picture of the Earliest Church

So, if you could travel back in time to the year 100 and visit several of the small Christian communities scattered across the Mediterranean world, what would you actually find? Numerous Christian communities, each with its own corporate personality, shared a common sense of belonging to something bigger than themselves. Each church viewed itself as a sort of nuclear family that belonged to an extended family of fellow Christian communities from places as far-flung as Egypt, Syria, Greece, and Rome. Despite some real diversity, they held the most central aspect of their faith in common: their self-conscious identity as "Christians" centered on what we call the "incarnational narrative."

For example, Ignatius of Antioch (c. 110), affirmed the central beliefs of Christians in the following terms:

---

[5]   Irenaeus, *Demonstration of the Apostolic Preaching 7*, in *St. Irenaeus: The Demonstration of the Apostolic Preaching*, trans. J. Armitage Robinson (London: SPCK, 1920), 74–75.

Totally convinced with regard to our Lord that he is truly of the family of David with respect to human descent, Son of God with respect to the divine will and power, truly born of a virgin, baptized by John in order that all righteousness might be fulfilled by him, truly nailed in the flesh for us under Pontius Pilate and Herod the tetrarch (from its fruit we derive our existence, that is, from his divinely blessed suffering), in order that he might raise a banner for the ages through his resurrection for his saints and faithful people.[6]

Likewise, Aristides of Athens (c. 125) described Christians this way:

The Christians, then, trace the beginning of their religion from Jesus the Messiah; and he is named the Son of God Most High. And it is said that God came down from heaven, and from a Hebrew virgin assumed and clothed himself with flesh; and the Son of God lived in a daughter of man. This is taught in the gospel, as it is called, which a short time was preached among them; and you also if you will read therein, may perceive the power which belongs to it. This Jesus, then, was born of the race of the Hebrews; and he had twelve disciples in order that the purpose of his incarnation might in time be accomplished. But he himself was pierced by the Jews, and he died and was buried; and they say that after three days he rose and ascended to heaven. Thereupon these twelve disciples went forth throughout the known parts of the world, and kept showing his greatness with all modesty and uprightness. And hence also those of the present day who believe that preaching are called Christians, and they are become famous.[7]

No, the earliest Christians were not confused about orthodoxy—the correct view of creation and redemption from the Father, through the Son, and by the Holy Spirit. Their shared faith was so early, widespread, and foundational to their beliefs and practices that we can reasonably conclude the worldwide Christian communities received this one Christianity from the previous generation—from the original apostles and prophets themselves.

---

[6]   Ignatius *Smrynaeans* 1.1–2 (Holmes, 249).

[7]   Aristides, *Apology* 2, in J. Rendel Harris, ed., *The Apology of Aristides on Behalf of the Christians*, 2nd ed., Texts and Studies, ed. J. Armitage Robinson (Cambridge, UK: Cambridge University Press, 1893), 36–37.

This was the faith into which they were baptized. This was the faith they proclaimed. This was the faith for which they lived and died.

Application

The situation of the early church wasn't all that different from that of the diverse denominations of Christians around the world today. Despite what has become popular to parrot in the public square, the earliest Christians, like far-flung Christians today, anchored their common identity on the person and work of the same Jesus—the good news of the incarnation of the God-man, who died for our sins, rose from the dead, ascended on high, and will come as Judge and King. This gospel has always formed the center and source of our Christian identity.

Today, we honor this legacy of the faith when we "major on the majors" and refuse to allow differences of agreement on less central doctrines to divide us. All conservative, orthodox, Protestant Christians hold to the same *Regula Fidei* as Ignatius of Antioch, Irenaeus of Lyons, and, indeed, all believers of the early church. If we add our own opinions to the center and demand allegiance to every minor doctrine or idiosyncratic teaching unique to our own church or tradition, we will find ourselves guilty of schism rather than unity. And if we downplay or decry any of those central truths that have always united orthodox Christians, we will be guilty of the same kinds of heresies against which the saints contended in the earliest churches. In this regard, the ancient dictum should prevail: "In essentials, unity; in nonessentials, liberty; in all things, charity."

Resources

Hartog, Paul A., ed. *Orthodoxy and Heresy in Early Christian Contexts: Reconsidering the Bauer Thesis*. Eugene, OR: Wipf and Stock, 2015.

Robinson, Thomas A. *The Bauer Thesis Examined: Geography of Heresy in the Early Christian Church*. Studies in Bible and Early Christianity. Lewiston, NY: Edwin Mellen, 1988.

Svigel, Michael J. *The Center and the Source: Second Century Incarnational Christology and Early Catholic Christianity*. Piscataway, NJ: Gorgias, 2016.

———

CHAPTER 6

An Emperor, Pope, or Church Council Canonized the Bible

The Legendary Story

Somebody in the early church—the emperor, a pope, or a church council—selected the books of the New Testament canon. In the best-case scenario, they based their decision on reasonable criteria like antiquity (Is it old?), apostolicity (Is it written by an apostle?), and orthodoxy (Does it teach the truth?). In the worst case, they chose the books based on prejudice, power, and personal preference. In light of the fact that human authorities chose the books of the Bible, a strong case can be made that the church's authority is at least equal to that of Scripture, because without the church, there would be no Bible.

Introduction: Unraveling the Legend

No church council, influential pope, ecclesiastical body, or even powerful emperor selected the books of the Bible—either the Old Testament or the New. Though various regional gatherings called "synods" published lists of Old and New Testament books they held sacred, no ecumenical (worldwide) council ever voted on the canon. And there is no record of church fathers or councils sorting through dozens of books to select the books of the Bible. Criteria such as antiquity, apostolicity, and orthodoxy were sometimes used to settle doubts or disputes about the status of a small handful of books or to explain why certain books had always been received as canonical and why others had not, but they were never used as tests to determine the canon from scratch.

The Canonizing Conundrum

How did the books in our Bible actually get there? Statements like the following, from the website of an Eastern Orthodox Church, are typical: "The Orthodox Church actually produced the Bible. The Church also lived Christian life to the fullest for centuries before the canon of the New Testament was even recognizable (AD 367). As such, the Bible is always understood within the life of the Church, not above or apart from it. The Bible is the Church's book."[1] Similarly, a popular Roman Catholic apologetic website states, "There was no canon of scripture in the early Church; there was no Bible. The Bible is the book of the Church; she is not the Church of the Bible."[2]

Even Protestants have fueled this kind of thinking. In a discussion on the role of tradition in theological method, one author noted, "The biblical canon of 27 New Testament books was not set by Christian church authorities until after Athanasius (d. 373). This single historical fact suggests that the role of tradition in theological method is decisive."[3] Then, of course, there's the extremely influential urban legend made popular by fiction, such as Dan Brown's *The Da Vinci Code*:

> Teabing paused to sip his tea and then placed the cup back on the mantel. "More than *eighty* gospels were considered for the New Testament, and yet only a relative few were chosen for inclusion—Matthew, Mark, Luke, and John among them."
>
> "Who chose the gospels to include?" Sophie asked.
>
> "Aha!" Teabing burst in with enthusiasm. "The fundamental irony of Christianity! The Bible, as we know it today, was collated by the pagan Roman emperor Constantine the Great."[4]

All of these accounts share the notion that the various books of the Bible were "canonized" sometime after the first century because they measured up to

---

[1]   St. Paul Antiochian Orthodox Church, "For Evangelical Protestants: Quick Questions & Answers on Orthodoxy," accessed February 10, 2019, https://saintpaulemmaus.org/for-visitors/for-evangelical-protestants.

[2]   Paul Flanagan and Robert Schihl, "The Canon of the Bible," Catholic Biblical Apologetics, last updated July 17, 2004, http://www.catholicapologetics.org/ap030700.htm.

[3]   Paul L. Allen, *Theological Method: A Guide for the Perplexed* (New York: T&T Clark, 2012), 19.

[4]   Dan Brown, *The Da Vinci Code: A Novel*, 2nd mass market ed. (New York: Anchor Books, 2009), 303–4.

an established external standard—certain "checks" or "marks" of inspiration, the authority of a council, a church hierarchy, or even an emperor!

Canonical Truth

The term *canon* comes from a Greek word meaning "standard" or "rule." Canonical books of the Bible are those regarded by Christians as the standard or rule of the faith—the final written authority in all matters of faith and practice. Gregory of Nyssa (335–395) once noted, "We always use holy Scripture as the canon and rule of all our doctrine. So we must necessarily look towards this standard and accept only that which is congruent with the sense of the writings."[5] It is important to emphasize that a book of the Bible is not deemed "canonical" because it measures up to some outside standard or rule set by the church; rather, a book of the Bible is deemed canonical because *it is itself the standard and rule for the church*. The church did not *decree* the books of the Bible to be canonical; rather, the church *received* the books of the Bible as canonical.

But how, why, and when did the whole church identify and receive all of the Old and New Testament books as canonical? With regard to the Old Testament canon, its development spans almost two millennia, from the time of Moses and the Pentateuch (c. 1500 BC) to the beginning of the medieval period (c. AD 500). We have very little direct testimony concerning how, why, and when the books of the Hebrew Scriptures came to be accepted by all Jews. We do, however, have the final result of that process. Throughout history, the church debated whether the Old Testament should include the books called the "Apocrypha." We will address this issue more directly in chapter 24.

Regarding the New Testament, we have a much clearer picture. Because the first-century apostles and prophets were teaching and writing from their God-given authority as the foundations of the church (Eph 2:20; 4:11), their official writings carried absolute authority among their recipients. As writings such as Matthew, Romans, or 1 Thessalonians were written, sent to churches, and received by them as apostolic and prophetic, those recipients would have immediately treated those writings as authoritative—that is, as *canonical*. There would have been no decision-making process, no hesitancy, no questioning whether those writings should be treated as the standard and rule of faith

---

[5]   Gregory of Nyssa, *On the Soul and the Resurrection* 3, in St. Gregory of Nyssa, *On the Soul and the Resurrection*, trans. Catharine P. Roth (Crestwood, NY: St. Vladimir's Seminary Press, 2002), 50. (Also see NPNF 2.5:98).

and practice. As Paul himself said, "Stand firm and hold to the traditions you were taught, whether by what we said or what we wrote" (2 Thess 2:15).

During the apostolic period, as these official apostolic and prophetic writings were sent and received, the growing number of churches began copying, passing around, and collecting them as the standards of doctrine and practice alongside the Old Testament books. Already around the year AD 65, the apostle Peter was aware of a collection of Paul's writings that he equated to "the Scriptures" (2 Pet 3:16). Then, just a few decades later, around the year 96, a disciple of the apostles, Clement of Rome, wrote to the church in Corinth, "Take up the epistle of the blessed Paul the apostle. . . . Truly he wrote to you in the Spirit."[6]

About a decade after that, Ignatius of Antioch (c. 110) alluded to or quoted from several New Testament writings: Matthew, possibly Luke, John, Romans, 1 Corinthians, Galatians, Ephesians, Philippians, 1 Timothy, and 2 Timothy.[7] His contemporary Polycarp of Smyrna (c. 110), who was himself a disciple of the apostle John, wrote a short letter to the church in Philippi and mentioned Paul's book of Philippians (Polycarp, *Philippians* 3.2). He also quoted from Eph 4:26, calling it "holy Scripture" (Polycarp, *Philippians* 12.1). In fact, Polycarp's letter—written just a decade or so after the end of the apostolic era—contains quotations from or allusions to numerous New Testament books: Matthew, Luke, Romans, 1 Corinthians, Galatians, Eph, Philippians, 1 and 2 Timothy, 1 Peter, and 1 John, and also possibly 2 Corinthians, 1 and 2 Thessalonians, and the Gospel of John.[8]

By the end of the second century, just 100 years after the close of the apostolic period, a disciple of Polycarp, Irenaeus of Lyons (c. 180), wrote a series of books against the heresies threatening the church of his day. Throughout those books he quoted from or alluded to all of the writings of the New Testament with the exception of James, Jude, 3 John, Philemon, and perhaps 2 Peter and Hebrews. Ignatius, Polycarp, and Irenaeus are just a few examples of the many second-century writers who evidenced the New Testament books' authority among the churches.[9]

---

[6]   *1 Clement* 47.1, 3 (Holmes, 189).
[7]   Michael J. Kruger, *Canon Revisited: Establishing the Origins and Authority of the New Testament Books* (Wheaton, IL: Crossway, 2012), 214–16.
[8]   See discussion in Kruger, 216–19.
[9]   See Michael J. Kruger, *The Question of Canon* (Downers Grove, IL: IVP Academic, 2013), 155–203.

MINI MYTHS

"Dozens of Potential Gospels Vied for Inclusion in the New Testament Canon"

Popular mythmakers in academia, fiction, and film have pushed the idea that numerous equally viable contenders for the status of "canonical Gospel" were considered in the early church. These include various "lost" or "rejected" gospels, such as the *Gospel of Truth*, the *Gospel of Thomas*, the *Gospel of the Egyptians*, the *Gospel of Mary*, the *Gospel of Philip*, and even the *Gospel of Judas*—yes, *that* Judas. The truth is, all scholars agree that these "gospels" were all forgeries deceptively attributed to apostles who had been long dead by the time the fakes were even written. The fact is that none of these so-called gospels was ever universally accepted by orthodox Christians or considered a reasonable candidate for inclusion in the canon. Only Matthew, Mark, Luke, and John enjoyed early, widespread acceptance as foundational reports of the person and work of Jesus.[10]

Canonical Conclusions

As far as we can tell from the evidence available to us, during those first 100 years after the apostles, the pastors and teachers of local churches faithfully received the writings of the Old and New Testaments, then copied, distributed, and passed them down to the next generation of leadership. Those who did the copying and collecting were either original disciples of the apostles or the successors of those disciples. Thus, they had a unique perspective to know which writings had come down from the authoritative apostles and prophets themselves. As long as they knew the writings had come from the apostles and prophets, those books functioned canonically in all the churches.

During the first two centuries, however, false teachers forged their own fake writings to compete with the authentic Scriptures of the apostles and

---

[10]   See Darrell L. Bock, *The Missing Gospels: Unearthing the Truth behind Alternative Christianities* (Nashville: Thomas Nelson, 2006).

prophets. They also produced edited versions of canonical writings and eventually produced their own collections of authoritative books to lead people astray. This prompted the true Christians to clarify which writings had been received as authoritative and used in the churches since the time of the apostles. So, around the year 180, the church in Rome produced a document describing the New Testament writings officially used in their teaching and preaching. This document, the Muratorian Canon, survives today in a poorly preserved Latin translation of an original Greek text, but it gives us some indication that the churches of the second century officially accepted the great majority of New Testament writings found in our own Bibles and rightly rejected heretical books.[11]

While the church of the second and third centuries enjoyed strong unity over most New Testament books, a handful of books that are part of the canon were doubted by some people in some places at some times. These include Hebrews, James, 2 Peter, 2 and 3 John, Jude, and—later—Revelation. At the same time, a small group of early Christian writings that are not apostolic and prophetic were wrongly regarded as Scripture by some people, in some places, at some times. These included the *Didache*, *Epistle of Barnabas*, *Shepherd of Hermas*, *Apocalypse of Peter*, and *Wisdom of Solomon*. However, doubts about the inclusion or exclusion of these books were never universal, and by the end of the fourth century, these questions were resolved through careful study, discussion, and consensus.

By the end of the patristic period, all churches throughout the world shared the exact same canon of twenty-seven New Testament books we have today. No ecumenical council ever debated or voted on the books. No pope ever decreed which books should be excluded or banned. No emperor made an arbitrary selection from among dozens of viable options. By the time several local churches and regional councils published their official lists describing (not prescribing) the books of the Bible in the fourth century, even the doubted books had been settled through an organic process of corporate discernment, not through an official affirmation or denunciation.

---

[11]　This dating of the Muratorian fragment and its role in establishing a second-century canon have not gone unchallenged. See Geoffrey Mark Hahneman, *The Muratorian Fragment and the Development of the Canon*, Oxford Theological Monographs (Oxford: Clarendon Press, 1992). However, the certainty of a second-century canon is based on much more than this fragment, particularly the authoritative use of New Testament writings by church leaders throughout the second century. See a positive appraisal of the Muratorian fragment in Charles E. Hill, "The Debate over the Muratorian Fragment and the Development of the Canon," *Westminster Theological Journal* 57 (1995): 437–52.

Application

Don't buy into the myth that the Catholic Church or Eastern Orthodox Church canonized the Bible or granted authority to the writings. They didn't. The books had inherent authority long before the production of official lists. The fact that the apostolic and prophetic books were "handed down" from generation to generation through the leaders of the churches does not imply that tradition has equal authority with Scripture. It was the authority of the apostles and prophets who spoke and wrote by the inspiration of the Holy Spirit that rendered the books of the Bible canonical—not the ecclesiastical authority of church leaders.

Even when we hear about the small handful of "disputed" books that took a couple of centuries to be accepted by all Christians (though they were always accepted by some), we should be encouraged. The dispute demonstrates that early church leaders were extremely cautious and not willing to simply accept any writing that carried an apostle's name, because they knew that forgeries were being written by heretics. However, once the leaders of the second and third centuries were able to establish the origins of doubted books and confirm they were, in fact, authentically apostolic and prophetic, all churches throughout the world reached a consensus on which books should be excluded and included. Therefore, we can have confidence in the books of the Bible as they have come down to us—not because some church council, pope, or emperor made a good choice, but because the churches throughout the world very early on knew which books had been written by apostles and prophets, upon which foundation the church was built (Eph 2:20; 4:11).

Resources

Bruce, F. F. *The Canon of Scripture*. Downers Grove, IL: InterVarsity Press, 1988.

Kruger, Michael J. *Canon Revisited: Establishing the Origins and Authority of the New Testament Books*. Wheaton, IL: Crossway, 2012.

Metzger, Bruce M. *The Canon of the New Testament: Its Origin, Development, and Significance*. Oxford: Oxford University Press, 1987.

CHAPTER 7

Pagan Philosophy Contaminated Christian Theology

The Legendary Story

The church has long struggled against an onslaught of philosophical fallacies and cultural cover-ups. Listening to sources such as these—rather than listening to the Bible—has led us into divisive doctrinal debates. To see examples, we need look no further than unbiblical doctrines inspired by philosophical speculations, such as the Trinity and the hypostatic union in Christology. The problem began way back in the early church, when certain Christians became enamored with Greek philosophy. These so-called Christians led the church away from the purity of its Jewish roots and instead developed cumbersome doctrines that complicated the simple faith and practice of Jesus's earliest followers. The result has been a lengthy captivity in the church to pagan ideas about God's nature, human nature, salvation, and other basic doctrines.

Introduction: Unraveling the Legend

Multiple contemporary groups—from Mormons and Jehovah's Witnesses to the Hebrew Roots movement and theological liberals—have sounded warnings about the allegedly hyper-philosophical nature of historic Christian doctrine. Most of the concern points back to creedal statements and councils of the fourth and fifth centuries. For instance, the Council of Nicaea adapted a Greek term—*homoousios*, meaning "of the same essence"—to describe the relationship between God the Father and God the Son. The doctrinal development in creeds and definitions such as Nicaea and Chalcedon has struck many as overly indebted to a desire within the Greek philosophical tradition to define everything—even the undefinable.

However, early Christians did not distort the gospel or capitulate to philosophical and cultural movements. For more than 1,500 years, classic Christians of all stripes—Catholic, Orthodox, and Protestant—have confessed the Nicene Creed as a faithful expression of Christian fundamentals. We should not, therefore, reject trinitarian and Christological doctrine from this era in order to set the Christian faith free from pagan ideas. Rather, we should see these core doctrinal developments as faithful expressions of classic Christian doctrine borne out by scriptural study and consensus.

Extreme Suspicions

Once the Reformation broke open the Christian world in the sixteenth century, believers began to reflect more directly on the beliefs and practices they had received from their Roman Catholic forebears. While much of the resulting recalibration was helpful and needed, the potential for harmful and extreme overreactions has remained a reality up to the present day.

In 1531, just ten years after Luther's excommunication, Michael Servetus (c. 1509–1553) published *On the Errors of the Trinity*.[1] Servetus interacted with much Scripture as he railed against a church "led astray"[2] by "metaphysical philosophers" who "invented"[3] the persons of the Trinity. The essence of Servetus's argument against the traditional Christian doctrine of God was precisely that it had gotten tangled up with pagan Greek philosophy. What began as legitimate questioning of the Roman Catholic tradition with Martin Luther (1483–1546) was quickly pushed to the extreme of denying a fundamental doctrine of the Christian faith, and all on the basis of "pagan philosophy."

This trend of questioning core Christian doctrine on the basis of its connection to Greek philosophy continued into the United States of the nineteenth century when a series of movements left behind classic Christian doctrines. The most striking of these movements is Mormonism, founded

---

[1]   Michael Serveto, *The Two Treatises of Servetus on the Trinity*, trans. Earl Morse Wilbur. Harvard Theological Studies, bk. 16 (Cambridge, MA: Harvard University Press, 1932).
[2]   *On the Errors of the Trinity* 1.23, in Serveto, 20.
[3]   *On the Errors of the Trinity* 1.30, in Serveto, 24.

by Joseph Smith in the 1820s. As Mormon theology has developed, it has consistently denied classic trinitarian theology. Mormons reason that Greek philosophy negatively influenced a proper Jewish-Christian reading of the Scriptures. Mormon theologian Richard Hopkins argues that "the Hebrews knew nothing of metaphysics," and that the "Greek" Christian apologists of the second century "failed to understand the significance of the fact that the scriptures were revealed to the Jews, not the Greeks."[4] For Hopkins and the Mormons, this means that later doctrinal developments related to trinitarian and Christological doctrine were wedded to philosophy rather than to the Bible, and should therefore be rejected.

Finally, the late nineteenth and early twentieth centuries produced an influential scholarly treatment of these issues in the spirit of theological liberalism. Adolf von Harnack (1851–1930) argued in his *History of Dogma* that early Christian use of Greek philosophy compromised Jesus's gospel message. Harnack wrote, "We perceive also in the doctrine of faith on which this commonwealth [the church] is based, the philosophic spirit of the Greeks."[5] Therefore, Harnack argued, modern Christians should peel off the philosophical aspects of Christian dogma to discover the seed of the true Jesus buried within.[6]

In each of the above cases, we find a decided impulse of distrust toward the early church's use of philosophy. This led to a complete reworking of doctrine by these scholars and groups, even down to their understanding of the Christian gospel. However, these approaches ignore some significant historical features.

Living in a Greek World

Much has been made of early Christianity's Jewish roots. Indeed, there seems to have been significant, continuous interaction between Jews and Christians even up to the fourth century.[7] And Jewish Christianity endured for several centuries, continuing to exercise some influence on the church's doctrinal

---

[4]   Richard R. Hopkins, *How Greek Philosophy Corrupted the Christian Concept of God* (Springville, UT: Horizon, 2009), 114.

[5]   Adolf von Harnack, *The History of Dogma*, vol. 1, trans. Neil Buchanan (Boston: Little, Brown, 1901), 46.

[6]   Adolf von Harnack, *What Is Christianity?*, trans. Thomas Bailey Saunders (New York: G. P. Putnam's Sons, 1902), 11–13.

[7]   Oskar Skarsaune, *In the Shadow of the Temple: Jewish Influences on Early Christianity* (Downers Grove, IL: IVP Academic, 2008).

identity.[8] So, the popular narrative that Christianity began as "Jewish" and sometime later was corrupted by becoming "Greek" is oversimplified.

Judaism in the time of Jesus had long taken on key features of Greek culture and thought—even for as long as 300 years before Christ. Many Jews of Jesus's day had adopted the Greek language and ways of education.[9] But this doesn't mean Judaism lost its essential character either. As historian G. W. Bowersock argues, "Hellenism, which is a genuine Greek word for Greek culture (*Hellenismos*), represented language, thought, mythology, and images that constituted an extraordinarily flexible medium of both cultural and religious expression. It was a medium not necessarily antithetical to local or indigenous traditions. On the contrary, it provided a new and more eloquent way of giving voice to them."[10] Every aspect of Greek culture didn't stand in opposition to Jews or Christians. Rather, many elements of Greek culture helped both Jews and Christians better express their religious views, a fact we find as we look at early Christians and their use of Greek language and philosophy.

Unmistakable Greek Influence

Early Christians used Greek language and thought to communicate the Christian faith to their culture, just as we use modern language and thought to communicate the gospel to our own. Though a few thinkers went overboard in adopting Greek ideas (e.g., Origen of Alexandria [184–253]), most theologians understood the limits of philosophy and worldly thinking and often warned of their potential dangers.

A great and early example of a Christian making use of philosophy was second-century apologist Justin Martyr (c. 100–165). After spending his early adulthood pursuing truth in various philosophical schools of thought, Justin eventually came to believe in Jesus, calling Christianity the "only sure and useful philosophy."[11] As he developed his theology, he identified the Greek

---

[8]   See Oskar Skarsaune and Reidar Hvalvik, eds., *Jewish Believers in Jesus: The Early Centuries* (Peabody, MA: Hendrickson, 2007).

[9]   Martin Hengel, *Judaism and Hellenism*, repr. ed. (Eugene, OR: Wipf and Stock, 2003), 70–78.

[10]   G. W. Bowersock, *Hellenism in Late Antiquity* (Ann Arbor: University of Michigan Press, 1996), 7.

[11]   Justin Martyr, *Dialogue with Trypho* 8, trans. Michael Slusser (Washington, DC: Catholic University of America Press, 2002), 15.

concept of the *logos* (word or reason) with Jesus.[12] Justin's use of this identification created a bridge of understanding between his Christian faith and the pagan philosophy of the ancient Greeks. Since Justin knew the philosophical systems of his day, he understood that they included pieces of the truth, and he knew where to find points of contact between pagan philosophy and true Christian faith.[13]

But Justin did not simply embrace everything in Greek culture and philosophy. He made clear that Christians did not follow in the idolatry of Greek religion.[14] Even more to the point, he saw Christianity as surpassing Greek philosophies in fundamental ways,[15] always recognizing that on some points Christians taught a "fuller and more divine" doctrine than the philosophers ever would.[16] This balanced approach, recognizing both strengths and weaknesses of Greek thought, was much more indicative of Christian approaches to philosophy in the early church.

Another period of early church history in which philosophy is said to have done significant damage was during the development of the doctrine of the Trinity (see chapter 8). Anti-trinitarians sometimes allege that church leaders imported Greek philosophical jargon when they adopted the term *ousia* ("essence"/"nature") to describe the relationship between the Father and the Son and the term *hypostasis* ("substance"/"person") to denote their distinction. The truth is, in Greek philosophy, those terms are not clearly distinguished. In adopting these terms from the Greek language, Christians had to adapt the meanings of the words and give them theological (*not philosophical*) meanings.

Though some, like Origen of Alexandria, may have taken engagement with philosophy to an extreme, most walked the careful path of Justin Martyr and the champions of trinitarian orthodoxy. Philosophy could (and should) be used fruitfully in defining and defending the faith, especially in a culture asking questions not directly answered in Scripture.

---

[12] Justin Martyr, *First Apology* 5, trans. L. W. Barnard (Mahwah, NJ: Paulist Press, 1997), 26. The Greeks identified the *logos* with divine reason at work in the world. Justin's use of the term in relation to Jesus draws a connection between that Greek idea and the apostle John's use of the term for Jesus in the opening of his Gospel (John 1:1).

[13] Justin Martyr, 20, 35.

[14] Justin Martyr, 9, 27.

[15] Justin Martyr, 18, 33. In this passage, Justin suggests that while the philosophers got some things right, he believes Christian faith in the one true God to be superior because we believe in the resurrection to come.

[16] Justin Martyr, 20, 35.

MINI MYTHS

"Saint Nicholas (aka 'Santa Claus') Punched Arius in the Face at the Council of Nicaea"

Around Christmas countless memes float and social media posts push the idea that Santa Claus (originally known as Saint Nicholas of Myra) was so enraged with the anti-trinitarian heretic Arius at the Council of Nicaea in 325 that he punched Arius in the face. This legend is so much a part of Christian lore that churches have icons and artwork depicting the violent scene. Though it is possible that Saint Nicholas attended the Council of Nicaea and joined in the condemnation of Arianism in favor of orthodoxy, it is highly unlikely that he punched Arius in the nose. This legend developed a good 1,000 years after Nicholas of Myra died.[17]

Application

To philosophize or not to philosophize, that is the question. Debates about whether fourth-century Christians made a mistake in their posture toward philosophy seem far distant from anything we are dealing with today. But the question actually remains as pertinent as ever. Christians continue to feel angst over our relationship to the world around us. Some believers argue that we should remove ourselves from the broader world of ideas to protect the sanctity of our faith. Others argue that we must engage with that same world of ideas, so that our voices will be heard.

Our study in this chapter has shown us that we cannot escape the cultural realities around us. Just like water in a swimming pool, culture surrounds us. If culture is, as Andy Crouch says, "what we make of the world,"[18] then we should see ourselves not simply as passive recipients of culture, but as active participants in it. As such, culture always has a voice in our thoughts and actions. The

---

[17] See Steven D. Greydanus, "Let's Stop Celebrating St. Nicholas Punching Arius," *National Catholic Register*, December 6, 2016, http://www.ncregister.com/blog/steven-greydanus/lets-stop-celebrating-st.-nicholas-punching-arius.

[18] Andy Crouch, *Culture Making: Recovering Our Creative Calling* (Downers Grove, IL: IVP Academic, 2008), 23.

way we think and the values we hold come to us wrapped in cultural realities such as language. This means that Christians in an ancient world dominated by Greek language and thought inevitably drew upon that language and thought to express their ideas. The same is true for Christians today—North American Christians think and express themselves in particular ways, African Christians in vastly different ways. Just like fourth-century Christians at Nicaea working on how best to express trinitarian doctrine, we seek to speak clearly about God in our own cultural contexts. Faithful language about God provides a basis for the simple life of faith, hope, and love that Christians seek to embody.

This subject also reveals a harmful dividing line that has cropped up in the past couple of centuries—the stark dividing line between theology and philosophy. Christians often assume that theology is good while philosophy is bad. History shows us, however, that philosophers and theologians are more alike than they are different, and that Christians have regularly made use of philosophy in their books, treatises, and sermons. Rather than an antagonist, then, philosophy can serve as a partner to Christians, helping us to see more clearly—in our own language and thought patterns—the shape of God's redemptive work in the world.

Resources

Morris, Thomas V. *God and the Philosophers: The Reconciliation of Faith and Reason.* Oxford: Oxford University Press, 1994.

Pearcey, Nancy. *Total Truth: Liberating Christianity from Its Cultural Captivity.* Wheaton, IL: Crossway, 2004.

CHAPTER 8

The Doctrine of the Trinity
Developed Centuries after Jesus

The Legendary Story

Not only is the word *Trinity* not found in the Bible, but the doctrine of the Trinity itself took several centuries to develop. Not until the great controversies and debates leading up to the Council of Nicaea in 325 did the church finally decree the doctrine of the Trinity to be the orthodox view. From that time forward, the Roman emperor enforced this teaching of "one God in three persons," requiring that Christendom adopt the deity of Christ and the Holy Spirit.

Introduction: Unraveling the Legend

Jehovah's Witnesses deny the doctrine of the Trinity as an unbiblical teaching that was centuries in the making. On their official website, they declare quite confidently, "FACT: The Trinitarian dogma is a late fourth-century invention."[1] Other anti-trinitarians attempt to make the same argument (see chapter 7). However, the doctrine of the Trinity is as old as the Christian faith itself. Though the word *Trinity* isn't used in the New Testament, every generation of Christians since the first century confessed Father, Son, and Spirit as one in power and divinity but three in personhood and in their distinct roles

---

[1] Watchtower Bible and Tract Society, "Myth 4: God Is a Trinity," JW.org, November 2009, https://www.jw.org/en/publications/magazines/wp20091101/myth-god-is-a-trinity/.

in creation, revelation, and redemption. Though the Councils of Nicaea in 325 and Constantinople in 381 settled on specific technical *language* to best describe the relationship of the Father, Son, and Holy Spirit, they did not invent the *doctrine* of the Trinity.

The Trinity before Nicaea

It is sloppy (and inaccurate) to speak of the "development" *of* the doctrine of the Trinity. Rather, it would be more appropriate to discuss the development *within* the doctrine of the Trinity. The basic understanding regarding the full deity, unity, and distinction of the Father, Son, and Holy Spirit were in place from the first through fourth centuries. However, the development of more refined language in light of misunderstandings occurred over the course of several generations, and these developments became enshrined in the classic language of the Niceno-Constantinopolitan Creed (AD 381).

A handful of direct quotations from early church fathers from the first through fourth centuries demonstrates that even though the church had not yet hammered out a universally accepted, dogmatic articulation of the Trinity, they agreed on the substance of the doctrine.

> First Clement (c. AD 96): "Do we not have one God and one Christ and one Spirit of grace which was poured out upon us?"[2]

> Ignatius of Antioch (c. 110): "For our God, Jesus the Christ, was conceived by Mary according to God's plan, both from the seed of David and of the Holy Spirit."[3]

> "Be eager, therefore, to be firmly grounded in the precepts of the Lord and the apostles, in order that 'in whatever you do, you may prosper,' physically and spiritually, in faith and love, in the Son and the Father and in the Spirit, in the beginning and at the end."[4]

---

[2]   *1 Clement* 46.6 (Holmes, 107).
[3]   Ignatius, *Ephesians* 18.2 (Holmes, 197).
[4]   Ignatius, *Magnesians* 13.1 (Holmes, 211).

Justin Martyr (c. 160): "He [the leader of the brethren] . . . sends up praise and glory to the Father of the Universe through the name of the Son and of the Holy Spirit, and offers thanksgiving."[5]

Polycarp of Smyrna (c. 155): "I praise you, I bless you, I glorify you, through the eternal and heavenly High Priest, Jesus Christ, your beloved Son, through whom to you with him and the Holy Spirit be glory both now and for the ages to come. Amen."[6]

Theophilus of Antioch (c. 180): "The three days which were before the luminaries, are types of the Trinity, of God, and His Word [Christ], and His wisdom [the Spirit]."[7]

Athenagoras of Athens (c. 180): "For we speak of His Word as God too and Son and of Holy Spirit likewise, united into one by power and divided in order thus, the Father, the Son, the Spirit, the Son being mind, word, or wisdom of the Father and the Spirit an effulgence as light from fire."[8]

Irenaeus of Lyons (c. 180): "For with Him were always present the Word and Wisdom, the Son and the Spirit, by whom and in whom, freely and spontaneously, He made all things, to whom also He speaks, saying, 'Let Us make man after Our image and likeness.'"[9]

Tertullian of Carthage (c. 200): "We have been taught that He proceeds forth from God, and in that procession He is generated; so that He is the Son of God, and is called God from unity of substance with God. For God, too, is a Spirit. Even when the ray is shot from the sun, it is still part of the parent mass; the sun will still be in the ray, because it is a ray of the sun—there is no division of substance, but

---

[5]   Justin Martyr, *1 Apology* 65.3, in Leslie W. Barnard, ed., *St. Justin Martyr: The First and Second Apologies*, Ancient Christian Writers (New York: Paulist, 1997), 56:70.

[6]   *Martyrdom of Polycarp* 14.3 (Holmes, 323).

[7]   Theophilus, *To Autolycus* 2.15 (ANF 2:100–101).

[8]   Athenagoras, *Embassy for the Christians* 24.1, trans. Joseph Hugh Crehan, *Athenagoras: Embassy for the Christians, The Resurrection of the Dead*, ed. Johannes Quasten and Joseph C. Plumpe, Ancient Christian Writers, vol. 23 (Westminster, MD: Newman, 1956).

[9]   Irenaeus, *Against Heresies* 4.20.1 (ANF 1:487).

merely an extension. Thus Christ is Spirit of Spirit, and God of God, as light of light is kindled."[10]

Hippolytus (c. 230): "A man, therefore, even though he will it not, is compelled to acknowledge God the Father Almighty, and Christ Jesus the Son of God, who, being God, became man, to whom also the Father made all things subject, Himself excepted, and the Holy Spirit; and that these, therefore, are three. But if he desires to learn how it is shown still that there is one God, let him know that His power is one. As far as regards the power, therefore, God is one. But as far as regards the economy there is a threefold manifestation."[11]

Origen of Alexandria (c. 230–240): "The apostles related that the Holy Spirit was associated in honour and dignity with the Father and the Son."[12]

Dionysius of Rome (c 260): "[Sabellius] blasphemes in saying that the Son Himself is the Father, and vice versa; but these [other heretics] in a certain manner announce three gods, in that they divide the holy unity into three different substances, absolutely separated from one another. For it is essential that the Divine Word should be united to the God of all, and that the Holy Spirit should abide and dwell in God; and thus that the Divine Trinity should be reduced and gathered into one, as if into a certain head—that is, into the omnipotent God of all."[13]

Lactantius (c. 305): "When we speak of God the Father and God the Son, we do not speak of them as different, nor do we separate each: because the Father cannot exist without the Son, nor can the Son be separated from the Father, since the name of Father cannot be given without the Son, nor can the Son be begotten without the Father."[14]

---

[10] Tertullian, *Apology* 21 (ANF 3:34).
[11] Hippolytus, *Against Noetus* 8 (ANF 5:226).
[12] Origen, *On First Principles* Preface 4 (ANF 4:240).
[13] Dionysius of Rome, *Against the Sabellians* 1 (ANF 7:365).
[14] Lactantius, *Divine Institutes* 4.29 (ANF 7:132).

MINI MYTHS

"The Church Historian Eusebius Was an Arian"

Actually, the fourth-century church had three somewhat prominent "Eusebiuses" at the same time. Two of them—Eusebius of Emesa (c. 300–360) and the famous church historian Eusebius of Caesarea (263–339)—were more focused on church unity than on choosing sides in the debate over Arius's theology. However, the third Eusebius, Eusebius of Nicomedia (d. 341), was indeed an ally of Arius. While Eusebius of Nicomedia did sign the Nicene Creed, he felt that Arius had been misunderstood and misrepresented, so he continued to support Arius in the years following Nicaea. That meant leading a group of bishops to oppose the defender of Nicaea, Athanasius, by filing false charges against him and eventually getting Athanasius exiled from his church and home country. On the other hand, the church historian Eusebius of Caesarea rejected the many elements of Arian teaching but also failed to completely embrace Athanasius's strong Nicene Christology. The church historian was technically neither an Arian nor an Athanasian. Though we would not follow the church historian Eusebius in his ambiguous Christology, we should not confuse him with Eusebius of Nicomedia, the Arian who baptized Constantine on his deathbed.[15]

From Doctrine to Dogma

Generation after generation, from the first century to the fourth, we see consistent teachings from the leaders of the church:

There is one God.
The Father is God.
The Son is God.

---

[15] See Khaled Anatolios, *Retrieving Nicaea: The Development and Meaning of Trinitarian Doctrine* (Grand Rapids: Baker, 2011); John Tyson, *The Great Athanasius: An Introduction to His Life and Work* (Eugene, OR: Wipf and Stock, 2017).

The Spirit is God.
The Father is not the Son.
The Son is not the Spirit.
The Spirit is not the Father.
There is only one God, not three gods.

Sometimes these early fathers attempted to clarify, explain, illustrate, and defend these basic assertions against tritheism (overemphasizing the distinction of the persons) or unitarianism (overemphasizing the unity of the persons).

However, in the fourth century we see a clear, consistent, unified, and refined use of technical language to describe what all Christians believed and taught about the Father, Son, and Holy Spirit. In other words, we see all elements of the *doctrine* (basic teaching) of the Trinity taught throughout the early centuries, but we don't see a finalized *dogma* (official decreed language) adopted universally until the fourth century.

Although the raw material of trinitarian theology was present in the New Testament and echoed in the following centuries, "no steps had been taken . . . to work all these complex elements into a coherent whole. The Church had to wait for more than three hundred years for a final synthesis, for not until the Council of Constantinople (381) was the formula of one God existing in three co-equal Persons formally ratified."[16] In other words, the councils of Nicaea (325) and Constantinople (381) did not invent the doctrine of the Trinity but provided technical language used to define and defend the Trinity in ways that would avoid misunderstanding and combat error.

One nineteenth-century scholar, after surveying the trinitarian thought of the first three centuries, concluded, "It only remains for me to remark concerning the Nicene and Constantinopolitan Creed, that all the clauses of it, which relate to the divinity of the Son and the Holy Ghost, may be supported by the writings of the Ante-Nicene [pre-Nicene] fathers."[17]

No, the doctrine of the Trinity was not invented in the fourth century. It was the teaching of the church from the first century onward.

---

[16]   J. N. D. Kelly, *Early Christian Doctrines*, 5th rev. ed. (New York: HarperOne, 1978), 87–88.
[17]   Edward Burton, *Testimonies of the Ante-Nicene Fathers to the Doctrine of the Trinity and of the Divinity of the Holy Ghost* (Oxford: Oxford University Press, 1831), 144.

Application

When Christians say *God*, we don't mean merely the philosophers' "First Cause" or the moralists' "Divine Lawgiver." The word *God* for Christians doesn't signify a generic "Supreme Being," a subjective "Ground of Being," or the folksy "Man Upstairs." When Christians refer to "God," they mean God the Father, God the Son, and God the Holy Spirit. The great Princeton scholar B. B. Warfield put it well: "There is one only and true God, but in the unity of the Godhead there are three coeternal and coequal Persons, the same in substance but distinct in subsistence."[18]

From the time Christians began baptizing in the name of the Father, Son, and Holy Spirit (Matt 28:19), they had at least a rudimentary understanding that God existed in three persons. All things are *from* the Father, *through* the Son, and *by* the Holy Spirit—creation, revelation, and redemption. They prayed to the Father, through the Son, by the Spirit. They worshipped and glorified the Father with the Son and the Spirit. They understood that salvation came only by faith in the Son, sent by the Father, through the regenerating work of the Spirit. To worship any other concept of "God" that is not Father, Son, and Holy Spirit is to worship a false god. To deny the Trinity in thought, word, or practice is to commit blasphemy, idolatry, and heresy.

The important thing to realize is that the one true God did not *become* a Trinity; he always has been one God in three persons. We can be thankful that Christians of the first three centuries wrestled with how to best articulate and defend the doctrine they believed. Today, about 1,600 years since the work of Nicaea and Constantinople, we have time-tested, ready-at-hand language to summarize what we mean by "God"—"one nature in three persons."

Resources

Barnes, Michel René. "Latin Trinitarian Theology." In *The Cambridge Companion to the Trinity*, edited by Peter C. Phan. Cambridge: Cambridge University Press, 2011.

McGuckin, John Anthony. "The Trinity in the Greek Fathers." In *The Cambridge Companion to the Trinity*, edited by Peter C. Phan, Cambridge: Cambridge University Press, 2011.

Olson, Roger E., and Christopher A. Hall. *The Trinity*. Guides to Theology. Grand Rapids: Eerdmans, 2002.

---

[18] Benjamin B. Warfield, "The Biblical Doctrine of the Trinity," in Warfield, *Biblical and Theological Studies* (Philadelphia: P&R, 1952), 35.

CHAPTER 9

The Emperor Constantine Made Christianity the Official State Religion

The Legendary Story

In the early years of the Roman emperor Constantine's life (272–337), the burgeoning Christian movement had rooted itself in the midst of the most powerful empire the world had ever known—this, despite the fact that these Christians had no semblance of earthly power and suffered persecution by overzealous pagan officials. While Christianity's numbers were growing despite these earthly limitations, the Roman Empire faced a crisis of leadership. In the first decade of the fourth century, four emperors vied for sole rulership over the region around the Mediterranean Sea. Who would be the last one standing?

Faced with the battle of his life, the pagan emperor Constantine shrewdly considered his position. The Christian movement was on the ascent. What if he aligned himself with it, in contrast to his pagan co-emperors? Not only might this help him gain the victory over his rivals, but it would give him a banner under which to unify the empire. Therefore, Constantine adopted Christianity before a decisive battle against one of his co-emperors at Milvian Bridge (AD 312). When he finally gained sole governing power, he made Christianity the religion of the whole empire (324).

Introduction: Unraveling the Legend

Even a cursory reading of Christian history reveals a union between church and state in Europe for centuries throughout the Middle Ages. There is little doubt that Christians regularly abused their power under this arrangement, resulting in great damage to people in that day and age, as well as compromising the image of the church for centuries afterward. However, a careful reading of history shows that this "Christian empire" did not begin with Constantine. The evidence paints a more nuanced portrait, one that acknowledges Constantine's favor toward Christianity but that also stops short of asserting that Constantine declared Rome Christian.

Decree to Be Free

Once Constantine gained power over the western half of the Roman Empire, he joined with the eastern emperor (and Constantine's brother-in-law), Licinius (c. 263–325), to issue the so-called Edict of Milan (313).[1] The edict is "so-called" because, while Constantine and Licinius did meet in Milan to discuss imperial policy toward Christians, no official edict was issued from Milan. Rather, the emperors cosigned two different letters, one in Latin, the other in Greek, that were sent at two different times to two different people in the empire.[2]

This meeting at Milan convinced the two co-emperors that it was in their best interest to offer at least some religious freedom to people of all faiths in the empire. Earlier imperial policy had presumed that "deviant" religious expressions, such as Christianity, were responsible for the difficulties in the empire. People believed that if only everyone would offer proper devotion to the Roman gods, the empire would remain strong and free from ills such as famine and invasion. Repeated incursions from armies outside the empire and strife between Romans themselves convinced Constantine and Licinius to try something different.[3]

The letters outlining imperial policy made explicit that "each one, and the Christians among the rest," should "have the liberty to observe the religion of his choice."[4] Practically, this meant the co-emperors advocated restoring

---

[1]　For the text of the entire edict, see Eusebius of Caesarea, *Ecclesiastical History* 10.5, trans. C. F. Cruse (Peabody, MA: Hendrickson, 1998), 372. The version preserved in Lactantius contains some key differences. See Lactantius, *On the Death of Persecutors* 48, trans. William Fletcher (New York: Cosimo Classics, 2007), 320.

[2]　Peter J. Leithart, *Defending Constantine: The Twilight of an Empire and the Dawn of Christendom* (Downers Grove, IL: IVP Academic, 2010), 99.

[3]　An earlier decree, the Edict of Toleration, issued by the emperor Galerius, had outlawed persecution of Christians two years before Constantine and Licinius's "edict" was published. Constantine was far more committed to this process than Licinius. The latter reneged on the edict and persecuted Christians in the eastern portions of the empire in the years after this agreement had been publicized.

[4]　Eusebius of Caesarea, *Ecclesiastical History* 10.5.2, 372.

church property that had been seized from Christians under previous Roman administrations. Despite the favorable conditions for Christians under this new policy, it did not make Christianity the official religion of Rome. Rather, it stated that all people should be free to worship as they pleased in the places of worship they set up for themselves. Therefore, the edict of AD 313 served as an important nod to religious freedom more than an embrace of state-sponsored religion.

An Emperor's Encouragement

Claims that Constantine made Christianity the religion of Rome usually point to a decree he issued to his eastern provinces in AD 324, as well as to the subsequent unification of Christianity at the Council of Nicaea in 325. For instance, theologian John Howard Yoder asserted Constantine's shift to state religion by linking him to Charlemagne (742–814). Pope Leo III (795–816) crowned Charlemagne Holy Roman Emperor on Christmas Day, AD 800, marking a clear link between church and state. Yet Yoder seemed to equate the church/state views of Constantine and Charlemagne, calling for rejection of "the decision by Constantine and Charlemagne that every European must be Christian."[5]

The type of claim Yoder made has seeped into the popular imagination as well. In Dan Brown's best-selling novel *The Da Vinci Code*, the "wise" Professor Teabing suggests that Constantine sought to unify the empire under Christianity in 325. Teabing believes that Constantine operated out of clever politicking, recognizing the ascent of Christianity and choosing to support the group he believed would ultimately gain control of the world. Constantine, Teabing argues, fused "pagan symbols, dates, and rituals into the growing Christian tradition" and "created a kind of hybrid religion that was acceptable to both parties."[6] Not only does such logic call into question the very essence of Christianity, but it also plays fast and loose with the facts as they have come down to us.

Constantine's edict of AD 324 offered the clearest vision yet of his dreams for the empire. The emperor clearly hoped that his tolerance of all Roman citizens would result in nonbelieving people coming to the "right way" of

5   John Howard Yoder, "The Disavowal of Constantine: An Alternative Perspective on Interfaith Dialogue," in *The Royal Priesthood: Essays Ecclesiological and Ecumenical*, ed. Michael G. Cartwright (Grand Rapids: Eerdmans, 1994), 254.

6   Dan Brown, *The Da Vinci Code* (New York: Doubleday, 2003), 232.

Christianity: "Let those in error, as well as the believers, gladly receive the benefit of peace and quiet. For this sweetness of fellowship will be effective for correcting them and bringing them to the right way."[7] Despite this hope for his people, Constantine followed with another affirmation of his tolerance: "Those who hold themselves back, let them keep if they wish their sanctuaries of falsehood."[8] While the emperor publicly disagreed with the views and practices of traditional Roman paganism, he was convinced that his people needed to have the right to worship as their consciences directed them.[9]

One other event sometimes connected to Constantine's supposed "Christianizing" of the empire was his call for the Council of Nicaea in 325. He had been disturbed by the division he witnessed among Christians and sought to use his influence to find a solution to the problem. While this certainly reveals Constantine's support for Christianity (an emperor antagonistic to Christians would have reveled in the fractures of controversy), it does not reach the level of "Christian empire." Of course, Constantine's posture toward religion does not mean he embraced the notion of a complete separation of church and state, as many do today. In some respects, he favored Christianity over other religions. For example, he engaged in an extensive, state-funded building program to celebrate important Christian sites, such as supposed locations of Jesus's birth and resurrection. Constantine also placed Christian imagery on coins and granted bishops authority to adjudicate legal disputes. Though he supported Christianity in these ways, Constantine's encouraging posture toward Christianity is not the same as declaring the empire Christian.

A Religion of Rome

Constantine's work as emperor certainly benefited Christians in their social context, and a number of other fourth-century emperors followed suit. However, only under the reign of Theodosius I (379–395) did the empire become "Christian" in any official sense.

In February 380, Theodosius I, along with his two co-emperors, released the Edict of Thessalonica, a statement that fundamentally changed the

---

[7] Eusebius of Caesarea, *Life of Constantine* 2.56.1, trans. Averil Cameron and Stuart George Hall. Clarendon Ancient History Series (Oxford: Oxford University Press, 1999), 113.

[8] Eusebius of Caesarea, 2.56.2.

[9] It is also worth noting that Constantine, while proclaiming himself a Christian, likely continued his devotion to the Roman god of the sun long after his stated conversion to Christianity. See Martin Walraff, "Constantine's Devotion to the Sun after 324," in *Studia Patristica* 34, ed. M. F. Wiles and E. J. Yarnold (Leuven, BE: Peeters, 2001), 256–69.

relationship between the government and Christianity. In it, the emperors enjoined their subjects to "live by that religion which divine Peter the apostle is said to have given to the Romans, and which it is evident that Pope Damasus and Peter, bishop of Alexandria, a man of apostolic sanctity, followed; that is that we should believe in the one deity of the Father, Son, and Holy Spirit with equal majesty, and in the Holy Trinity according to the apostolic teaching and the authority of the gospel."[10]

This edict makes no provision for worship of other kinds in the Roman Empire. Everyone should believe in the Trinity, a doctrine that had been given its mature form in 325 at the Council of Nicaea, and had continued to spur debate and conversation between Christians and others into the 380s.

However, the work of Theodosius was not yet complete. He and his co-regents issued another statement later in 380, which declared that law courts and legal proceedings such as debt collections cease on Sundays—"the Lord's Day."[11] Violators would be considered "not only infamous but sacrilegious" for their refusal to serve and observe "holy religion on that day."[12] Words such as "infamous" and "sacrilegious" might not mean much to us today, but in the Roman world, the criminal act of sacrilege could lead to citizens losing some privileges in society.

That Theodosius I and his coregents put the muscle of the law behind their edict reveals a new approach to Christianity in the empire. This was not merely a reversal from the situation of earlier Christians under the harsh rule of the emperor Diocletian.[13] The Christian emperors insisted not just on the offering of a sacrifice or worship on the Lord's Day (analogous to the older Roman system's pagan requirements), but also that people *believed* a certain way. Whereas old Rome staked its claim on the external actions of the people, the new and "improved" Christian Rome claimed the minds of its people as well.[14]

Where Christians had once been charged with crimes for religious practice, the late fourth century saw a 180-degree shift, leaving Christians as the ultimate insiders with the attendant positions of power while their pagan neighbors increasingly found themselves powerless, outsiders in danger of persecution.

---

[10]   *Codex Theodosianus* 16.1.2, trans. Oliver J. Fletcher, in *The Library of Original Sources*, vol. 4, *Early Mediaeval Age* (Milwaukee: University Research Extension, 1907), 70.

[11]   *Codex Theodosianus* 11.7.13, 69.

[12]   *Codex Theodosianus* 11.7.13, 69.

[13]   Hermann Doerries, *Constantine and Religious Liberty*, trans. Roland Bainton (New Haven, CT: Yale University Press, 1960), 52.

[14]   Doerries, 54.

Application

One popular outcropping of the mythological narrative is that Christians in power, by nature, oppress others. On the other hand, if Constantine, a Christian, stuck to the principles outlined in Milan, then that reveals that Christians can indeed wield power in responsible and humane ways that preference freedom over control.[15] The Constantine of Milan presents a vision of tolerance in the best sense of that term (Rom 12:10, 16). People of radically different faiths can indeed live and worship under common national banners. That Constantine encouraged this as an avowed Christian makes his overtures toward freedom that much more meaningful for believers who sit in positions of power—governmental, ecclesiastical, or otherwise.

The state of the church in the empire under Constantine and beyond him also provides for us a warning. When the emperor issued a decree that encouraged his people to become Christians, many came to the church out of a misguided notion to go along with the earthly power rather than as a result of any commitment to Christ's message. Not only did this fundamentally change the experience of Christian community in churches all over the empire, but Christians began to lose their prophetic voice in the midst of a government that favored them. The loss of that prophetic voice led to a "Christianizing" of the empire that compromised freedom, coerced Christian participation, and associated Christians with the acts of a self-serving nation-state. Rather than seeking political favor or coerced conversion, we should recommit ourselves to loving our [pagan, Hindu, liberal, conservative, etc.] neighbors as ourselves.

Resources

Doerries, Hermann. *Constantine and Religious Liberty*. Translated by Roland Bainton. New Haven, CT: Yale University Press, 1960.

Eusebius of Caesarea. *Life of Constantine*. Translated by Averil Cameron and Stuart George Hall. Clarendon Ancient History Series. Oxford: Oxford University Press, 1999.

Leithart, Peter J. *Defending Constantine: The Twilight of an Empire and the Dawn of Christendom*. Downers Grove, IL: IVP Academic, 2010.

---

[15] Leithart, *Defending Constantine*, 107.

CHAPTER 10

Women Never Served as Church Officers in the Early Church

The Legendary Story

When Jesus chose his Twelve, he chose men. When Paul appointed leaders in the churches he planted, he chose men. The Christian church has always limited all its offices to men. Specifically, the offices of pastor/elder and deacon historically have been filled by men.

None of this denies the contribution of women to God's work throughout the church's early history. Women often worked on God's behalf in the early church. However, the work of women was never as church officers. God loves both men and women equally, and by the power of his Spirit has gifted men and women. However, the early church evidences that God has reserved appointed offices like elders and deacons for men alone.

Introduction: Unraveling the Legend

Human beings suffer from shortsightedness. Christians are no exception, often taking their own situation or circumstance and assuming it has been the church's norm throughout history. When a person has seen something practiced only one way, a kind of mental inertia takes over and roots us in our perspective. When that perspective is right and true, this can be a profound and helpful experience. However, when a perspective is not sufficiently informed by historical facts, Christians can end up arguing for ideas that are false.

This has been the case in many churches regarding the ministry roles of women. An examination of the New Testament read in the context of the earliest historical sources will show that women likely held the office of deaconess in the first century and beyond.

New Testament Roots of the Early Church's Branches

Several New Testament texts indicate that women were prominently involved in various ministries of the earliest church. Acts 21:9 mentions Philip's four daughters, "who prophesied." This identification indicates a general characteristic about these women rather than a onetime action. Luke's account of the early church also mentions Lydia, a woman whose house became a place for believers to worship (Acts 16:40). Paul mentioned Nympha, who also had a church meeting in her house (Col 4:15). Does prophetess count as an "official" ministry position? Were the women whose homes were used for church gatherings merely hostesses of means? The scant textual evidence does not tell us one way or the other, but clearly, women played a vital part even in the basic organization and workings of the church in some places.

The most significant biblical example of a woman in ministry comes from the final chapter of Paul's letter to the church at Rome. Paul began his list of greetings in that chapter with, "I commend to you our sister Phoebe, who is a servant of the church at Cenchreae" (Rom 16:1). The Greek word translated "servant" is *diakonon*, which can also be rendered "deacon," as Paul used it in 1 Tim 3:8–13. Taken on its own, one might perceive ambiguity in the word *diakonon*. However, in the context of the phrase "a *diakonon* of the church," the term becomes much more revealing. The construction "a/the _____ of the church" appears numerous times in the Bible and in early Christian literature. Every time, the word in the blank refers to an office (e.g., deacon) rather than a simple function (e.g., servant). Acts 20:17 mentions "the elders of the church," Eph 5:23 pictures Jesus as "the head of the church," and Jas 5:14 exhorts believers to call for "the elders of the church."[1]

Casting a wider net brings in several more examples from the second century AD. Ignatius of Antioch (c. 35–110), writing in the first decade of the

---

[1]   This construction also occurs several times in Revelation: "the angel of the church" (Rev 2:1, 8, 12, 18; 3: 1, 7, 14). In that case, the "angel" or "messenger" in question is most likely a human representative of the specific church tasked to take Christ's message back to his individual church. In other words, these seven individuals each received a message from the Lord in an official capacity on behalf of his church. See Robert L. Thomas, *Revelation 1–7: An Exegetical Commentary* (Chicago: Moody, 1992), 127–28.

second century, referred to deacons as "ministers of God's church."[2] We also find in the early second-century references to the "the council of presbyters of the church,"[3] "bishop of the Church,"[4] and "bishop of the catholic church in Smyrna,"[5] all of which adopt the same basic formula and refer to office holders in the church. Linguistically, then, the evidence seems to point to the phrase in Rom 16:1 as an official (and apostolic) designation in reference to Phoebe as a deacon.

Fulfilling Specific Needs in the Church

New Testament hints at the possibility of the office of deaconess are greatly strengthened when we look at the on-the-ground situation in the early church. While it may not have been a universal practice, enough evidence exists to suggest deaconesses were not completely out of the norm for orthodox Christianity from its earliest days.

A writing from the late first and early second century called the *Shepherd of Hermas* (c. 90–140) contains the following instructions: "Therefore you will write two little books, and you will send one to Clement and one to Grapte. Then Clement will send it to the cities abroad, because that is his job. But Grapte will instruct the widows and orphans."[6] Early testimony informs us that a man named Clement was a prominent leader of the church of Rome in the late 90s—at the twilight of the apostolic era. One of his responsibilities at that time was to correspond with other churches. At the same time, Grapte (a female) was tasked with instructing "widows and orphans." Later in the *Shepherd of Hermas*, we learn that looking after the widows was a responsibility given to the "deacons."[7] Thus, at the very end of the apostolic period, we have historical evidence of a female deacon, Grapte, functioning in an official capacity in a prominent church (Rome).

Another early testimony of the presence of deaconesses comes from a different region of the church: northern Asia Minor. Around AD 111 (a decade after the apostolic period), a Roman governor, Pliny the Younger, wrote a famous

---

[2]   Ignatius, *Trallians* 2.3 (Holmes, 217). The term for servant there is not the standard one for "deacons," but the context makes it clear that Ignatius was talking about office-holding deacons who serve God's church.

[3]   Ignatius, *Philadelphians* 5.2 (Holmes, 241).

[4]   Ignatius, *Polycarp*, inscription (Holmes, 263).

[5]   *Martyrdom of Polycarp* 16.2 (Holmes, 325).

[6]   *Shepherd of Hermas*, Vision 2.4.3 (Holmes, 469).

[7]   *Shepherd of Hermas*, Similitude 9.26.2 (Holmes, 667).

letter to the emperor Trajan (AD 53–117).[8] In this letter Pliny consulted the emperor regarding the punishment of Christians, the beliefs and practices of whom Pliny had investigated. He claims to have learned details of Christian beliefs and worship by capturing and torturing two female Christians called *ministra* in Latin, a translation of the Greek term for "deaconess." Thus, shortly after the end of the apostolic period, we have additional historical evidence of female deacons in Asia Minor.

Clement of Alexandria (c. 150–215) represents another witness to the ministry of deaconesses in the early church. Ministering and writing for much of his adult life from one of the most significant centers of Christianity in the ancient world, this teacher of Alexandria wrote, "We also know the directions about women deacons which are given by the noble Paul in his second letter to Timothy."[9] This clear reference to "women" in 1 Tim 3:11 offers not only evidence of church practice in Alexandria, but that church leaders were actively rooting their practices in biblical reflection and interpretation.[10]

Another document from the early third century, the *Teaching of the Apostles (Didascalia Apostolorum)*, suggests a practical reason for the presence of female deacons in the church: "Send a Deaconess for many things. The office of a woman Deaconess is required, first, when women go down to the water, it is necessary that they be anointed by a Deaconess."[11] In other words, since baptism involved disrobing, female deacons needed to be present to complete the anointing when a newly baptized woman rose up out of the water. Church leaders who employed female deacons sought to protect the purity and holiness of the baptismal moment.

Turning to the fourth century, Epiphanius, bishop of the church at Salamis on the Mediterranean island of Cyprus, affirmed the office of deaconess. As he said, "It is plain, too, that there is an order of deaconesses in the church. But this is not allowed for the practice of priesthood or any liturgical function, but for the sake of female modesty, at either the time of baptism or of the examination of some condition or trouble, and when a woman's body

---

[8]   *Letter* 10.96, *Plinius Traiano Imperatori.*

[9]   Clement of Alexandria, *Stromata* 3.6. Translation from Henry Chadwick and J. E. L. Oulton, eds., *Alexandrian Christianity: Selected Translations of Clement and Origen*, Library of Christian Classics, Ichthus ed. (Louisville: WJK, 1977), 2:65.

[10]   The CSB (along with the ESV, NET, and KJV) renders the Greek word *gunaikas* as "wives" rather than "women." Other translations choose to translate it as "women" (NASB, NIV, and NLT), or provide "women" as an alternative in a footnote (CSB).

[11]   *Didascalia* 16. Translation from *The Didascalia Apostolorum in English*, ed. and trans. Margaret Dunlop Gibson (Cambridge: Cambridge University Press, 1903), 78.

may be bared."[12] Interestingly, Epiphanius makes this point in contrast to the practice of a heretical Christian sect that he criticizes for embracing too much female leadership. It seems, then, that this bishop recognizes a line within church leadership, but that in the office of the deaconess, there is clearly a space for women.

Another fourth-century document, the *Apostolic Constitutions*, also makes provision for female deacons to baptize women: "Let also the deaconess be honored by you in the place of the Holy Ghost, and not do or say anything without the deacon."[13] Such a passage suggests a developing hierarchy within the diaconate, where men took the lead among all the male and female deacons. Later, the same document calls for women to be appointed as deaconesses and for deaconesses to receive any women coming for baptism.[14]

One final document deserves mention, for rather than an individual or localized perspective, this one stands with the authority of the ancient church alongside some of the most important creedal language in the church's history. Alongside the Nicene Creed, attendees at the council released numerous additional statements or canons. After describing how a group of schismatic Christians can reenter the orthodox, catholic church, one of the canons says, "Likewise in the case of their deaconesses."[15] If the church at that time didn't allow deaconesses, this group of deaconesses would not have been marked out on their own. By mentioning them explicitly, the canon suggests that these women would continue in their role as deaconesses once they returned to the fold of the true church.

Summary of Evidence

The foregoing evidence suggests that by the end of the apostolic age, the church office of deaconess was in existence, having developed throughout the apostolic period and quite possibly established by apostolic authority. Such an office would involve training, testing, and official appointment. It would also involve real responsibility as deacons and deaconesses worked together in assisting the elders in the work of church ministry.

---

[12]   Epiphanius of Salamis, *The Panarion of Epiphanius of Salamis, Books II and III. De Fide*, trans. Frank Williams, 2nd rev. ed. (Leiden: Brill, 2012), 639.
[13]   *Constitutions of the Holy Apostles* 2.4.2, trans. Irah Chase (New York: D. Appleton, 1848), 43.
[14]   *Constitutions of the Holy Apostles*, 90.
[15]   Henry R. Percival, "The Canons of the 318 Holy Fathers Assembled in the City of Nice, in Bithynia," in *The Seven Ecumenical Councils*, ed. Philip Schaff and Henry Wace, A Select Library of the Nicene and Post-Nicene Fathers of the Christian Church (New York: Charles Scribner's Sons, 1900), 14:40.

However, a few caveats are in order. First, although there appears to us to be good evidence in the early church for the presence of deaconesses, there is no evidence for the presence of female elders. Second, the role of deaconesses appears to have been limited to the care of widows and orphans—women and children, but it seems to have included their catechetical instruction, baptism, and discipleship—all under the oversight of the church elders. Similarly, the role of male deacons was also generally limited to the catechesis, baptism, and discipleship of men. Third, early churches appear to have exercised some sensibility regarding the compatibility between a woman's stage of life and her responsibilities for church ministry. Married women in child-rearing years do not appear to have been primary candidates to serve as deaconesses, who tended to be older women—often widows—who in any case had enough time and energy to commit to full-time Christian service. Similarly, unmarried women ("virgins") also engaged in official ministry as "deaconesses." Nevertheless, it is clear that in many places, very early, women held the official ministry position of deaconess in the local churches.

Application

When the early church perceived specific needs for ministry in their midst, they often appointed those best suited—male and female—to the office of deacon/deaconess. Many contemporary churches take a different tack—encouraging men and women to do the work of deacons without giving women the official title. While this could help democratize the work of the ministry and get a wider group of people involved, it has downsides as well. By keeping things unofficial, churches often lack the structure for accountability that comes with an office. This can lead to dangerous situations where people who have not been vetted properly take on the responsibility for delivering spiritual guidance or distributing financial resources.

Furthermore, refusing women any kind of church office can lead us to think about the work of the ministry as the exclusive territory of males. Rather, the witness of the early church suggests that the focus should be on looking for opportunities for all of the church's members to serve the family of God.

Resources

Hübner, Jamin. *A Case for Female Deacons.* Eugene, OR: Wipf and Stock, 2015.
Witherington, Ben, III. *Women in the Earliest Churches.* Cambridge: Cambridge University Press, 1988.

PART II

Urban Legends
of the Medieval Period
(500–1500)

Medieval Church Time Line
(Some of the dates below are approximate.)

570–632: Muhammad

589: Third Council of Toledo

622: Birth of Islam

673–735: Bede the Venerable

675–749: John of Damascus

680–681: Council of Constantinople III

712–766: Chrodegang of Metz

726–842: The Iconoclastic Controversy

742–814: Charlemagne

785–865: Paschasius Radbertus

787: Council of Nicaea II

795–816: Pope Leo III

800: Crowning of Charlemagne

810–893: Photius I of Constantinople

910: Founding of Cluny Monastery

999–1088: Berengar of Tours

1000–1059: Michael Keroularios

1000–1061: Cardinal Humbert

1002–1054: Pope Leo IX

1020–1085: Pope Gregory VII

1033–1109: Anselm of Canterbury

1054: Great Schism between East and West

1079–1142: Peter Abelard

1090–1153: Bernard of Clairvaux

1096–1141: Hugh of St. Victor

1098: Founding of monastery at Citeau

1100–1160: Peter Lombard

1140–1205: Peter Waldo

1150–1241: Pope Gregory IX

1160–1216: Pope Innocent III

1181–1226: Francis of Assisi

1215: Fourth Lateran Council

1225–1274: Thomas Aquinas

1244–1334: Pope John XXII

1250–1307: Fra Dolcino

1272–1274: Second Council of Lyons

1288–1348: William of Ockham

1290–1349: Thomas Bradwardine

1300–1358: Gregory of Rimini

1300–1700: Renaissance Period

1325–1384: John Wycliffe

1340–1384: Gerard Groote

1347–1380: Catherine of Siena

1369–1415: John Huss

1383–1447: Pope Eugenius IV

1383–1471: Thomas à Kempis

1405–1464: Pope Pius II

1412–1431: Joan of Arc

1414–1417: Council of Constance

1420–1495: Gabriel Biel

1447–1510: Catherine of Genoa

1450: Printing press invented

1452–1498: Girolamo Savonarola

1478: Spanish Inquisition begun

CHAPTER 11

Nothing Good Came from the "Dark Ages"

The Legendary Story

Shortly after the golden age of the early church, between about 100 and 500, a disease set in that eventually brought the church to its deathbed. Because of its close relationship with the state, the Roman Catholic Church defected in both doctrine and practice. The pure, simple devotion to Christ that had been exemplified by the blood of the martyrs gave way to a deep-seated decadence and dogmatism that decimated Christianity until the Reformation. For centuries, the church of the Middle Ages had no spiritual vitality, rendering most of this period uninspiring and useless. Thus, nothing good, nothing worthy of praise, and certainly nothing but bad examples can be seen during the Middle Ages. It's probably just best to skip it altogether and jump from the early church to Martin Luther.

Introduction: Unraveling the Legend

Though the period between 500 and 1500 certainly saw its share of dark and disturbing moments, we must not overlook a number of examples of faithfulness and fruitfulness during this period. When corruption set in, men and women pushed for reform. When doctrinal deviation occurred, reformers spoke out. When wickedness and sin stained church and society, preachers called for repentance. All the while, remnants of true believers strove to maintain purity and piety in the midst of turbulent events. One author rightly notes that though many have called the Middle Ages an era of darkness, "in this period the church of Christ was ever endeavoring to lift a light which the darkness did not overcome."[1]

Post Tenebras Lux!

In a peaceful corner on the grounds of the University of Geneva in Switzerland stands a monument to the Reformation known as the "Reformation Wall." The wall features statues of prominent figures of the Reformation, including William Farel (1489–1565), John Calvin (1509–1564), Theodore Beza (1519–1605), and John Knox (1513–1572). Engraved in the wall, flanking these four individuals on either side, is the motto of the Reformation: *POST TENEBRAS LUX*—"After Darkness, Light!" This Latin phrase illustrates perfectly the typical Protestant perception of most—if not all—of the Middle Ages.

The typical picture of the medieval period, often dubbed the "Dark Ages," comprises deterioration, corruption, ignorance, brutality, poverty, disease, and a spiritual blindness among church leaders and members alike. Modern Protestant evangelicals sometimes portray Christendom between the years 500 and 1500 as having nothing positive to offer. Dead dogmatism, coupled with tepid traditionalism, led to a severely ill bride of Christ devoid of true spiritual life and devotion.

Is this an accurate characterization of the medieval period? Did nothing good come from these allegedly godforsaken centuries?

Shedding Light on the "Dark Ages"

Characterization of the medieval period as the "Dark Ages" began about the time of the Renaissance (1300–1700), when scholars viewed the flourishing of art, literature, and architecture in the classical Roman and Greek periods as "bright" compared to the decline in culture and learning in the West after the fall of Rome. One historian of the Middle Ages notes, "People spoke of a dark time because of the sins of humankind, in particular of Christians, and especially of the clergy," while "the Renaissance became an identification with classical antiquity and in part also with Christian antiquity."[2] Nostalgia for

---

[1]   George E. McCracken, "General Introduction," in *Early Medieval Theology*, ed. George E. McCracken and Allen Cabaniss, The Library of Christian Classics, repr. (Louisville: WJK, 2006), 15.

[2]   Adriaan H. Bredero, *Christendom and Christianity in the Middle Ages: The Relations between Religion, Church, and Society*, trans. Reinder Bruinsma (Grand Rapids: Eerdmans, 1994), 72–73.

a brighter "golden age" of the forgotten past began a process of retrieval and reform that eventually led to the Reformation.

Certainly things had gone wrong since the early church. Even Roman Catholic scholars, who believe the Reformation was a "revolt" against the true church, admit this. Catholic historian Philip Hughes recounts several "abuses," "evils," "shortcomings," and "scandals," concluding that "the period 1270–1517 is, then, one of steady decline."[3] Bernard of Clairvaux's "denunciation of the church as a 'den of thieves,'" church historian Jaroslav Pelikan noted, "found many echoes in this period."[4]

Yet along with critics of the Catholic Church came attempts to restore or preserve doctrinal and practical purity. Let's survey a few positive points of light shining in the medieval period that not only kept alive authentic faith, hope, and love during those centuries but also may serve as inspiring examples for us.

The Carolingian Renaissance and Beyond

The crowning of Charlemagne (742–814), or "Charles the Great," in the year 800 is often bedeviled as a sign of the disastrous wedding of church and state that sent the Roman Catholic Church in a trajectory of disaster. However, the Holy Roman Empire and the Carolingian dynasty (named after "Carol," a variation of "Charles") ushered in a number of positive reforms. To combat corruption in the churches, Charlemagne enacted many far-reaching reforms affecting the training and behavior of the clergy.[5] He also urged that priests should teach children to read and write for free, believing that an educated citizenry was a blessing to the state and the church.[6] Many of the Carolingian reforms continued to influence the church and society for generations.

Regarding the period between 1050 and 1300, R. W. Southern notes, "It was above all an age of rational and coherent advance. . . . We can observe this in law, natural science, and in the practical art of government no less than in theology and philosophy; and the great artistic achievements of the age are a

---

[3]   Philip Hughes, *A Popular History of the Catholic Church* (Garden City, NY: Image Books, 1954), 134.

[4]   Jaroslav Pelikan, *The Christian Tradition: A History of the Development of Doctrine*, vol. 4, *Reformation of Church and Dogma (1300–1700)* (Chicago: University of Chicago Press, 1984), 87.

[5]   Margaret Deanesly, *A History of the Medieval Church 590–1500*, 9th corr. ed. (London: Routledge, 1972), 58–59.

[6]   Deanesly, 60–61.

reflection of the same confident spirit."[7] The generally stable social order established during this period bettered the lives of common people. And advances in academics, theology, philosophy, art, and architecture contributed to this stability. These positive elements of medieval society both benefited from and provided a safe haven for religious devotion in the Middle Ages.

Medieval Spirituality

Because common people generally did not keep written journals, we have very few windows into the spiritual and religious life of everyday men and women in the Middle Ages. However, numerous centers of religious devotion emerged in this period, a fact we should not quickly dismiss. Southern notes, "Turn where we will in the later Middle Ages, we find towns and countryside sprinkled with communities of *religiosi* of many different kinds," which "reflect the society from which they sprang."[8]

The kind of spiritual life that characterized these movements is usually called "mysticism," though medieval mysticism isn't the same as modern esoteric occultism typical of Far Eastern religions or new age religion. Jeffrey Bingham explains: "The mysticism of the Middle Ages was a quest for a deeper, more authentic devotional life." Mystics in that period were known for "withdrawing from the public arena and concentrating instead on inner reflection, morality and a simple life."[9]

Monastic communities in particular served many purposes, but one of their major emphases was prayer, especially prayer as a form of spiritual warfare against Satan and his kingdom on behalf of society. Of course, even monasteries were subject to corruption and decay, simply because they were human institutions. Yet when such degeneration did occur, reform movements often followed, either rousing existing communities to devotion or establishing new communities that would take their commitments to prayer and service more seriously.

Orders of traveling friars also contributed to the spiritual revitalization of many sectors of Christian society. Some of these were itinerant preachers who called men and women to conversion, commitment, and a higher spiri-

---

[7]   R. W. Southern, *Western Society and the Church in the Middle Ages*, Penguin History of the Church (New York: Penguin, 1970), 2:42.

[8]   Southern, 214–15.

[9]   D. Jeffrey Bingham, *Pocket History of the Church* (Downers Grove, IL: InterVarsity Press, 2002), 104.

tual life.[10] Groups dedicated to spiritual revitalization sprang from the soils of medieval Europe to reinforce simple devotion to Jesus. One of these was the Brethren of the Common Life, founded by Gerard Groote (1340–1384), who, after a "conversion experience," urged men and women to a simple life of devotion.[11]

MINI MYTHS

"The Roman Catholic Church Once Had a Female Pope"

The legend of "Pope Joan" involves a brilliant woman who disguises herself as a man, distinguishes herself in the study of theology, enters the priesthood, and eventually rises to become pope in the ninth century. After only two years, she gives birth to a child in the midst of a procession in the streets of Rome and dies shortly thereafter. Though some have attempted to defend the story either to point out the scandalous nature of the papacy or the precedent for female clergy, the story is almost certainly a myth. The first actual accounts of Pope Joan appear four centuries after the alleged events, and details of the accounts vary considerably and become more embellished with the telling. Thus, it's almost certainly a fanciful fiction.[12]

Early Protest and Reform Movements

In the late medieval period (1000–1500), as the general health of the church steadily declined, numerous scholars and preachers cried foul and attempted to set the church on the right path. These included university professors, priests, and lay preachers such as Peter Waldo (c. 1140–1205), Thomas Bradwardine (c. 1290–1349), Gregory of Rimini (c. 1300–1358), John Wycliffe (1325–1384), John Huss (1369–1415), and William Savanarola

---

10   Southern, *Western Society and the Church*, 273–74.
11   See Albert Hyma, *The Brethren of the Common Life* (Grand Rapids: Eerdmans, 1950).
12   See Alain Boureau, *The Myth of Pope Joan* (Chicago: University of Chicago Press, 2001).

(1452–1498).[13] The fact that so many noticed problems in the doctrines and practices of the church indicates that a remnant of "true believers" always remained, even if their voices were sometimes silenced or their messages unheard.

The reality is that the Protestant Reformation, often believed to have been ignited single-handedly in 1517 by Martin Luther (1483–1546), culminated centuries of medieval revival and reform movements that had been slowly simmering throughout the Middle Ages. Martin Luther himself had been an Augustinian monk and university professor, taught at a young age by a school run by the Brethren of the Common Life, and influenced by currents of German medieval mysticism. Those roots bore fruit especially in his conversion experience and his belief in a personal relationship with God.

A Balanced View of the Middle Ages

Rather than viewing the entire period from about 500 to 1500 as a dark and decrepit alley of church history best avoided, it would be better to see the period as a long country road of varying quality. At times we experience pitfalls, potholes, rough patches, sudden turns, and certainly ups and downs. It would be safe to say that one experiences a general decline in overall quality on the medieval road, though the route is never so bad that it can't serve as a faithful thoroughfare between the early church and the Reformation.

Instead of viewing the medieval period as the "Dark Ages," then, it would be best to view those centuries as sometimes brighter, sometimes dimmer, but never without guiding lights to shine on the way (see chapter 14). Perhaps Bingham puts it best:

> People in the Middle Ages were faced with the problems that can occur when a "Christian culture" is confused with conversion of the heart, when institutions and hierarchies are confused with church and leadership, and when theology is of concern to the clergy but not the laity. But in the Middle Ages we can also gaze on brilliant

---

[13] See Justo L. Gonzalez, *Church History: An Essential Guide* (Nashville: Abingdon, 1996), 63–64; John D. Hannah, *Invitation to Church History: World*, Invitation to Theological Studies (Grand Rapids: Kregel, 2018), 255–63; Stephen Lahey, "Wyclif and Lollardy," in *The Medieval Theologians: An Introduction to Theology in the Medieval Period*, ed. G. R. Evans (Oxford: Blackwell, 2001), 334–54.

examples of Christian leadership, prayer, the right use of the mind and the practice of the devotional life.[14]

Application

Nobody believes the centuries between 500 and 150 were pure gold. As in every era, the church of the Middle Ages had its share of severe problems. Yet to neglect legitimate contributions to theology and spirituality during this time would be to turn up our noses at vital insights and to condemn the genuine faith and faithfulness of true brothers and sisters in Christ. Yes, Protestants can learn important lessons even from the voices of the Middle Ages.

It is also important to recognize that even in the midst of spiritual decline and corruption, God preserves his remnant. Never is the world left without a witness to the gospel preached and lived. This is true in the universal church as well as at the local church level. As we see our own local churches go through a decline toward spiritual malaise, look for the elements of spiritual vitality that haven't succumbed. And even when we experience the harmful effects of worldliness or corruption in our churches, align with those who still carry the torch of truth to shine light in the growing darkness.

Resources

Deanesly, Margaret. *A History of the Medieval Church 590–1500*. 9th corr. ed. London: Routledge, 1972.

Pelikan, Jaroslav. *The Christian Tradition: A History of the Development of Doctrine*. Vol. 2, *The Spirit of Eastern Christendom (600–1700)*. Chicago: University of Chicago Press, 1974.

———. *The Christian Tradition: A History of the Development of Doctrine*. Vol. 3, *The Growth of Medieval Theology (600–1300)*. Chicago: University of Chicago Press, 1978.

Southern, R. W. *Western Society and the Church in the Middle Ages*. Penguin History of the Church. Vol. 2. New York: Penguin, 1970.

---

[14] Bingham, *Pocket History of the Church*, 62.

CHAPTER 12

The Substitutionary Atonement First Appeared in the Middle Ages

The Legendary Story

Anselm of Canterbury (1033–1109) was the first person to articulate substitutionary atonement. His writing *Cur Deus Homo* (*Why God Became Man*) originally voiced the doctrine that Christ suffered and died as a penal substitute for sinners. Until that time, earlier church fathers and medieval theologians held to the *Christus Victor* ("Christ as Victor") theory or some other nonpenal substitutionary view of the atonement.

Introduction: Unraveling the Legend

Substitution—and even penal substitution—is one of several explanations of the atonement that go all the way back to the earliest centuries of the church. These various explanations were not mutually exclusive. Christians often held and taught several explanations simultaneously in a holistic approach to the work of Christ. Amid this diversity of explanations, numerous Fathers and theologians of the early church and medieval period refer to Christ's death as a sacrificial substitute, by which he experienced the penalty of death in place of sinners.

Mystery of the Atonement

Early in my teaching career, as I (Mike) was sitting in my office on campus with the door propped open, I overheard a conversation between two students as they passed. One line that I caught midsentence jarred me: ". . . church didn't teach the doctrine of penal substitution until Anselm of Canterbury . . ." Since then I have heard the same type of claim from various sources.

For example, one contributor to a popular website for converts to Eastern Orthodoxy argues, "Penal Substitution has its origin in Anselm of Canterbury. . . . His seminal work, *Cur Deus Homo*, expressed for the first time in the history of the church the Satisfaction Theory of the Atonement."[1] The same writer points to this historical "fact" as a major influence in his own road to Orthodoxy: "If in 1,000 years no Christian had held to this model of the atonement, how could I believe it was the true gospel? . . . How could an entire millennium of Christians have been so wrong?"[2]

A bit more nuanced, but still misleading approach goes like this: "This doctrine of substitutionary atonement, articulated most clearly in the late eleventh century by Anselm of Canterbury, became the dominant doctrine of atonement adopted by the church by the end of the Middle Ages."[3] Though the author says Anselm "most clearly" articulated substitutionary atonement, statements like this can make it sound as if the whole notion of substitution had only a fuzzy or unclear history before the work of Anselm. (Anselm's view of the atonement is actually regarded as "satisfaction," which we explain more clearly in chapter 18.)

So, what had Christians allegedly believed instead of penal substitution-ary atonement? Most critics point to something called the *Christus Victor* model, classically articulated in 1931 by Gustaf Aulén. He suggested, "It is the dominant idea of the Atonement throughout the early church period," which "was gradually ousted from its place in the theological teaching of the church."[4] Simply put, the *Christus Victor* theory emphasizes Christ's victory over (and thus believers' liberation from) sin, Satan, and death through his person and work.

---

[1] Matt Ferdelman, "Why I'm Becoming Orthodox: Part 2 of 3," *Journey to Orthodoxy* (blog), December 29, 2014, https://journeytoorthodoxy.com/2014/12/why-im-becoming-orthodox-2-of-3/.

[2] Ferdelman.

[3] Pamela Cooper-White, "Suffering," in *The Wiley-Blackwell Companion to Practical Theology*, ed. Bonnie J. Miller-McLemore (Oxford: Blackwell, 2012), 28.

[4] Gustaf Aulén, *Christus Victor: An Historical Study of the Three Main Types of the Idea of Atonement*, trans. A. G. Herbert (London: SPCK, 1931; Eugene, OR: Wipf and Stock, 2003), 6. Citations refer to the Wipf and Stock edition.

Substitution before Anselm

The idea that Christ's death paid the debt of sin owed by humanity was present throughout the patristic period. In fact, "typically Anselmian concepts, such as satisfaction and a concept of sin as debt, were already well developed in Athanasius."[5] You don't have to take my word for it. Consider the following quotations spanning several centuries up to the time of Anselm, from influential Christians of both the Eastern and Western churches:

Clement of Rome (c. AD 95): "On account of the Love he bore for us, Jesus Christ our Lord gave His blood for us by the will of God; His flesh for our flesh, and His soul for our souls."[6]

Epistle to Diognetus (c. 160): "He Himself took on Him the burden of our iniquities, He gave His own Son as a ransom for us, the holy One for transgressors, the blameless One for the wicked, the righteous One for the unrighteous, the incorruptible One for the corruptible, the immortal One for them that are mortal. For what other thing was capable of covering our sins than His righteousness? By what other one was it possible that we, the wicked and ungodly, could be justified, than by the only Son of God? O sweet exchange! O unsearchable operation! O benefits surpassing all expectation! That the wickedness of many should be hid in a single righteous One, and that the righteousness of One should justify many transgressors."[7]

Irenaeus of Lyons (c. 180): "Redeeming us by His own blood in a manner consonant to reason, He gave Himself as a redemption for those who had been led into captivity. . . . The Lord thus has redeemed us from His own blood, giving His soul for our souls, and His flesh for our flesh."[8]

Tertullian of Carthage (c. 208): "That you should ransom with money a man whom Christ has ransomed with His blood, how unworthy is it of God and His ways of acting, who spared not His own Son for you, that He might be made a curse for us, because cursed is he that hangeth on a tree,—Him who was . . . delivered up to death, nay, the death of the cross. All this took place that He might redeem us from our sins."[9]

---

[5]   Ben Pugh, *Atonement Theories: A Way through the Maze* (Eugene, OR: Cascade Books, 2014), 51.
[6]   *1 Clement* 49 (ANF 1:18).
[7]   *Epistle to Diognetus* 9 (ANF 1:28).
[8]   Irenaeus, *Against Heresies* 5.1.1 (ANF 1:527).
[9]   Tertullian, *De Fuga in Persecutione* 12 (ANF 4:123).

Athanasius of Alexandria (c. 318): "And thus taking from our bodies one of like nature, because all were under penalty of the corruption of death He gave it over to death in the stead of all, and offered it to the Father."[10]

John Chrysostom (c. 390): "And what hath He done? 'Him that knew no sin He made to be sin, for you.' For had He achieved nothing but done only this, think how great a thing it were to give His Son for those that had outraged Him. But now He hath both well achieved mighty things, and besides, hath suffered Him that did no wrong to be punished for those who had done wrong. But he did not say this: but mentioned that which is far greater than this. What then is this? 'Him that knew no sin,' he says, Him that was righteousness itself, 'He made sin,' that is suffered as a sinner to be condemned, as one cursed to die. 'For cursed is he that hangeth on a tree.' (Gal. iii. 13.)"[11]

Augustine of Hippo (c. 420): "This same death of ours, which had originated in sin, He had taken upon Himself, and hung on the Tree. . . . He shows then that the Son of God died a true death, the death which was due to mortal flesh: lest if He were not 'accursed,' you should think that He had not truly died. But since that death was not an illusion, but had descended from that original stock, which had been derived from the curse, when He said, 'Ye shall surely die:' and since a true death assuredly extended even to Him, that a true life might extend itself to us, the curse of death also did extend to Him, that the blessing of life might extend even unto us."[12]

Leo the Great (c. 450): "Weakness and mortality, which were not sin, but the penalty of sin, were undergone by the Redeemer of the World in the way of punishment, that they might be reckoned as the price of redemption. What therefore in all of us is the heritage of condemnation, is in Christ 'the mystery of godliness.' For being free from debt, He gave Himself up to that most cruel creditor."[13]

John of Damascus (c. 740): "Since our Lord Jesus Christ was without sin . . . He was not subject to death, since death came into the world through sin. He dies, therefore, because He took on Himself death on our behalf, and He makes Himself an offering to the Father for our sakes."[14]

---

10   Athanasius, *On the Incarnation* 8.4 (NPNF 2.4:40).
11   John Chrysostom, *Homilies on 2 Corinthians* 11.5 (NPNF 1.12:333).
12   Augustine, *Exposition on the Psalms* 38.25 (NPNF 1.8:111).
13   Leo the Great, *Sermons* 72.2 (NPNF 2.12:184–85).
14   John of Damascus, *An Exact Exposition of the Orthodox Faith* 27 (NPNF 2.9:72).

The Place of Penal Substitution

Anselm of Canterbury was not the first theologian to suggest that Christ died in our place to accomplish for us what we could not accomplish for ourselves. However, though substitution appears to be a recurring theme when church fathers describe the "how" of the atonement, *penal* substitution isn't the only explanation presented in the writings of the church. The great historian of the early church, J. N. D. Kelly, summarizes three tendencies in the patristic period:

> First, there was the so-called "physical" or "mystical" theory . . . which linked the redemption with the incarnation. According to this, human nature was sanctified, transformed and elevated by the very act of Christ's becoming man. . . . Secondly, there was the explanation of the redemption in terms of a ransom offered to, or a forfeit imposed on, the Devil. . . . Thirdly, there was the theory, often designated "realist," which directed attention to the Savior's sufferings. Making more of sin and the punishment due for it than of its tragic legacy, this placed the cross in the foreground, and pictured Christ as substituting Himself for sinful men, shouldering the penalty which justice required them to pay, and reconciling them to God by His sacrificial death.[15]

Substitution was one of several explanations of how Christ's death on the cross saves us. Again, Kelly provides important insight here: "These various theories . . . should not be regarded as in fact mutually incompatible. They were all of them attempts to elucidate the same great truth from different angles."[16]

It should also be noted that Anselm's purpose in *Cur Deus Homo* was not to make a case for substitutionary atonement per se, but to present a rational argument for the necessity of the incarnation without appealing to divine revelation in Scripture. When he relied on the argument that God's honor must be satisfied by the payment of a debt (the honor owed to God by humans), Anselm did so in order to show that the one who paid the price for atonement had to be the God-man: "For God will not do it, because he has no debt to pay; and man will not do it, because he cannot. Therefore, in order that the God-man may perform this, it is necessary that the same being should be perfect God and perfect man, in order to make

---

[15] J. N. D. Kelly, *Early Christian Doctrines*, 5th rev. ed. (New York: HarperOne, 1978), 375–76.
[16] Kelly, 376.

this atonement."[17] Anselm's writing on the atonement is rightly honored as a classic work of theology for its unique clarity and apologetic value. But he was not the first proponent of substitutionary atonement.

Application

The apostle Peter wrote, "For Christ also suffered for sins once for all, the righteous for the unrighteous, that he might bring you to God" (1 Pet 3:18). And the apostle Paul wrote, "He made the one who did not know sin to be sin for us, so that in him we might become the righteousness of God" (2 Cor 5:21). For centuries Christians understood that the death of Christ accomplished substitutionary atonement—that Christ died in the place of sinful humanity, paying the price of sin on our behalf, that is, death. This wasn't a late medieval, Protestant, or modern invention, but a view that can be traced throughout the history of the church.

However, it's important for us to remember that substitutionary atonement is an *explanation of how Christ's death saves us*. It is not itself the object of saving faith. To be saved, we must accept the message of the gospel—who Jesus is and what he has done for us. He is the God-man who died for our sins and rose from the dead. We must accept the revealed fact *that* Christ's death saves us; we do not have to comprehend exactly *how* it saves us. In any case, substitutionary atonement is a biblically, theologically, and historically sound answer to the "how" question. It's an explanation for the atonement that enjoys a long history in the church. Yet it isn't the only description of what Christ's death accomplishes for us. We should not reject it; nor should we reduce the work of Christ merely to his functioning as a stand-in. It is much more than that.

Resources

Allison, Gregg. "A History of the Doctrine of the Atonement." *Southern Baptist Journal of Theology* 11, no. 2 (Summer 2007): 4–19.
Johnson, Junius. *Patristic and Medieval Atonement Theory: A Guide to Research*. Lanham, MD: Rowman & Littlefield, 2016.
Vlach, Michael. "Penal Substitution in Church History." *Masters Seminary Journal* 20, no. 2 (Fall 2009): 199–214.

---

[17] Anselm of Canterbury, *Cur Deus Homo* 1.3, trans. Sidney Norton Deane, in *St. Anselm: Proslogium; Monologium; An Appendix in Behalf of the Fool by Gaunilon; and Cur Deus Homo*, repr. ed. (Chicago: Open Court, 1926), 246.

CHAPTER 13

The Roman Catholic Church Ruled Europe with Uniformity

The Legendary Story

As the Roman Empire crumbled at the end of the fifth century, a diverse group of smaller rulers and principalities developed in Europe. Into this situation of competing interests stepped a unified institution—the Roman Catholic Church. The Catholic Church spoke into every area of people's lives. As the centuries rolled on, the papacy grew so strong that the Holy Roman emperor—a political ruler over a wide swath of Europe—was expected to submit to the authority of the pope. In turn, the singularity of the Roman Catholic Church brought stability—political, cultural, intellectual—to the budding nation-states of Europe. None of this would have happened had the Roman Catholic Church not been a unified, well-defined, and well-run institution that exercised steel-fisted control over European life, culture, and thought.

Introduction: Unraveling the Legend

Without a doubt, the Roman Catholic Church carried the outward appearance of unity. Despite earlier breaks with the Coptic Church (after Chalcedon in AD 451) and the Eastern Orthodox churches in 1054, the Roman Catholic Church continued to position itself as the singular ecclesiastical entity in the world. A single hierarchical structure of leadership, with the pope at its head, contributed to this idea.

However, the church of the Middle Ages—whether the Roman Catholic Church in the West or Eastern Orthodoxy in the East—was a diverse collection of groups and individuals, with differing theological positions and practices. Despite Roman Catholic attempts at instituting uniformity, the diversity eventually broke free from ecclesiastical structures in the form of the Protestant Reformation. Therefore, "the stereotype that the Roman Catholic Church had emerged from the Middle Ages" as "a monolithic and corrupt institution" that only became more so after the Reformation stands as an inaccurate portrait of medieval Catholic faith and practice.[1]

Worship Wars

Christians have been wrestling with the nature of communal worship for almost as long as the church has been around. Throughout much of the church's history, she has practiced liturgy, a term that refers to a particular form of public worship. When it comes to liturgies of the early Middle Ages, there was "a diversity of practice across Europe."[2]

During this period, as churches in the former Roman Empire became increasingly linked together and dependent on guidance and direction from the bishop of Rome, church leaders made a number of attempts to bring uniformity to the church's liturgy. One of the earliest was made by Chrodegang (712–766), bishop of the city of Metz in the kingdom of the Franks (modern-day eastern France). Deeply impressed by a visit to Rome, Chrodegang brought Gregorian chant into the Frankish churches. He also wanted Frankish churches to imitate the liturgy of the church at Rome. To that end he developed a series of prescriptions, called the *Rule of Chrodegang*, which gave directions on life and corporate worship to the priests and monks under his purview.[3] Assessing the impact of Chrodegang on the church's liturgy, Julia Barrow argues, "Chrodegang's influence on ecclesiastical institutions in the Carolingian and post-Carolingian period was

---

[1]   J. Michael Hayden, *The Catholicisms of Coutances: Varieties of Religion in Early Modern France, 1350–1789*, McGill-Queen's Studies in the History of Religion 63 (Montreal: McGill-Queen's University Press, 2013), 12.

[2]   Nicholas Bell, "Liturgy," in *The Routledge History of Medieval Christianity: 1050–1500*, ed. R. N. Swanson (London: Routledge, 2015), 126.

[3]   Jerome Bertram, ed. and trans., *The Chrodegang Rules* (London: Routledge, 2017).

profound, not so much because of his own Rule, which only had a very narrow circulation, as because of the Rules which were created from it or in imitation of it."[4] The impulse toward liturgical uniformity grew strong as the profile of Rome and the authority of the papacy continued to grow throughout the Middle Ages.

In line with the efforts of Chrodegang, the Holy Roman Emperor Charlemagne (742–814) "sought to impose political and theological uniformity across his expansive realm."[5] Charlemagne's vast political power allowed him to communicate his desires far and wide. However, he could not easily or successfully institute uniformity. Instead, as the Roman liturgy (called the Roman Rite) became common across Europe, the way people practiced the liturgy varied considerably.[6]

One innovation that eventually came into the church's worship caused consternation among many traditional-minded people: polyphonic music. Gregorian chant, a form of music that had long been incorporated into medieval liturgy, was monophonic—following a single musical line, and using only voices. Eventually, the harmonies of polyphonic music found their way into the church.

In 1324, Pope John XXII (1244–1334) issued a decretal (the fancy papal word for "decree" or "order") on the subject of music called *Docta Sanctorum Patrum (Teaching of the Holy Fathers)*. In the statement, the pope criticized certain polyphonic (melody plus harmony) compositions, and the musicians who played them, for "running without pausing." Instead of promoting devotion, John said, these composers prevented it by creating a "sensuous atmosphere."[7] While later popes eventually allowed the practice of polyphonic music, conflict clearly existed, leading to an undeniable diversity in the worship of the medieval church.

---

[4]　Julia Barrow, "Review Article: Chrodegang, His Rule and Its Successors," *Early Medieval Europe* 14.2 (2006): 205

[5]　Bell, "Liturgy," 126.

[6]　Bell, 126.

[7]　Bryan R. Simms and Craig M. Wright, *Music in Western Civilization* (Stamford, CT: Thomson, 2006).

MINI MYTHS

"Peter was the First Pope"

Though the apostle Peter was almost certainly executed in Rome around the year AD 67, it is almost impossible that he ever served as the first "bishop of Rome," let alone the first "pope" of the Roman Catholic Church. It is plausible that he appointed leadership in the church of Rome toward the end of his life, though throughout the first century, church leadership in Rome appears to have consisted of a plurality of elders, perhaps with a "presiding elder" similar to a modern-day senior pastor. The idea that the bishop of Rome was also the bishop of the whole church universal was a much later development in history—and one never actually embraced by the Eastern Orthodox Churches.[8]

Diverse Doctrine

At the heart of every significant doctrinal difference in the medieval Catholic Church was a disagreement on the proper interpretation of Scripture. In this, contemporary Christians are not far from our forebears. The Bible was at the center of reflection for most medieval Catholic theologians, but they also felt the impulse to systematize their findings, drawing on the interpretive insights of earlier commentators and theologians.

While the Christianity of Europe was dominated by the Roman Catholic Church, European Christians held diverse beliefs on a number of significant issues. One prominent myth of the medieval era suggests that popes reigned with unchecked power and received unchecked devotion from the legions of European Catholics. While medieval popes were undeniably powerful, the reality is much more complex. One scholar notes, "Popes did not enjoy their supremacy over history without near constant competition and criticism."[9]

---

[8]   See George E. Demacopoulos, *The Invention of Peter: Apostolic Discourse and Papal Authority in Late Antiquity* (Philadelphia: University of Pennsylvania Press, 2013).

[9]   Brett Edward Whalen, "The Papacy," in *The Routledge History of Medieval Christianity: 1050–1500*, ed. R. N. Swanson (London: Routledge, 2015), 6.

Diverse views of the papacy were impossible to ignore then; we shouldn't ignore them now.

One of the great challenges to papal power in the medieval era came in the form of a movement called *conciliarism*. This group grew in adherents and power from the twelfth through the fifteenth centuries, believing that matters of faith and practice should ultimately be decided not just by one man in the privacy of his study or by a pope *ex cathedra*, but by a plurality of leadership at meetings called ecumenical councils.[10] The Council of Constance (1414–1417) issued a strong conciliar statement, recognizing that any council "has its power immediately from Christ, and every one, whatever his state or position, even if it be the Papal dignity itself, is bound to obey it in all those things which pertain to the faith."[11]

Unfortunately for the conciliarists, their designs failed when, at the Council of Basel (1439), they elected a second pope because of their disagreements with the existing pope, Eugenius IV (1383–1447). The problem? Conciliarists believed in plurality of leadership precisely to avoid having multiple popes elected by small splinter groups of cardinals (Roman Catholic officeholders responsible for electing each new pope). When the conciliarists elected a second pope themselves, they broke one of their core principles, which led to a loss of support churchwide. Eventually, in 1460, Pope Pius II (1405–1464) issued a papal bull (or decree) that "condemned the notion that councils were superior to the papacy."[12]

Another doctrinal difference that marked the medieval church involved a theologian named Berengar of Tours (999–1088). He found himself at the center of controversy in 1050 when he wrote a letter affirming a "memorial" view of the Eucharist (Lord's Supper)—that the bread and wine were merely figures or symbols of Christ's body and blood. By this time, the memorial interpretation had been floating around the church for about 200 years,[13] but had, during that time, been overshadowed by the more popular view: the bread and wine

---

[10]   Much of the energy behind this conciliar movement stemmed from opposition to an untenable situation with the popes of the late fourteenth and early fifteenth centuries, when, for about fifty years, there were two—and eventually three—men claiming the title of pope. Many of those who elected popes in the church—officeholders called cardinals—believed the best way to resolve this conflict was to give more power to a plurality of leaders.

[11]   Kevin Madigan, *Medieval Christianity: A New History* (New Haven: Yale University Press, 2015), 380.

[12]   Madigan, 385.

[13]   This memorial view goes back at least as far as John Scotus Erigena, who appeared on the historical scene around AD 850. The mainstream view of the Roman Catholic Church that the bread and wine transform into the body and blood of Jesus was most famously proposed by Paschasius Radbertus (785–865) in his work *The Body and Blood of the Lord* (831).

actually transformed into the body and blood of Jesus. The issue remained a contentious one for much of the next two centuries, with a number of writings against Berengar's position, before the current Roman Catholic view of transubstantiation was codified at the Fourth Lateran Council (1215).

Reformation on the Horizon

Despite the efforts of many throughout the medieval period, the church could never shake the diversity of belief and practice from its ranks. As Gary Macy has written, the church is "better described as a set of common traditions rather than as an institutional monolith."[14] Those traditions united churches throughout Europe in a broad sense. But differences in applying the specifics ensured a decided lack of uniformity throughout Europe. That diversity of specific views and practices within an outward hierarchy eventually boiled over into what we know as the Reformation.

Application

Thinking of the medieval church as a singular entity with theological agreement and homogenous worship does not line up with the historical facts. Ironically, in many evangelical communities and denominations today, the goal seems to be to re-create a version of this mythological medieval church, a place where everyone agrees on everything and where unity equals uniformity. This has never been the reality in—or the goal for—the church.

Even the church of Acts, the church run by the apostles themselves, suffered from disagreements—think, for example, of Paul and Barnabas disagreeing over John Mark (Acts 15:36–41). The Roman Catholic Church's attempt to enforce doctrinal uniformity in the medieval period should serve as a cautionary tale for believers today. Not only did the Catholic Church fail to achieve the goal of uniformity, but even in making the attempt, the Catholic Church turned away from its historic roots. From the earliest days of the church's life, diversity of practices and ideas around a common belief in the person and work of Jesus was the norm.

A corresponding lesson concerns our response to controversy and disagreement. The church's attempt to establish an ever-growing set of doctrines

---

[14] Gary Macy, "Was There a 'the Church'?" in *Unity and Diversity in the Church*, Studies in Church History 32, ed. R. N. Swanson (Oxford: Blackwell, 1996), 107.

and practices that identified what it meant to be truly Christian left many faithful believers in the person and work of Jesus on the outside. The church needs a clear distinction between her core dogma that makes God's people identifiably Christian and all other doctrine and practice, which, while interesting and sometimes even important, should never be used to exclude people from the church.

Resources

Bredero, Adriaan Hendrik. *Christendom and Christianity in the Middle Ages: The Relations between Religion, Church, and Society.* Translated by Reinder Bruinsma. Grand Rapids: Eerdmans, 1994.

Cannon, William Ragsdale. *History of Christianity in the Middle Ages.* Reprint. Grand Rapids: Baker, 1983.

Madigan, Kevin. *Medieval Christianity: A New History.* New Haven, CT: Yale University Press, 2015.

CHAPTER 14

The Christian Faith Was Lost during the Middle Ages

The Legendary Story

During the period known as the "Dark Ages," the bright light of Christian truth flickered and dimmed. As the Catholic Church increasingly turned inward on itself to strengthen its growing political power, the Catholic Church's grasp on the true gospel weakened. The Catholic Church of the Dark Ages gave up its commitment to Scripture. Instead, the theologians and pastors of this era charted a path that followed tradition into a morass of bad theology and misguided practice. Thus, it's probably best to view the Protestant movement of the sixteenth century more as a "restoration" than a "reformation." The Christian faith was lost during the Middle Ages. It had to be rediscovered.

Introduction: Unraveling the Legend

Many kids have a strong—and often irrational—fear of the dark. What is simple and straightforward in the light becomes twisted and dangerous once the lights go out. Shadows on the walls become monsters and inky black corners are hiding places for wicked creatures. As a result, many children take whatever measures necessary to avoid being in dark rooms: don't be the last one in a room at night, set up a night-light before bedtime, or just leave lights on in every room!

The popular myth of the "Dark Ages" works on our minds in a similar way. The hints of knowledge we have about this era become monstrous shadows, suggesting a completely corrupted Roman Catholic Church in which the light of the Christian faith was stamped out. This narrative sits at odds with a host of historical facts. Turning a spotlight on the Middle Ages reveals a stream of careful expositors of the Scriptures and faithful witnesses to the gospel. Nevertheless, the myth persists. Let's turn our lights onto this important period of history.

Painting with a Broad Brush

Historical myths often say more about the contemporary situation than they do about the past. What kind of cultural and religious situation among Protestant Christians contributes to this "Dark Ages" myth? The church has tended to overstate its own progress in faith and its nearness to the truth, using previous generations as a foil for new directions or more fully developed teachings. While believers can use this approach to bring understanding and clarity, when Christians take it to an extreme, it can get out of hand.

For instance, one popular Bible handbook described the church of the Middle Ages this way: "The Church had Changed its Nature, had entered its Great Apostasy, had become a Political Organization in the Spirit and Pattern of Imperial Rome, and took its Nose-Dive into the millennium of Papal Abominations. . . . In its ambition to Rule it lost and forgot the spirit of Christ."[1] This paints a picture of a church that had not simply lost its way on some issues, but had left the very core of its identity—Jesus Christ himself.

The Work of the Spirit

In Acts 2, the Spirit descended on the believers, an event the Bible calls the day of Pentecost (Acts 2:1). From that moment on, followers of Jesus were indwelt by the Holy Spirit. Each new believer received the Spirit, in every case for the entirety of their lives. This echoes the prediction of Jesus, which he made to his disciples the night before he was betrayed: "I will ask the Father, and he will give you another Counselor to be with you forever" (John 14:16).

Some have argued that the Bible predicts a great apostasy, in which the church will essentially disappear for more than 1,000 years. This argument is typical of heretical Christian groups such as Mormonism.[2] Even true

---

[1]   Henry H. Halley, *Halley's Bible Handbook: An Abbreviated Bible Commentary*, 24th ed., The Bible Handbook Series (Grand Rapids: Zondervan, 1965), 760.

[2]   James E. Talmage, *Jesus the Christ* (Salt Lake City: Covenant Communications, 2006), 745.

Christians have been taken in by this "great apostasy" argument. But when scrutinized, this argument doesn't hold up, because we believe that Jesus, by his Spirit, is going to be with us always, even to the end of the age (Matt 28:20). Any suggestion that the church lost the gospel compromises the faithfulness of Jesus to remain in the world, by his Spirit, until he returns. If we believe in the ministry of the Spirit that began in Acts 2, we have to presume that the Spirit has continued to work redemptively in the world, that he didn't simply cease working for 1,000 years.

An Unbroken Thread

Who remained faithful during these so-called Dark Ages? To assess someone's faithfulness to true Christian teaching requires seeing how they spoke about the person and work of Jesus and their effects on us. While this is by no means an exhaustive list of the faithful during this period, it serves as an excellent starting point in the search for light amid this "dark" era of history.

Gregory the Great (540–604), who served as the bishop of the church at Rome from 590 to 604, took on an increasingly powerful role in leading the church worldwide. Many Protestants consider Gregory to have been the first true "pope," largely for the way he was able to apply his many administrative gifts to his church office. Gregory also wrote a lengthy series of reflections on the book of Job, where he commented on the redemptive work of Jesus, saying, "Thereupon in our behalf the Son of God came into the womb of the Virgin; there for our sakes He was made Man. Nature, not sin, was assumed by Him. He offered a sacrifice in our behalf, He set forth His own Body in behalf of sinners."[3] The narrative that Jesus was born of a virgin and that he, being God and man, sacrificed himself for sinners stands at the very center of orthodox Christian faith.

Further along in these "Dark Ages," a monk and theologian named Anselm of Canterbury (1033–1109) brought together the person of Jesus—namely, that he is the God-man—with the death of Jesus to better explain how God saves. To this end, Anselm wrote, "If it be necessary, therefore, as it appears, that the heavenly kingdom be made up of men, and this cannot be effected unless the aforesaid satisfaction be made, which none but God can make and none but man ought to make, it is necessary for the God-man to

---

[3] Gregory the Great, *Morals on the Book of Job* 17.46, Library of the Fathers of the Holy Catholic Church 21 (Oxford: J. H. Parker, 1845), 309.

make it."[4] In other words, if heaven will be populated by human beings whose sin debt has been paid, but only God has the ability to pay the human debt of sin, then Jesus had to be both divine and human. Anselm's focus on this important core truth of Christian teaching shows the gospel alive and well in the eleventh and twelfth centuries.

One other impressive witness to the gospel in the Middle Ages was a theologian who stood as the most significant figure in the church at that time (and for a long time afterward): Thomas Aquinas (1225–1274). In his masterwork, the *Summa Theologica*, Aquinas asserted that "the truth of faith is contained in Holy Writ [Scripture]."[5] Aquinas also wrote a commentary on the book of Romans, which includes extensive quotations from all over the Bible. In his treatment of Romans 1, Aquinas wrote well on the importance of the gospel, arguing that it is through believing the gospel that we receive forgiveness of sins, sanctification, and eternal life. He argued that the gospel "confers salvation . . . through faith."[6] Aquinas understood well the central importance of Scripture and the gospel in drawing people to Christ.

Other significant figures in the Roman Catholic Church of the Middle Ages stood up to what they believed were extremes in doctrine and abuses in practice. In so doing, these individuals lit the way to the gospel as they highlighted the shortcomings of the church in certain areas. Two prime examples stood for the truth of Christianity against doctrinal corruption in the Catholic Church. When the English professor John Wycliffe (c. 1325–1384) witnessed egregious abuses of power among the clergy, he found himself drawn back to the Bible (rather than church leadership) for guidance from God. Wycliffe translated the Bible into English, believing Scripture to be sufficient for salvation and a life of godliness. Similarly, the university professor John Huss (c. 1369–1415), who lived and ministered around Prague in what is now the Czech Republic, lamented abuses in spiritual practice such as the buying of indulgences and the veneration of relics. Like Wycliffe, he also affirmed the Bible as the chief spiritual authority in the lives of believers. Huss was eventually executed by the Roman Catholic Church for his views.[7]

We should also not forget that throughout the Middle Ages, the Apostles'

---

[4]   Anselm of Canterbury, *Cur Deus Homo* [Why God Became Man] 2.6 (Chicago: Open Court, 1903), 58.

[5]   Thomas Aquinas, *Summa Theologica* II-II, q. 1, art. 9, response 1, trans. Fathers of the English Dominican Province (London: Burns Oates & Washbourne, n.d.).

[6]   Thomas Aquinas, *Commentary on Romans* 1.100.

[7]   Erwin Lutzer, *Rescuing the Gospel: The Story and Significance of the Reformation* (Grand Rapids: Baker, 2016), 7–21.

Creed and Nicene Creed preserved the basic doctrines of the Christian faith. These creeds affirmed repeatedly—in simple language that common people could understand—the truth about the triune God as well as the person and work of Christ, who died for our sins and rose from the dead. Yes, medieval theology and practice in the official church tended to muddle the basic melody of the gospel of Jesus Christ, but God made sure the essential truths of the faith continued to be proclaimed from the early church through the Middle Ages. And the work of the Holy Spirit could clear out the clutter so people could respond in faith to the simple truth of the Christian faith.

Application

God has always ensured the presence of faithful believers, people who serve as a witness to the truth of God's redemptive work in the world. When it comes to the church, then, we can trust that God has always had a group of people indwelt by the Spirit. The Spirit has continued to work through gifted people across the church's history. Dispelling this myth of "dark ages" should serve as a great encouragement to the believer today. The Holy Spirit is at work in his people. He never ceases his ministry of drawing people to the Father this side of Christ's return.

Second, we would do well not to overestimate our own proximity to the truth, while so easily rejecting entire eras. Considering others well (whether they are alive or have been long dead) requires a sense of humility in us that the world desperately needs. The temptation to dismiss the unknown remains a real danger for believers, for we end up reacting out of an ignorance that we suppose is knowledge. May we recommit ourselves to knowing those who have gone before us, that we might learn from them, sometimes differ with them (and their actual views), and at other times receive support from them or their followers.

Resources

Brooke, C. N. L., and R. B. Brooke. *Popular Religion in the Middle Ages: Western Europe 1000–1300*. London: Thames & Hudson, 1984.

Christian Spirituality 1: Origins to the Twelfth Century. Edited by Bernard McGinn, John Meyendorff, and Jean Leclercq. New York: Crossroad, 1985.

Christian Spirituality 2: High Middle Ages and Reformation. Edited by Jill Raitt. With an introduction by Bernard McGinn and John Meyendorff. New York: Crossroad, 1987.

CHAPTER 15

The One True Church Went Underground during the Dark Ages

The Legendary Story

When the apostles were spreading the gospel and starting churches around the Mediterranean and beyond, they brought real light to the world through the hope of Christ. However, as these faithful men passed away, the churches they founded began to falter and abandoned their first love. Indeed, the apostles even warned of such things, believing apostasy would characterize the generations following them. The apostle John taught that "even now many antichrists have come" (1 John 2:18), while Paul warned Timothy that people would want to have their ears tickled, accumulating teachers that accord with their own desires (2 Tim 4:3).

But thanks be to God, a few believers remained. To preserve the truth, the true church founded by the apostles had to go "underground" shortly after the first century and especially during the Dark Ages. They appear occasionally on the radar of history as "heretics" persecuted by the official Roman Catholic Church and mainline Protestant denominations.

Introduction: Unraveling the Legend

When plants and trees grow to maturity, they develop seeds that eventually fall into the soil below. This process, a natural sowing, ensures that there is always more vegetation to come when the plants currently in bloom eventually wither and die. Therefore, even during the winter season, when plant life may have died off above ground, there are seeds underground preparing to bloom when spring arrives.

Some have used this type of thinking to claim there were long periods of "winter" in the church's history, where no believers existed "above ground," but that all were forced "underground," or outside the institutional and visible church. However, the Spirit has never failed to leave believers "above ground," shining the light of the gospel into the world. God has always continued to work through believers in the church as a testimony to himself. While the number of the faithful has grown and shrunk depending on the era and the circumstances around the church, they have never disappeared or gone fully "underground."

An Underground Church?

What are the specifics of this myth of an underground church, and how should we evaluate these specifics? On the surface, the view might seem compelling because supporters refer to multiple historical groups across different eras. One early proponent of this view, James Robinson Graves (1820–1893), believed that the true church, Baptist by nature, could be found in an unbroken line throughout church history. Graves described the historical origins and development of this underground church, asserting that "these uncorrupted witnesses of Jesus were called 'Cathari' at first, the Pure, and afterwards by the names of their most prominent ministers and leaders, as Novatians, Donatists; and after they fled to the valleys of the mountains from the face of their implacable persecutors, where for ages they were hid as in a 'wilderness,' they received the general name of 'Waldenses' and 'Vaudois,' which mean the inhabitants of the 'valleys' or 'valley-men.'"[1]

Another voice sympathetic to this myth was Hugh Tully, who made clear that this true underground church was essentially Baptist. He wrote, "All denominations that have come into existence since the days of Christ do not have Scriptural authority to baptize. . . . New Testament Churches were Baptist Churches. . . . Baptists alone have continued from days of Christ, and consequently alone have authority to baptize."[2] This movement, called Landmarkism, denies that "pedobapist [infant baptizing] societies are Scriptural

---

[1]   James Robinson Graves, *Old Landmarkism: What Is It?* 2nd ed. (Ashland, KY: Calvary Baptist Church Bookshop, 1965), 108.

[2]   Hugh L. Tully, *A Brief History of Baptists with Chapters on Baptism, Lord's Supper, Etc.* (Ensley, AL: Jefferson Printing, 1938), 38.

churches."[3] In the context of this myth, true churches that practiced believer's baptism were present "underground" throughout church history. It all sounds impressive and historically informed, but the details reveal quite the opposite.

The "Cathari," a name likely derived from a Greek word meaning "pure," were mentioned at the Council of Nicaea in AD 325, a significant council that helped Christians better articulate the relationship between God the Father and God the Son. Canon 8 of the council allowed for "Cathari" clergy to return to the church after having left during earlier persecutions.[4] The "Cathari" refers to a group often called "Novatians" by church historians,[5] which Graves also mentioned. Both the Novatians and another group, called the Donatists, had split from the broader church over the issue of holy living in the midst of persecution. Both of these groups wanted to deny church membership to anyone who had denied Christ during periods of persecution, even when those who had denied later repented. The Novatians and the Donatists believed God honored their purity and didn't want to see the church tainted by those who had fallen into sin. There is no indication that the Novatians or the Donatists practiced believer's baptism.

Graves also mentioned the "Waldenses," a group associated with one Peter Waldo (1140–1205). Waldo lived in Lyons, France, during the latter half of the twelfth century, during which time he sold all his possessions—he was a rich merchant—and devoted himself to preaching the gospel. Waldo had become concerned about his eternal salvation, so he paid two scholars to translate the Bible from Latin into his native French. Eventually, Waldo and his group (the Waldensians) found themselves at odds with the church leadership, largely over their authority to preach and a concern from the clergy that these new preachers were making mistakes and leading people astray. The Waldensians took the apostolic motto upon themselves: "Obey God rather than people" (Acts 5:29).[6] The movement eventually developed an antagonistic relationship with the Roman Catholic Church, criticizing abuses in the clergy and the Catholic dogma of the Lord's Supper, transubstantiation. However, once again, no evidence exists that this group practiced believer's baptism.

In the end, there is a decided lack of evidence that the true church (practicing believer's baptism or otherwise) existed secretly throughout the centuries.

---

[3]   William Cathcart, ed., "Old Landmarkism," in *The Baptist Encyclopedia* (1881), 867–68.

[4]   William Bright, *The Canons of the First Four General Councils of Nicaea, Constantinople, Ephesus and Chalcedon,* 2nd ed. (Oxford: Clarendon, 1892), xi–xii.

[5]   Bright, 29.

[6]   Gabriel Audisio, *The Waldensian Dissent: Persecution and Survival, c. 1170–c. 1570,* trans. Claire Davison (Cambridge: Cambridge University Press, 1999), 6–25.

When confronted with this lack of historical evidence, some advocates of this myth say persecutors destroyed the evidence. Though a great plot for historical fiction writers, the idea of an unbroken line of independent churches outside either the Western and Eastern organized catholic churches is simply not true.

Recognizing the Remnant

Throughout the Bible, God has always preserved a remnant of elect believers. This principle explicitly operated as far back as the time of Joseph, whom God sent to Egypt "to establish [them] as a remnant within the land" (Gen 45:7). During the era of the judges, when so many in Israel had fallen away, Deborah sang of how "the remnant of the noble" marched for her in battle (Judg 5:13 ESV). Maybe most powerfully in the Old Testament, when Elijah felt so desperately alone in the face of Ahab and Jezebel's attacks, the Lord assured his prophet that 7,000 in Israel had not become idolaters (1 Kings 19:18).

In the New Testament, Jesus offered a parable that speaks to this very topic—the story of the wheat and the weeds (Matt 13:24–30). In the parable, which Jesus told in reference to the kingdom of God, a man sowed a field of wheat while his enemy later sowed weeds in the same field. But notice the solution Jesus offered through the master's advice to his servants: "Let both grow together until the harvest" (Matt 13:30). In other words, Jesus recognized that God's people would exist with unbelievers in their midst.

This biblical emphasis on the remnant, when combined with the continuous ministry of the Holy Spirit described in the previous chapter, provides both a biblical and theological backdrop for God's continued ministry in the visible church. All of this stands against the idea of an underground church that existed outside visible churches.

Denominational Division

One of the impulses that drove Landmarkists such as Graves to propose an underground church involved the presence of denominations that denied core teachings and practices of the church, including rightly administered baptism and communion. This led the Landmarkists to deny the status of "authentic church" not just to Catholics and Orthodox believers who were encumbered by their devotion to man-made traditions, but also to Protestant denominations that developed after the Reformation. The Landmarkists believed that since even these denominations affirmed false doctrines such as infant baptism, they could not be part of the remnant.

However, if we take a closer look at history, even Baptists of the Landmark variety developed as a result of the denominational freedom that was born out of the Reformation. Every denomination has within it a mixture of truth and error. As the Westminster Confession (1646) says, "This catholic Church hath been sometimes more, sometimes less visible . . . The purest churches under heaven are subject both to mixture and error."[7] The (small-*c*) "catholic church" speaks to the universality of the true church across a variety of denominations, wherever Christians with true faith and practice gather around their confession and pursue the person and work of Jesus Christ. This has always been an invisible reality in visible church communities of all kinds.

While several individuals and groups throughout the Middle Ages claimed the Roman Church had become corrupt (e.g., Waldo, Wycliffe, Huss), the church nonetheless had not gone underground. The universal church, which is manifest in local congregations, was at all times and in all places above ground.

Application

Throughout history, people have enjoyed a good conspiracy theory. The idea that the church wasn't actually the church throughout most of Christian history would be one of the most far-reaching conspiracies known to humanity. The problem? This conspiracy theory, just like most that float around contemporary society, is simply not true. The evidence leads to a more complex conclusion.

Rather than propose alternative histories suggesting there is somewhere a pure, "underground" church, we need to take seriously the lesson of Jesus's parable of the wheat and the weeds. While the church contains a mixture of truth and error in this age, God will protect the church and sort out the wicked from the righteous at the end of all things. The lesson for us is striking. We should not see ourselves as floating in a singular bubble of pure doctrine and practice—one that sets us apart from the rest of the whole history of the visible church. Instead, we live and move and have our being in churches that mix both truth and error, because we ourselves are a mixture of truth and error. The real temptation of this myth lies most strongly in our desire to see ourselves as the people who have finally figured it all out.

---

[7]　John H. Leith, ed., "Westminster Confession XXV," in *Creeds of the Churches: A Reader in Christian Doctrine from the Bible to the Present*, 3rd ed. (Louisville: WJK, 1982), 222.

Resources

Audisio, Gabriel. *The Waldensian Dissent: Persecution and Survival, c. 1170–c. 1570.* Translated by Claire Davison. Cambridge: Cambridge University Press, 1999.

Kidd, Thomas S., and Barry G. Hankins. *Baptists in America: A History.* Oxford: Oxford University Press, 2015.

Patterson, James A. *James Robinson Graves: Staking the Boundaries of Baptist Identity.* Nashville: B&H Academic, 2012.

CHAPTER 16

The Medieval Catholic Church Completely Abandoned Salvation by Grace

The Legendary Story

Jesus first introduced the clear water of life—salvation by grace—which then flowed into the infant church from the New Testament teaching of the apostles (Eph 2:8–9). This fresh stream of living water turned into a mighty river in the early church as the community of faith expanded both numerically and in spiritual maturity. In the fifth century, this glorious river streamed into the deep waters of Augustine of Hippo (354–430)—salvation came by God's grace, not as a result of human works.

However, as the church entered the Middle Ages, her leaders focused on exerting power over people rather than empowering people to do the work of the gospel by the Spirit. This misplaced focus led to a change in the quality of that water of grace. What once had been clear and fresh was now muddied and polluted. Where once grace had been the centerpiece of salvation, human works took center stage in the medieval church.

Introduction: Unraveling the Legend

Place a stick in a rushing river and the small piece of wood becomes subject to the water current. The clear "salvation-by-grace" soteriology of the apostles, the early church, and Augustine became subject to the flow of the theological waters in the church of the Middle Ages. Theology that developed over this

113

time period pushed Augustine's teaching out of the river's center, the theological core of the Roman Catholic Church.

Offering alternatives to Augustine's teaching or developing ideas related to its key questions is much different from completely abandoning salvation by grace. The truth is, many of the medieval church's most influential theologians retained a strong emphasis on grace as the means to salvation. And while there were some voices who overemphasized humanity's role in salvation, the church as a whole never abandoned a fundamental conviction that salvation was by grace.

Grace Alone

Simply stated, Augustine of Hippo believed salvation to be the result of God's free and unmerited gift of grace. In describing the origins of saving faith, Augustine argued that "the spirit of grace, therefore, causes us to have faith, in order that through faith we may, on praying for it, obtain the ability to do what we are commanded."[1] Later in the same treatise, Augustine made the point even more clearly, arguing that good works do not prepare the way for grace and faith. Rather, unbelieving people engage in evil and rebellious works. Quoting from Ezek 36:22, where Israel was confronted for profaning the name of the Lord, Augustine noted that "there were not only no good merits of theirs, but the Lord shows that evil ones actually preceded."[2] When saving faith comes, according to Augustine, it comes only as a result of God's grace.

A century after Augustine's death, the church continued to affirm his teaching on the subject of grace in salvation. The Second Council of Orange (AD 529), held in the south of France, spoke decisively on these subjects. Canon 4 of the council stated it clearly: "If any one contends that God to cleanse us from sin waits for our will, and does not rather allow that our very wish to be cleansed is put into us by the infusion and operation of the Holy Spirit, he resists the Spirit Himself."[3] In other words, people desire salvation only when the Spirit, by grace, has brought us to the point of desiring his salvation. A bit later, the council took issue with those who believe grace is merely a supplement to human virtues "instead of acknowledging that obe-

---

[1]   Augustine of Hippo, *A Treatise on Grace and Free Will*, 28 (NPNF 1.5:455).

[2]   Augustine of Hippo, 28 (NPNF 1.5:456).

[3]   Second Council of Orange, Canon 4. F. H. Woods, *Canons of the Second Council of Orange, A.D. 529: Text, with an Introduction, Translation, and Notes*, Oxford Study Guides, ed. F. S. Pulling (Oxford: James Thornton, 1882), 21.

dience and humility are the gift of grace itself."[4] A person's salvation simply does not depend upon good works, such as humility or obedience. While this meeting at Orange did not carry the explicit doctrinal authority of a major ecumenical council, Pope Boniface II affirmed the council's findings only two years later in 531, making the canons of Orange part of the official doctrine of the church.[5]

Profit from Penance?

While Augustine set the tone for the church's views on the necessity of "grace through faith" for salvation, the myth that the church shifted entirely to salvation by works has persisted in a post-Reformation world. For instance, in describing the system of confession and penance that developed in the Middle Ages, one scholar has noted that "ecclesiastical penance was thus confounded with Christian repentance, without which there can be neither justification nor sanctification. Instead of looking to Christ for pardon through faith alone, it was sought for principally in the Church through penitential works."[6]

The medieval church did indeed require believers to practice the sacrament of penance, meant to bring about confession, forgiveness, and reconciliation after believers had committed sins. The penance usually focused on pointing the sinner toward contrition over his or her sin, confession (to a priest), and performing certain acts to repair the harm. But is this a complete denial of salvation by grace?

Two points are worth making here. First, the medieval church regularly emphasized that salvation was an ongoing process.[7] They emphasized passages such as 1 Cor 1:18, which refers to believers as those "who are being saved." At times, sanctification was the primary lens through which they saw salvation. Second, some in the medieval church taught that humans attain salvation as righteousness is infused into them by their faith-filled participation in the sacraments. The infused merit, while given entirely by grace, causes its recipient to merit salvation, according to this teaching.[8] These phenomena help to

---

[4]   Second Council of Orange, Canon 6 (Woods, 25).

[5]   F. L. Cross and Elizabeth A. Livingstone, eds., *The Oxford Dictionary of the Christian Church* (Oxford, UK: Oxford University Press, 2005), 1193.

[6]   Jean Henri Merie d'Aubigné, *History of the Reformation of the Sixteenth Century,* vol. 1, trans. Henry Beveridge (Glasgow, UK: William Collins, 1853), 30.

[7]   Protestants have historically emphasized the reality of salvation as having occurred at some point in the past of the believer's life, in the spirit of Eph 2:8–9.

[8]   Gregg R. Allison, *Historical Theology* (Grand Rapids: Zondervan, 2011), 504–9.

explain the way penance or "works" end up being connected with the language of "salvation."

However, the medieval church continued to affirm the primacy of grace, where penance only followed after God's saving grace. Therefore, penance became a tangible way of expressing the believer's fight against sin. In confession, "the penitent was supposed to understand he or she was confessing to God, as well as to the priest." Completing one's penance "required true contrition and making satisfaction" for the sin.[9] This entire process only made sense in the context of believing people. Interestingly, it rests on an important distinction rooted back in Augustine (354–430) and elaborated upon by Aquinas (1225–1274).

In the fifth century, Augustine described the relationship between God's operation and our cooperation with him. Augustine wrote, "He operates, therefore, without us, in order that we may will; but when we will, and so will that we may act, He co-operates with us."[10] In other words, God's work of saving grace gives believers the ability to choose. Once God has made that possible, he expects his people to cooperate with him in following after Christ. Or to use the language of Paul, God calls believers to work out their salvation (Phil 2:12), though it is God working in them to both will and work (2:13).

Thomas Aquinas explained that Augustinian distinction in more detail, noting that "operating grace" involves God as the "sole mover" while "cooperating grace" speaks of God helping us to do some particular act.[11] Aquinas made the primacy of operating grace abundantly clear elsewhere: "God does not justify us without ourselves, since when we are justified we consent to his justice by a movement of our free will. This movement, however, is not the cause of grace, but the result of it. The whole operation is therefore due to grace."[12] Another important medieval theologian, Hugh of St. Victor (1096–1141), predated Aquinas in making the same point, as he wrote, "Know, then, that at no time, whatever, from the beginning of the world till its end, there either was or is a truly good man save him who is justified by grace, and that no one could ever obtain grace except through Christ."[13]

---

9   Thomas M. Izbicki, "Sin and Pastoral Care," in *The Routledge History of Medieval Christianity: 1050–1500*, ed. R. N. Swanson (London: Routledge, 2015), 150.

10   Augustine of Hippo, *A Treatise on Grace and Free Will* 33 (NPNF 1.5:458).

11   Thomas Aquinas, *Summa Theologica*, trans. Fathers of the English Dominican Province (London: Burns Oates & Washbourne, n.d.).

12   Thomas Aquinas, *On Nature and Grace*, ed. A. M. Fairweather (Philadelphia: WJK, 1954), 168.

13   Hugh of Saint Victor, *A Scholastic Miscellany: Anselm to Ockham*, ed. Eugene R. Fairweather (Philadelphia: WJK, 1956), 312.

Preparation for Pardon?

The late medieval church (fourteenth–fifteenth century) did, in fact, have a prominent strand of thought in contrast to Augustine and Aquinas, represented by theologians such as William of Ockham (1288–1348) and Gabriel Biel (c. 1420–1495). Biel believed that people, if they were going to be saved, needed to do their best in order to receive God's gracious gift of salvation.[14] As Biel argued, "God has established the rule [covenant] that whoever turns to Him and *does what he can* will receive forgiveness of sins from God. God infuses assisting grace into such a man, who is thus taken back into friendship."[15]

Biel's ideas not only placed him directly at odds with Augustine and Aquinas, but they left the salvation of humanity rooted in the decision of people to turn toward God on their own. In the decades after Biel, the Reformers reacted to this tradition of "human effort first, God's grace second," offering a much more rigorous view of salvation by grace alone that extends beyond the emphasis of Aquinas and even Augustine.

Despite this stream of thought represented by Biel, the medieval church remained a home for the clear distinctions offered by Augustine and Aquinas—that God is the sole operator in bringing people to salvation, and that we cooperate with God in working out that salvation in a life of humility and obedience (which Protestants usually call "sanctification").

Application

Protestants have long emphasized salvation by grace alone, and rightly so. Recognizing that salvation comes as a result of God's action should humble us and keep us from thinking that we are better than we are or that we have anything to contribute in and of ourselves. God is good, and he has given sacrificially that we might benefit through faith in Jesus.

Seeing how much the medieval church testified to the reality of grace as the means to salvation can help us better appreciate the long tradition of grace in the church—Catholic and Protestant. And while there have been voices against the primacy of grace in salvation, we dare not make these voices the be-all and end-all of the medieval Catholic Church's theology, in the same

---

[14]   Matthew Barrett, "Can This Bird Fly?" *Southern Baptist Journal of Theology* 21, no. 4 (2017): 68.

[15]   Gabriel Biel, "The Circumcision of the Lord," in *Forerunners of the Reformation: The Shape of Late Medieval Thought Illustrated by Key Documents*, ed. Heiko Oberman (Philadelphia: Fortress, 1981), 173, emphasis added.

way we don't allow extreme Protestant views to mark the entirety of that movement either.

One danger of the Catholic strong focus on salvation as "in process" is it might give us the impression that our salvation in some way depends on our own efforts. This has been a pointed struggle in the church at least since the time of Augustine and his debates with Pelagius. That said, the Protestant view may tend toward the opposite extreme—seeing salvation as a past event that expects nothing from the believer post-conversion. Both of these extremes are incorrect caricatures of the views Protestants and Catholics hold on this all-important subject.

Resources

Allison, Gregg R. *Roman Catholic Theology and Practice: An Evangelical Assessment.* Wheaton, IL: Crossway, 2014.

McGrath, Alister E. *Iustitia Dei: A History of the Christian Doctrine of Justification.* 3rd ed. Cambridge: Cambridge University Press, 2005.

Pelikan, Jaroslav. *The Christian Tradition: A History of the Development of Doctrine.* vol. 3, *The Growth of Medieval Theology (600–1300)*, chapter 3, "The Plan of Salvation." Chicago: University of Chicago Press, 1978.

CHAPTER 17

The One True Church Is Marked by an Unbroken Chain of Apostolic Succession

The Legendary Story

Just before the beginning of the church on the day of Pentecost, the apostle Peter declared a need to replace the faithless Judas (Acts 1:21–22). Peter's appointment of Matthias to the apostolic office set a pattern that would extend beyond the New Testament and into the early church. Throughout the New Testament era, apostles and other leaders appointed men to succeed them, always by an official act—ordination via the laying on of hands (Acts 9:17–19, 13:3; 1 Tim 5:22).

The early and medieval church stated apostolic succession even more clearly, with bishops regularly highlighting it in order to show their people where to find the one true church. This historical pattern testifies to the reality that the Roman Catholic Church—or even the Eastern Orthodox Church, depending on one's perspective—is the true church because it can trace its leadership of bishops back to the apostles, who established the office of the bishop as the unfailing mark of the "one, holy, catholic, and apostolic Church."

Introduction: Unraveling the Legend

One of the great challenges in any organization—the church included—is establishing credibility and authority to those one is trying to reach. The Roman Catholic Church, with its emphasis on the unified and visible church, has long held to the principle of apostolic succession in order to ground the authority of its message. The allegedly tangible lineage from apostles to current leaders provides a measure of credibility to current leaders, serving to connect their ministry and message with that of the first leaders of the Christian church.

While this type of teaching carries a definite appeal for those seeking to validate a church's ministry and leadership, it also carries certain problems and questions. This view seems to suggest that the church is only ever true when connected to the universal, visible Roman Catholic (or Eastern Orthodox) Church. However, despite the lack of apostolic succession, we believe Protestant churches are not false churches. Protestants have gathered around the universal gospel message and preach the core Christian truth of salvation through Christ.

A Circular Argument

John Henry Newman (1801–1890), an Anglican convert to the Roman Catholic Church, offered a classic defense of apostolic succession, connecting the ecclesiastic descendants of the apostles to the visible church on earth:

> There is on earth an existing Society, Apostolic as founded by the Apostles, Catholic because it spreads its branches in every place; i.e. the Church visible with its Bishops, Priests, and Deacons. And this surely *is* a most important doctrine; for what can be better news to the bulk of mankind than to be told that Christ, when He ascended, did not leave us orphans but appointed representatives of Himself to the end of time?[1]

Newman also asserted that "though Peter, James, and John should be taken from the world, the true church should never be left without Apostles, but be guided by their successors to the end of time."[2] Contemporary Roman Catholic doctrine has followed suit, affirming the Roman Catholic Church as "the sole church of Christ."[3]

The claim of apostolic succession as the evidence of being the "true church" or the "sole church" has a fundamental problem, however. Neither the Eastern

---

[1]   John Henry Newman, "Tract 2: The Catholic Church," in *Tracts for the Times* (London: J. G. & F. Rivington, 1833), 1:2.

[2]   Newman, "Tract 29: Christian Liberty," in *Tracts for the Times*, 1:7.

[3]   Catholic Church, "811: The Church Is One, Holy, Catholic, and Apostolic," in the *Catechism of the Catholic Church*, 2nd ed. (Vatican: Libreria Editrice Vaticana, 2012).

nor Western traditions can validate their respective claims to be the one true church without circular reasoning—appealing to their own presupposed authority as the one true church in order to validate their particular mark of unique authenticity. In other words, the claim of apostolic succession presumes that the current leaders of their own church are the true representatives of the apostles on earth. Only if they already are assumed to be the true church would they have the apostolic authority to determine which branch—East or West—preserves the true succession and thus have such authority.

Furthermore, the claim of apostolic or episcopal succession is a misunderstanding of the second-century appeal to succession of bishops in the early church. Second-century fathers cited apostolic succession as a trustworthy means of authenticating orthodox doctrine and practice—not as a mark of the authentic institutional church. In the late first century, Clement (c. 35–99), the bishop (or head pastor) of the church at Rome, wrote to the church at Corinth regarding issues of division and disunity. Clement made much of the importance of proper leadership succession, noting that when the apostles "should die, other approved men should succeed to their ministry."[4] Clement was trying to solidify leadership in a post-apostolic church. Therefore, he argued that church members should not be removing duly appointed bishops. Most interesting for our purposes, however, is Clement's reasoning—it had nothing to do with the one true church. Rather, Clement pointed out that these bishops had served the church "blamelessly and in holiness."[5] A bishop's status as true successor to the apostles derived from his faithful service to God.

Later in the second century, Irenaeus (c. 120–200), bishop of the church at Lyons, also addressed the issue of leadership in the church. Referring to the succession of bishops from the apostles, Irenaeus wrote, "All, therefore, who wish to see the truth can view in the whole Church the tradition of the apostles that has been manifested in the whole world. Further, we are able to enumerate the bishops who were established in the Churches by the apostles, and their successions even to ourselves. These neither taught nor knew anything similar to what [the heretics] prate about."[6] Once again, an early Christian

---

[4] *1 Clement* 44.2 (Holmes, 103). Earlier in the same letter, Clement makes clear that the apostles "appointed their first fruits, when they had tested them by the Spirit, to be bishops and deacons for the future believers." *1 Clement* 42.4 (Holmes, 101).

[5] *1 Clement* 44.4 (Holmes, 105).

[6] Irenaeus of Lyons, *Against Heresies* 3.3.1., trans. Dominic J. Unger, *St. Irenaeus of Lyons: Against the Heresies (Book 3)*, Ancient Christian Writers, vol. 64 (Mahwah, NJ: Paulist Press, 2012), 32. Throughout *Against Heresies*, Irenaeus makes clear his argument for proper succession of leadership—both bishops and elders (presbyters) as a means of guarding the truth handed down from the apostles just a generation earlier. *Against Heresies* 3.3.2, 3.3.4, 3.4.1, 4.26.2, 4.33.8.

bishop wrote of succession, but not as a reference to finding or knowing the true church. In this case, Irenaeus's concern was that his people know where to find the truth itself—the gospel message (or, to use Irenaeus's term, the "Rule of Faith") about the person and work of Jesus.

For the early church (and for us), the core content of Christian truth reflects the teaching of the apostles. In the Niceno-Constantinopolitan Creed (381), one of the most important statements of faith to come out of the early church, Christians described the church as one, holy, catholic, and *apostolic*. That last term signifies that the truth of Christianity—preserved within the church—is founded on the apostles and prophets (Eph 2:20). The language of the creed was not intended to point us to the authenticity of an institution as much as it pointed us to the authenticity of the church's teaching.

We're Not Catholic, Are We?

Many Protestant and evangelical believers would not describe themselves or their doctrine as "catholic" due to the term's connection with the Roman Catholic Church. However, the early church used the term (which simply means "universal" or "whole") to describe both the extent and the nature of the truth they preached and taught. Early Christians believed that the church was teaching the truth throughout the world, making the church and the truth she taught "universal." However, historian D. H. Williams helps to broaden the concept of "catholic" in the early church:

> It is clear from the early Fathers that "catholic" meant much more than "universal" or "general." . . . On the one hand, catholic defines the church in space and time as that which is spread as a harmonious body throughout the world. . . . But just as important is Cyril's emphasis that the catholic church is comprehensive in its message in the sense that there is no saving doctrine that it fails to teach.[7]

In other words, the church wasn't simply universal in space and time—catholic also described the comprehensiveness of the gospel truth the church taught.

In the medieval era, the Roman Catholic Church affirmed its own status as

---

[7] D. H. Williams, *Retrieving the Tradition and Renewing Evangelicalism* (Grand Rapids: Eerdmans, 1999), 225.

the only true church by taking this notion of universality and applying it to the unique Roman Catholic expression of Christianity, in contrast to other communities—Coptic churches in Ethiopia, Orthodox churches in the East, and, eventually, Protestant churches in the West. The existence of the Protestant churches, however, prompts a rereading of the early church sources, revealing that the true church is gathered around an enduring gospel message derived from the apostles in Scripture and not from a specific, institutional leadership structure. In other words, the fundamental question to determine the truth of the message is not "Who ordained this teacher?" but "Does this teacher's message reflect the teaching we received from the apostles?" In this way, each local church can (and should!) ask itself whether its leaders are connected to that catholic/universal/whole truth spoken by the early church.

MINI MYTHS

"The Offices of Apostles and Prophets Continued throughout History"

Some approaches to church government today want to revive the offices of "apostle" and "prophet" as leaders of churches, usually defining these ministries as "missionaries" and "preachers." However, the second-century heirs of the apostles' leadership—elders/overseers and deacons—were in agreement that apostles and prophets were a limited and temporary number of eyewitnesses of Jesus and men and women endowed with revelatory prophetic gifts respectively. In fact, the late second-century "Muratorian Canon" claims *Shepherd of Hermas* was not accepted as canonical "either among the prophets, whose number is complete, or among the apostles, for it is after [their] time."[8] The fact is, apostles and prophets were unique offices of the early church, the foundation upon which we build (1 Cor 12:28; Eph 2:20).

---

[8]   Bruce M. Metzger, *The Canon of the New Testament: Its Origin, Development, and Significance* (Oxford: Clarendon Press, 1987), 307.

Visible or Invisible?

Understanding the apostolicity and catholicity of the church helps clarify the relationship between the visible and invisible church. The term *visible church* denotes the physical, visible expressions of the church in the world throughout history and today. Therefore, a believer's local church would constitute a portion of the visible church—a place where believers can hear the Word of God preached and participate in the administration of the sacraments or ordinances. The term *invisible church* is a theological concept that denotes the entire group of true believers from all ages—a group that won't exactly correspond to the members of the visible church (Matt 7:21–23).

This distinction pushes back against the idea of "one true church" that is only determined by a visible line of apostolic succession. Instead, the idea of the invisible church prompts believers to recognize that the fundamental issue is one's affirmation of and trust in the God who delivers to humanity the good news of Jesus. Therefore, while Protestant believers do not participate in the so-called one true church of Roman Catholicism or Eastern Orthodoxy, our own visible expressions of the faith in our churches can be expressions of true faith.

Application

If apostolic succession is not about protecting a line of leadership, but rather a line of teaching faithful to the apostolic witness, the ministry of Catholic, Orthodox, or Protestant and evangelical churches can be validated by the content of their teaching, rather than on their structure of leadership. This seems to place the emphasis in the right place for believers today. Believers of all kinds need to take the time to appreciate the fundamentals of the true Christian faith. And while faithful leadership passed on from generation to generation is certainly a help to that, it need not be an unbroken line of leaders to the apostles in order to provide God's people access to the unbroken line of true Christian doctrine and practice.

Secondly, the proper understanding of "catholic" Christianity also turns believers' attention to the content of the Christian faith in a particular way. Christians can be confident that a church that faithfully represents the apostolic preaching retains the fullness of the gospel. In teaching this gospel, believers should go out with boldness, knowing that God will use our faithful witness to his redemptive plan for the world.

Resources

Ehrhardt, A. *The Apostolic Succession in the First Two Centuries of the Church*. London: Lutterworth, 1953.

Southern, R. W. *Western Society and the Church in the Middle Ages*. The Penguin History of the Church. Vol. 2, chapter 5, "Bishops and Archbishops." New York: Penguin, 1970.

Williams, D. H. *Retrieving the Tradition and Renewing Evangelicalism*. Grand Rapids: Eerdmans, 1999.

CHAPTER 18

Abelard and Anselm Debated over the Atonement . . . and Anselm Won

The Legendary Story

At the dawn of the scholastic period in late medieval Europe, a great debate erupted in the universities. On the one side stood the dour and disciplined Anselm of Canterbury (1033–1109), who affirmed the classic "penal substitution theory" of the atonement—that Christ took the penalty for our sins on himself so we might be reckoned as righteous. On the other side the arrogant and unteachable Peter Abelard (1079–1142), who rejected Anselm's view and instead taught the "moral influence theory" of the atonement—that Christ's death was a picture of self-sacrificial love meant to motivate Christ followers to loving action. For good or ill, Anselm won, securing the position of penal substitution in the official teachings of the church all the way through the Reformation, while the moral influence view of the atonement was relegated to the backwaters of theology.

Introduction: Unraveling the Legend

Anselm of Canterbury and Peter Abelard never met. Nor, for that matter, were they ever perceived during their lifetimes as representing two diametrically opposed theories of the atonement. Besides this, Anselm's view of the atonement is best described as the "satisfaction theory" rather than "penal substitution," and Abelard's view was much more complex than simply a "moral influence theory" of the atonement framed in opposition to Anselm.

Pitting these two against each other is, in fact, a modern misrepresentation of both men.

An Anselm–Abelard Smackdown?

The idea that Anselm and Abelard engaged in some kind of dispute can be found on the lips of lay historians and professional theologians alike. For example, Louis Berkhof suggests a deep divide between the doctrines of the atonement in Anselm and Abelard.[1] He notes, "Abelard's theory has little in common with that of Anselm. . . . Abelard rejects the Anselmian view."[2] Another church historian notes, "The opinions of these two church leaders represent a general division of interpretive opinion. Abelard understood the atonement of Christ ethically (the essence being love), while Anselm focused upon judicial aspects."[3]

Similar characterizations abound in texts on soteriology that describe various theories of the atonement. Teachers of church history or the history of doctrine likewise pit Anselm and Abelard against each other—one the forefather of Reformed orthodoxy, the other the forerunner of liberalism. However, casting Anselm and Abelard in these two different roles as hero and heretic, conservative and liberal, misrepresents the facts.

It is true that Bernard of Clairvaux (1090–1153) severely criticized Abelard's soteriology (doctrine of salvation). Bernard regarded Abelard's view of Christ's work of redemption and the role of human free will in salvation as Pelagian, a kind of works righteousness. Yet Abelard's critics were probably as much turned off by his arrogance, jealous of his popularity, and disturbed by his critical approach to traditional authorities as they were leery of his soteriology. Jaroslav Pelikan concludes that Bernard's judgment of Abelard as a Pelagian "was itself an inadequate and an unjust reading of Abelard's thought, one that has been perpetuated also by many modern scholars."[4]

So, there was no theological throw-down, dogmatic duel, or even scholarly disputation between Anselm and Abelard over theories of the atonement. Though Abelard most likely was familiar with some of Anselm's writings,

---

[1] Louis Berkhof, *The History of Christian Doctrines*, Banner of Truth ed. (Edinburgh: Banner of Truth Trust, 1969), 171–75.

[2] Berkhof, 174.

[3] John D. Hannah, *Our Legacy: The History of Christian Doctrine* (Colorado Springs: NavPress, 2001), 163.

[4] Jaroslav Pelikan, *The Christian Tradition: A History of the Development of Doctrine*, vol. 3, *The Growth of Medieval Theology (600–1300)* (Chicago: University of Chicago Press, 1978), 129.

"it is improbable . . . that he knew his work thoroughly and accurately."[5] In fact, Abelard once praised Anselm of Canterbury as a "magnificent doctor of the Church," though it is possible that later in his life he mocked the revered archbishop, perhaps for what he regarded as a simpleminded approach to theology.[6] Nevertheless, Abelard and Anselm were never, in reality, the doctrinal nemeses they are sometimes portrayed to be when modern Christians pit their alleged atonement theories against each other. And, as we will see, even this understanding of their so-called contradictory atonement theories has been greatly exaggerated.

Anselm's Atonement

As we have seen in chapter 12, Anselm of Canterbury is sometimes mistakenly credited with having first articulated the doctrine of "penal substitutionary atonement." Not only is such an assertion misleading in its portrayal of when penal substitution emerged as an atonement theory, but it is also a misunderstanding of Anselm's presentation of the atonement in *Cur Deus Homo* (Why God Became Man). Though Anselm's view in that important work definitely includes Christ's death for the benefit of sinful humanity, we can more accurately describe it as the satisfaction theory of the atonement. Bruce Demarest describes the perspective this way: "Influenced by the concept of a feudal overlord whose dignity was injured by his serfs or private citizens, proponents suggested that Christ's death chiefly satisfies God's wounded honor. Although reflecting the seriousness of sin and the solidarity of the race, this theory focused more on God's injured honor and less on the penal and substitutionary nature of Christ's death."[7]

Scholars and historians regard Anselm's view as objective; that is, Christ's death actually accomplished something in itself. We should also regard it as a variety of substitutionary atonement in that Christ accomplished on our behalf and in our stead something that we fallen humans could not accomplish—the satisfaction of the infinite honor due God by humanity as well as the payment of a sacrificial death above and beyond what was necessary to reestablish that honor.

5　John Marenbon, *Abelard in Four Dimensions: A Twelfth-Century Philosopher in His Context and Ours* (Notre Dame, IN: University of Notre Dame Press, 2013), 95.

6　See M. T. Clanchy, "Abelard's Mockery of St. Anselm," *Journal of Ecclesiastical History* 41, no. 1 (January 1990): 1–23.

7　Bruce Demarest, *The Cross and Salvation: The Doctrine of Salvation*, Foundations of Evangelical Theology, ed. John S. Feiberg (Wheaton, IL: Crossway, 1997), 151.

However, we should not confuse Anselm's satisfaction theory with the penal substitution theory. One historian of the development of dogma goes so far as to assert that Anselm's theory presented in *Cur Deus Homo* is "no theory of penal suffering, for Christ does not suffer penalty; the point rather at which penalty is inflicted is never reached, for God declares Himself satisfied," and it is "no theory of vicarious representation in the strict sense of that term, for Christ does not suffer penalty in our stead, but rather provides a benefit, the value of which is not measured by the greatness of sin and sin's penalty, but by the value of His life."[8]

A simple summary of Anselm's satisfaction theory of the atonement worked out in his *Cur Deus Homo* would be the following: "God's honor demands restoration and reparation by humanity; however, humanity cannot satisfy the demand; the God-Man, Jesus, is able to make satisfaction on behalf of humanity, for He is both divine (able) and human (obligated)."[9] It should be remembered, though, that the purpose of *Cur Deus Homo* was not to establish a comprehensive theory of the atonement or give a clear explanation for how Christ's death on the cross saves humanity. Rather, in *Cur Deus Homo*, Anselm sought to demonstrate by reason alone—apart from appeal to biblical revelation—the logical necessity of the incarnation of the God-man. By establishing the problem of the Creator God to whom infinite honor is owed and a fallen, sinful humanity that has robbed God of that honor and is unable to pay it, Anselm provided the logical solution of a God-man who is responsible for restoring honor as man and able to restore honor as God. Anselm's purpose was primarily Christological, not soteriological; the resulting explanation of the atonement (satisfaction) was actually ancillary to his main purpose.

Abelard's Atonement

Abelard's view has been characterized as a precursor to—or the first articulation of—the moral influence theory of the atonement, a completely subjective view of the atonement that only leads to an emotional or volitional response in the believer to motivate moral reform.[10] Along these lines,

---

[8]   Adolf von Harnack, *History of Dogma*, vol. 6, trans. William M'Gilchrist (repr., Eugene, OR: Wipf and Stock, 1997), 68.

[9]   Nathan D. Holsteen and Michael J. Svigel, eds., *Exploring Christian Theology*, vol. 2, *Creation, Fall, and Salvation* (Minneapolis: Bethany House, 2015), 257.

[10]   See Harnack, *History of Dogma*, 6:78–79.

Demarest notes, "First advanced by Peter Abelard (d. 1142) in reaction to the classic and satisfaction views, the moral influence theory finds many adherents among modern, liberal theologians."[11] And Berkhof complains, "This theory robs the sufferings of Christ of their redemptive significance and reduced Him to a mere moral teacher, who influences men by His teachings and by His example."[12]

However, Abelard's actual teachings on the death of Christ are a bit more complex. Certainly, in his exposition of Romans, Abelard uses language that can be easily interpreted as advocating a moral influence theory:

> Now it seems to us that we have been justified by the blood of Christ and reconciled to God in this way: through this unique act of grace manifested to us—in that his Son has taken upon himself our nature and preserved therein in teaching us by word and example even unto death—he has more fully bound us to himself by love; with the result that our hearts should be enkindled by such a gift of divine grace, and true charity should not now shrink from enduring anything for him.[13]

This seems clear enough. But in a book titled *Know Thyself*, Abelard wrote, "The Lord Jesus 'bore our sins,' [1 Pet. 2:24] meaning that he endured the penalty for our sins, or the penalties springing from them."[14] Quite clearly, then, Abelard had room in his view of the death of Christ for a penal substitutionary atonement in which Christ endured the penalty of sin for us.

In any case, nothing like a showdown, debate, or disputation between Abelard and Anselm occurred during Abelard's lifetime. In fact, most treatments of Abelard's life, career, and theology make no mention of his apparently skewed or heterodox atonement theory.[15] In his 1970 work on the soteriology

---

[11]   Demarest, *The Cross and Salvation*, 153.

[12]   Berkhof, *History of Christian Doctrines*, 175.

[13]   Peter Abelard, *Exposition of the Epistle to the Romans*, 2.3, in *A Scholastic Miscellany: Anselm to Ockham*, ed. and trans. Eugene R. Fairweather, The Library of Christian Classics (Louisville: WJK, 1956), 283.

[14]   Peter Abelard, *Ethics or the Book Called "Know Thyself"* 14, in *A Scholastic Miscellany: Anselm to Ockham*, ed. and trans. Eugene R. Fairweather, The Library of Christian Classics (Louisville: WJK, 1956), 292.

[15]   See Adriaan H. Bredero, *Christendom and Christianity in the Middle Ages: The Relations between Religion, Church, and Society*, trans. Reinder Bruinsma (Grand Rapids: Eerdmans, 1994), 225–45; Margaret Deanesly, *A History of the Medieval Church 590–1500*, 9th corrected ed. (London: Routledge, 1972), 130–33; Lauge O. Nielsen, "Peter Abelard and Gilbert of Poitiers," in *The Medieval Theologians: An Introduction to Theology in the Medieval Period*, ed. G. R. Evans (Oxford: Blackwell, 2001), 102–14.

of Peter Abelard, Richard Weingart sought to set the record straight.[16] After a thorough examination of Abelard's doctrine of the work of Christ in salvation and drawing on far more than just a few isolated snippets, Weingart concludes that Abelard's soteriology includes elements of a more objective nature: "The cross is the altar on which Christ, the only true and perfect Priest and Victim, sacrifices himself for the sins of mankind. . . . The cross is the means whereby Christ bears man's sins, endures the curse of the Law, and assumes God's righteous judgement against sin in order to free sinners from the divine wrath."[17]

Application

In political debate it's easy to fall into the trap of oversimplifying issues into two opposing views squaring off against each other like heavyweight boxers in a ring. That approach to points of debate certainly makes it easy to pick sides, demonize opponents, and utterly misunderstand the complexity of the issues or the nuance of the arguments. Sadly, as in politics, so in theology. How easy it is to imagine a tidy objective "Anselmic" atonement theory pitted squarely against a subjective "Abelardian" theory—the one with allies like Calvin, Luther, and the Protestant tradition; the other with theological heirs like the Socinians, the Grotians, and a long line of liberal theologians.

Yet as Christians, we must learn to think more carefully, read more critically, and interact more charitably. Theological discourse and disagreements are almost always more complicated than what some pastor projects on a PowerPoint slide or some professor summarizes in a side-by-side comparison chart. Often, things aren't what they appear on the surface. Often champions of one theological position misunderstand or misrepresent the views of others. The best procedure in any case is to go straight to the original source rather than to rely on secondary or tertiary sources. This is true in the case of the alleged controversy between Anselm and Abelard. And it's true of many other "us" versus "them" debates in theology today.

---

[16]   Richard E. Weingart, *The Logic of Divine Love: A Critical Analysis of the Soteriology of Peter Abailard* (Oxford: Oxford University Press, 1970), vii.

[17]   Weingart, *Logic of Divine Love*, 204. See his more detailed description and examination of Abelard's writings especially on pp. 128–46.

Resources

Evans, G. R. "Anselm of Canterbury." In *The Medieval Theologians: An Introduction to Theology in the Medieval Period*, edited by G. R. Evans, 94–101. Oxford: Blackwell, 2001.

Nielsen, Lauge O. "Peter Abelard and Gilbert of Poitiers." In *The Medieval Theologians: An Introduction to Theology in the Medieval Period*, edited by G. R. Evans, 102–28. Oxford: Blackwell, 2001.

Weingart, Richard E. *The Logic of Divine Love: A Critical Analysis of the Soteriology of Peter Abailard*. Oxford: Oxford University Press, 1970.

CHAPTER 19

The Eastern and Western Churches Split over Just One Word in the Creed

The Legendary Story

The ancient church dwelt in harmony and unity. Attacks periodically came from outside the church—such as Emperor Diocletian's persecution in the early fourth century. More often, however, the church dealt with adversity from within its own ranks in the form of heretical teaching, as we see in the cases of people such as Arius and Nestorius. Through it all, the church remained unified . . . until everything changed in AD 1054.

In that year, the Eastern and Western churches split, going so far as to condemn each other to hell. The issue? A dispute over a single (Latin) word in the Nicene Creed. The Western churches had added the word to the creed without consulting the Eastern churches. Lingering bad feelings over the change flared up as leaders in each church excommunicated their rivals.

Introduction: Unraveling the Legend

On a recent visit to the Grand Canyon with my family, I (John) marveled at the lines that cut across the rock throughout the depth of the canyon. Geologists believe these layers of rock show us something about the passage of time in the canyon, indicating different historical eras when ocean water completely covered the canyon. The ground around the canyon—the very ground visitors stand on to see the canyon—is only the top layer of sediment, resting upon a whole series of layers beneath.

History works in much the same way. While there might be a significant "top layer" cause that leads to specific effects, that cause is usually only one among several other "layers" of causes buried beneath the surface. The split of the Eastern and Western churches fits this model. While the dispute over a single word in the Niceno-Constantinopolitan Creed (381) created much tension between the churches on the surface, the debate about the word had been going on for centuries before 1054. Furthermore, other causes contributed to the split in important ways. Any discussion of a split must reckon with the continued relationship between East and West even after 1054.

A Culture of Difference

While the New Testament was written in Greek, the Latin language was ascending in popularity throughout the Roman Empire. However, Rome's power weakened by the fifth century. The empire shrank, but Latin retained its hold on western Europe. The language had become entrenched in European culture, and, as such, the words spoken and sung in European church worship were in Latin. In the Eastern church, the lingua franca was Greek, not Latin. But more than that, the Eastern church had historically been much more open to linguistic variation as regional churches developed, each with its own linguistic tradition.[1] The language differences were an underlying contributor, though not a primary cause of the schism in 1054.

Distinctions in church practice and worship started early, with Eastern and Western churches disagreeing about when to celebrate Easter at least as far back as the second century. Eastern churches were also in the habit, from the beginning of the church's history, of using leavened bread in the Eucharist each week.[2] Indeed, this was the tradition throughout the church, with the use of unleavened bread developing in the West at some point later.[3]

---

[1]   Today, the Eastern Orthodox Church contains a number of linguistically unique traditions that claim their origins before 1054. Several of these were widely recognized at the time: the Greek Orthodox Church, the Antiochian Orthodox Church, the Coptic Orthodox Church, the Syriac Orthodox Church, the Georgian Orthodox Church, and the Armenian Orthodox Church. Several other orthodox communions, including the largest orthodox communion—the Russian Orthodox Church—claim their origins before AD 1054 as well.

[2]   Eastern churches point to the distinction between "bread" and "unleavened bread" in Scripture, and state that in the relevant "Eucharist passages" from the Gospels and 1 Corinthians, the Bible only uses "bread," indicating common or leavened bread.

[3]   George Galavaris, *Bread and the Liturgy: The Symbolism of Early Christian and Byzantine Bread Stamps* (Madison, WI: University of Wisconsin Press, 1970), 54.

However, not even these differences in core practices of the church seem to have been the primary reason for the split.[4]

While these differences ultimately weren't the specific issues that caused the schism, their presence contributed to a larger culture of difference between East and West. As a result, other issues of more importance to churchmen at the time played off this existing culture of difference, making it that much harder for the church to remain unified.

A Difference That Made a Difference

In April 1054, a papal ambassador (or legate), Cardinal Humbert (c.1000–1061), traveled from Rome to Constantinople in order to smooth over fractures in the relationship between Pope Leo IX (1002–1054) and Michael Keroularios (c. 1000–1059), the bishop of Constantinople. Within three months, Humbert issued a papal bull (official statement) excommunicating Keroularios from the church. A week later, Keroularios excommunicated Humbert (but not the pope, interestingly) and offered a response to his excommunication. Issues listed in this response are numerous and include the type of bread used, whether the clergy could be married (East) or not (West), and the *filioque* clause, the last of which will be discussed in more detail below.

However, the unifying theme running through all of the minor complaints involved Roman leadership. The Eastern churches believed in a plurality of leadership—even though Rome would be honored among the most significant churches. But the power of the papacy had grown considerably over the previous centuries, and the Eastern churches chafed at the domineering rule from Rome. As one Roman Catholic scholar suggests, "The eleventh-century reform in the Western Church called for the strengthening of papal authority, which caused the church to become more autocratic and centralized. Basing his claims on his succession from St. Peter, the pope asserted his direct jurisdiction over the entire church, East as well as West."[5] The East rejected the West's power play, and the single word added to the Creed served as a convenient representative of the more significant disagreement

---

[4] It is worth noting that in responding to his excommunication in AD 1054, the bishop of Constantinople, Michael Keroularios, mentioned the issue of bread among his concerns with the western church. See Andrew Louth, *Greek East and Latin West: The Church AD 681–1071* (Crestwood, NY: St. Vladimir's Seminary Press, 2007), 311.

[5] George T. Dennis, 1054: "The East-West Schism," in "The 100 Most Important Events in Church History," issue 28, *Christian History* magazine, 1990.

over leadership. As Gregg Allison has noted, "At the heart of the matter was the question of authority."[6]

What about That Single Word?

Popular understanding of the schism between East and West continues to presume the singular difference was over one word in the creed. The word, *filioque*, is a compound Latin term that means "and the Son." Many have oversimplified the controversy and pointed to this war of words as representing what was wrong with the medieval church. For instance, note the explanation on one "find-the-answer" website: "There was so much contention over this issue that it eventually led to the split between the Roman Catholic and Eastern Orthodox churches in A.D. 1054. The two churches are still not in agreement on the filioque clause."[7] With conflicts over such issues as clerical celibacy and papal leadership, there were clearly multiple factors that played into the schism. But exactly what role did *filioque* play?

Two key issues regarding the term were raised: (1) The addition of the word to the Nicene Creed,[8] and (2) the meaning of the word in the Creed. The first record of *filioque* in the Nicene Creed comes nearly 300 years after the creed's inception, at the Third Council of Toledo in 589. It took four more centuries, however, for the word to gain acceptance in the official worship of the church at Rome. When the schism of 1054 came around, the word had only been used in Roman Church worship for about thirty years.[9]

For some evangelical Protestants, a word change in the Nicene Creed might seem like small potatoes. However, throughout the majority of the church's history, the Nicene Creed has been the standard for expressing the fundamentals of the Christian faith, especially doctrines such as the Trinity and Christology. For the bishops of the West to make a change to the fundamentals of the Christian faith without consulting the Eastern churches was the height of impropriety.

The second key issue involved the meaning of the word *filioque*. It appeared

---

[6] Gregg Allison, *Historical Theology* (Grand Rapids: Zondervan, 2011), 440.

[7] "What Is the Filioque Clause / Filioque Controversy?," Got Questions, accessed January 22, 2020, https://www.gotquestions.org/filioque-clause-controversy.html.

[8] Actually, the word was added to a longer version of the original Nicene Creed. This longer version was also from the fourth century, a result of the First Council of Constantinople in AD 381. This creedal statement retained the language of Nicaea, but added language to the statement on the Holy Spirit, including language about the church. Sometimes, this creed is called the Niceno-Constantinopolitan Creed. For brevity's sake, this chapter uses the shortened title, the Nicene Creed.

[9] Wayne Grudem, *Systematic Theology* (Grand Rapids: Zondervan, 1994), 246.

in the statement on the Holy Spirit, "who proceeds from the Father [and the Son = *filioque*]." The language of "proceeds from the Father" is a direct quotation of John 15:26 and historically has addressed the nature of the eternal relationship between God the Father and God the Spirit. When the Western church added "and the Son" on the basis of John 16:7, they were, in the minds of the Eastern churches, playing fast and loose with Scripture, since John 16:7 speaks of "sending" rather than "procession." Nearly two centuries before the schism, an Eastern bishop from Constantinople named Photios I (c. 810–893) objected to the additional word on the grounds that this idea compromised the monarchy of the Father, leading to a kind of "ditheism." The idea also suggested that the Spirit's procession from the Father was somehow less than perfect if a procession from the Son was also required.[10] The Western churches, however, focused on the unity of the three persons in their work, explicitly rejecting any kind of "ditheism."

While the Roman Church started using the language only a few decades before 1054, the *filioque* clause became official church doctrine at the Second Council of Lyons in 1274.[11] Given that Pope Urban II sent armies to the East in 1095 to aid the Eastern churches against Muslim invasion, it seems clear that a sense of unity amid the strife and disagreement prevailed even after 1054. However, when the Western church issued a call for unity at Lyons in 1274, the Eastern church explicitly rejected it, a clear sign of separation.[12]

Application

Throughout the majority of the church's history, the Nicene Creed has functioned as the central statement of core Christian doctrine. As a result, Christians have recited it regularly—even weekly—in corporate church worship among Roman Catholics, Eastern Orthodox, and some Protestant churches. The creed was birthed in consensus. The church, East and West, North and South, gathered at Nicaea (and later, at Constantinople) to hammer out the language. Thus, when a small group of churches unilaterally decided to add language to the creed, it shouldn't surprise anyone that other churches might legitimately question the decision.

This historical reality offers a lesson for Christians today: when it comes

---

[10] Louth, *Greek East and Latin West*, 185.

[11] Allison, *Historical Theology*, 243.

[12] Recent decades have seen much progress made in the relationship between Rome and the Eastern churches, even as the East continues to reject papal authority and does not use the *filioque* clause.

to core Christian doctrine, seek out the ancient consensus of the historic church rather than the fresh invention of a contemporary individual. The core doctrine of the church ultimately points believers back to the apostolic preaching about the person and work of Jesus, which stands at the center of God's redemptive story in Scripture.

However, another lesson becomes apparent as a result of the split between East and West—unity requires humility and empathy. Christian leaders at the time exerted their power to excommunicate and divide rather than their patience to listen and understand. If they had made more effort to do the latter, empathy for the alternative perspective might have had time to develop. No doubt Christians throughout history would have continued to diverge on specific issues, but a sense of one's own limitations allows for continued fellowship despite doctrinal disagreements and varying customs.

Resources

Dennis, George T. 1054: "The East-West Schism." In "The 100 Most Important Events in Church History," issue 28, *Christian History* magazine, 1990.
Louth, Andrew. *Greek East and Latin West: The Church AD 681–1071.* Crestwood, NY: St. Vladimir's Seminary Press, 2007.

___

CHAPTER 20

The Roman Catholic Church Regularly
Burned Heretics at the Stake

The Legendary Story

The Roman Catholic Church has a lot of blood on its hands. Throughout its many centuries of dominance, it has been responsible for the deaths of countless critics conveniently labeled "heretics." When torture didn't work to turn the wayward back to blind submission to the pope and Mother Church, stiff-necked heretics were burned at the stake. As history progressed, the Roman Catholic Church used the crusades to slaughter infidels and employed the Spanish Inquisition to hunt down heretics. God only knows how many millions died at the hands of the Roman Catholic Church.

Introduction: Unraveling the Legend

The use of violence in dealing with heresy has a complex history. In both the medieval and Reformation periods (and in territories dominated by both the Roman Catholic and Protestant churches), the secular authority, not the church, was responsible for punishing criminals. However, because of the close relationship between church and state, when the church leaders found a person (or group) guilty of heresy, they would hand them over to the state to be dealt with according to the laws of the land. Technically, the church was not responsible for executing heretics. Their authority only allowed them to render them guilty of heresy and to excommunicate them from the church. In fact, church authorities officially appealed to the secular authorities to show mercy toward the condemned. Practically, however, the closeness of church and state in this period made the question of who was really responsible for the execution of heretics somewhat fuzzy.

Heresy-Hunting in the Middle Ages

Today the Vatican organization responsible for officially approving doctrinal truth and confronting doctrinal error is called "the [Sacred] Congregation for the Doctrine of the Faith." Between 1908 and 1965, this same congregation was called "The Congregation of the Holy Office" or simply "the Holy Office." And before that, from its founding in 1542, it was called "The Sacred Congregation of the Holy Roman and Universal Inquisition," or "the Inquisition" for short.[1] Its primary purpose was to oversee a coordinated anti-Protestant effort, reining in all forms of heresy and stopping its dangerous advancement in lands that had been bastions of the Roman Catholic Church for centuries.

The official "Holy Roman and Universal Inquisition," however, wasn't alone. Already in the twelfth and thirteenth centuries, the Roman Catholic Church had established bodies responsible for seeking out and suppressing heresy in Europe. The first major target of the medieval inquisition was the Cathar heresy. The Cathars likely entered France through the work of missionaries from eastern Europe sometime in the middle of the twelfth century. The Cathars, also known as the "Albigenses," held to deviant views similar to the earlier heresy of Gnosticism, likely denying the two natures of Christ, the authority of the Old Testament, and the practice of baptism, while affirming a dualistic view of God and the inherent evil of the material world.[2]

By 1200, Catharism had become so entrenched in certain regions of France that Pope Innocent III (1160–1216) called for a military crusade against the Cathar territories in 1209, called the "Albigensian Crusade" (1209–1255). French barons in the North answered the call and attacked the lands of Count

---

[1]   Cullen Murphy, *God's Jury: The Inquisition and the Making of the Modern World* (New York: Houghton Mifflin Harcourt, 2012), 2–3.

[2]   See Michael Frassetto, *The Great Medieval Heretics: Five Centuries of Religious Dissent* (New York: BlueBridge, 2008), 75–79.

Raymond VI, who had exercised tolerance toward the growing population of Cathars in his territory before being forced to repent and join the attack on the Cathars. One historian notes, "The mounted knights and foot soldiers indulged in a horrible slaughter, killing men, women, and children—Catholic and heretic alike. They plundered homes, invaded churches, burned large sections of the town, and indulged in wanton destruction and looting."[3] Thousands died in this long series of military campaigns designed to stamp out Catharism from France.[4]

Following the Albigensian Crusade, Pope Gregory IX (c. 1150–1241) established a tribunal with the specific task of seeking out and compelling heretics to repent. Frassetto notes:

> People accused of heresy were brought before the inquisitors, who often asked leading questions which forced the accused to prove their innocence. Torture was resorted to at times, but the inquisitors' goal was to discover the heretics and to recall them to the faith. Other inquiries followed, building on the precedents and procedures established at Toulouse [France], and in the great inquest of 1245–46 more than five thousand people were interrogated, many of whom were found guilty of heresy and thus subject to imprisonment, exile, or loss of property.[5]

Through the work of these inquisitors—mostly Dominican and Franciscan monks—and with the support of the secular authorities, the Cathar heresy in France was finally destroyed by the fourteenth century. In the course of the crusade and inquisition against the Cathars, many of its obstinate leaders, themselves sometimes guilty of violence and bloodshed, were executed through immolation—"burning at the stake."

Many of the procedures developed in the inquisition against the Cathars—including the use of torture—were duplicated in other inquisitions against Jews, Muslims, Waldensians, and other heretics and infidels. Often these methods of extracting confessions were cruel and unusual, leading to reports of injustice and brutality that sometimes led to attacks against the inquisitors, their assistants, and secular authorities that enforced their policies.

---

[3]   Frassetto, *Great Medieval Heretics*, 90.
[4]   John D. Hannah, *Invitation to Church History: World*, Invitation to Theological Studies (Grand Rapids: Kregel, 2018), 220.
[5]   Frassetto, *Great Medieval Heretics*, 104–5.

The Spanish Inquisition

Perhaps the greatest specter looming over any discussions regarding the brutal treatment of heretics is the Spanish Inquisition. Yet many have only a vague and inaccurate understanding of what the Inquisition actually was and what it really did. In 1478, the monarchs of Spain, Ferdinand and Isabella (known for bankrolling the voyage of Christopher Columbus), established the infamously rigorous and brutal operations of the Spanish Inquisition. Originally used to consolidate political and ecclesiastical power, the tribunal led to forced conversions of Jews and Muslims before turning their attention to the rise of Protestantism.

During the sixteenth century, the Spanish Inquisition led to the execution of hundreds of people found guilty of heresy—usually the heresy of "Protestantism." In the Netherlands, that number surpassed 1,300 by 1566.[6] In response to the brutal treatment by inquisitors, Protestant pamphleteers broadcast the details of the persecutions far and wide, including John Foxe's famous *Book of Martyrs* (1563). Though the executions in other lands often outpaced those in Spain, the stories of the "Spanish Inquisition" fueled both fear and hatred of the Spaniards for their allegedly barbarous cruelty.

Without denying the brutality and cruelty of the Inquisition—or downplaying the injustice and wickedness of its official actions—we need to acknowledge that the historical facts and figures have been frequently mixed with exaggerations and outright fictions. For example, a nineteenth-century account of the Inquisition suggested that the Spanish tribunal was responsible for burning "more than *three hundred thousand victims!*"[7] In fact, the actual number of victims was about 1 percent of that fanciful figure.[8] In a scathing review of an irresponsible work on the history of the Inquisition, Henry Kamen notes that the author overstated the number of people tried by the Inquisition "with errors of nearly one hundred per cent in some cases."[9]

---

[6]   Henry Kamen, *The Spanish Inquisition: A Historical Revision* (New Haven: Yale University Press, 1997), 377.

[7]   Juan Antonio Llorente, *The History of the Inquisition of Spain from the Time of Its Establishment to the Reign of Ferdinand VII*, abr. ed., trans. (London: Whittaker, 1826), xvi–xvii.

[8]   Kamen, *The Spanish Inquisition*, 383.

[9]   Henry Kamen, "Review of *The Spanish Inquisition* by Joseph Pérez," *Renaissance Quarterly* 59, no. 1 (Spring 2006): 165.

"Joan of Arc Was Burned at the Stake for Witchcraft"

Peasant revolutionary Joan of Arc (c. 1412–1431) was burned at the stake by French Catholics in league with English invaders of France. While Joan died under the banner of a church trial, this incident was actually inspired by a political end—the need to contain Joan's revolutionary tendencies. Many have argued that the French burned Joan for witchcraft. In reality, the crimes listed against her in the twelve charges read before her execution were more mundane—she wore men's clothes and listened to the voices of dead saints over and against the voices of church authorities. In the end, Joan died because her refusal to listen to correction from church leaders made her, in their eyes, a blasphemer and an idolater.[10]

Setting the Record Straight

There is no acceptable number of men and women persecuted or executed for their non-Christian religious beliefs—not 300,000, not 3,000, and not 3. In pointing out the gross exaggerations in common retellings of the Inquisition, we don't want to excuse its injustice, corruption, and depravity. However, we must take care that we deal with facts and figures as they are.

The numbers of those executed as a result of the various medieval inquisitions against Jews, Muslims, Cathars, Waldensians, and Protestants are nothing near the "millions" or "hundreds of thousands" promulgated by common urban legends. And Roman Catholic countries were certainly not alone in establishing laws against heresy, holding trials, and then carrying out sentences. Protestants were also guilty of heresy trials and executions. One immediately thinks of the execution of the anti-trinitarian heretic Michael Servetus (1509–1553) by the city council of Geneva after being found guilty in a heresy trial. John Calvin (1509–1564) himself supported the sentence of the secular authorities, though

---

[10]   See Helen Castor, *Joan of Arc: A History* (New York: Harper, 2015), 187.

he argued for a more humane execution than burning at the stake.[11] Lutherans, Presbyterians, Anglicans, Congregationalists, and Anabaptists were all guilty to some degree of countering heresy or establishing their orthodoxy by persecution, prosecution, execution, and even warfare.

But we must also recall the official position of the Roman Catholic Church that ecclesiastical power stopped short of the authority to execute a heretic. Canon 3 of the Fourth Lateran Council (1215) says, "We excommunicate and anathematize every heresy which exalteth itself against this holy, orthodox, and Catholic faith, which we have set forth. . . . Let such persons, when condemned, be left to the secular powers who may be present, or to their officers, to be punished in a fitting manner."[12] Thus, from a technical, legal perspective, the church was not itself responsible for punishment and execution. However, from a practical perspective, the situation is more complicated, because the same Canon decrees, "Let the secular powers, whatever offices they may discharge, be admonished and induced, and, if need be, compelled by ecclesiastical censure" to strive for the faith against heresy, and "if any temporal lord, being required and admonished by the church, shall neglect to cleanse his country of this heretical filth, let him be bound with the chain of excommunication by the metropolitan, and the other co-provincial Bishops."[13] So, though the church was not technically carrying out the sentences of execution, the secular authorities who did faced pressure from the church to do so.

Finally, we need to reckon with the historical realities and political complexities of the medieval world, in which the Christian church and the Christian state were practically inseparable. No, the Roman Catholic Church didn't "regularly burn heretics at the stake." From a technical legal perspective, they burned none, except, perhaps, in the rare case in which a single individual might have wielded religious authority in one hand and secular authority in the other. And in any case, the actual number that secular authorities executed was not as great as some have imagined, though one heretic burned over a difference of religious opinion is one too many.

One historian sums up well the growing consensus of modern scholarship on the Inquisition based on more recent research of available sources:

---

[11]   Hannah, *Invitation to Church History: World*, 317.
[12]   Canon III of the Fourth Lateran Council, in John Evans, *The Statutes of the Fourth General Council of Lateran* (London: L. and G. Seeley, 1843), 86.
[13]   Evans, *The Statutes of the Fourth General Council of Lateran*, 86–87.

Most people accused of heresy by the Inquisition were either acquitted or their sentences suspended. Those found guilty of grave error were allowed to confess their sin, do penance, and be restored to the Body of Christ. The underlying assumption of the Inquisition was that, like lost sheep, heretics had simply strayed . . . Unrepentant or obstinate heretics were excommunicated and given over to secular authorities. Despite popular myth, the Inquisition did not burn heretics. It was the secular authorities that held heresy to be a capital offense, not the Church. The simple fact is that the medieval Inquisition *saved* uncounted thousands of innocent (and even not-so-innocent) people who would otherwise have been roasted by secular lords or mob rule.[14]

Application

The phenomenon of official religious persecution against those perceived as heretics and infidels—apostates and unbelievers—should cause us to consider the serious flaws in a too-close relationship between church and state, especially when the secular authorities are urged or compelled by religious interests to enforce theology or morality on professed unbelievers. This is a danger that is too often left unheeded in history.

Without doubt, the persecution of heretics by church and state has left a major scar in the body of Christ. Though it may be easy for Protestants and free church evangelicals to distance themselves from the official Roman Catholic Church's Inquisition, most Christian denominations and traditions have had their own histories of persecution and brutality. We must all own up to the real history of injustices done in the name of Christ and his church. And we must make sure that we are not engaged in the same kinds of injustices in our own day.

Resources

Ames, Christine Caldwell. *Righteous Persecution: Inquisition, Dominicans, and Christianity in the Middle Ages.* Philadelphia: University of Pennsylvania Press, 2009.

Kamen, Henry. *The Spanish Inquisition: A Historical Revision.* New Haven, CT: Yale University Press, 1997.

---

[14] Thomas F. Madden, "The Real Inquisition," *National Review,* accessed June 18, 2004, https://www.nationalreview.com/2004/06/real-inquisition-thomas-f-madden/.

PART III

Urban Legends
of the Protestant Era
(1500–1700)

Protestant Era Time Line
(Some of the dates below are approximate.)

1469–1534: Cardinal Thomas Cajetan

1483–1546: Martin Luther

1484–1531: Ulrich Zwingli

1486–1541: Andreas Karlstadt

1488–1569: Myles Coverdale

1489–1525: Thomas Müntzer

1489–1565: William Farel

1491–1529: George Blaurock

1494–1536: William Tyndale

1495–1543: Melchior Hoffman

1496–1561: Menno Simons

1498–1526: Conrad Grebel

1498–1527: Felix Manz

1499–1543: Sebastian Franck

1500–1534: Jan Matthijs

1500–1536: Jacob Hutter

1504–1572: Pope Pius V

1509–1553: Michael Servetus

1509–1564: John Calvin

1513–1572: John Knox

1517: Luther's Ninety-Five Theses

1519–1605: Theodore Beza

1530: Augsburg Confession

1532–1612: Adrian Saravia

1536: Calvin's *Institutes* published

1545–1563: Council of Trent

1560–1609: Jacob (James) Arminius

1561–1626: Francis Bacon

1566: Second Helvetic Confession

1566–1625: King James I

1570–1612: John Smyth

1575–1616: Thomas Helwys

1585–1652: John Cotton

1588–1649: John Winthrop

1590–1676: Pope Clement X

1591–1643: Anne Hutchinson

1592–1679: John Wheelwright

1596–1650: René Descartes

1603–1683: Roger Williams

1605–1690: John Eliot

1611: King James Bible published

1618–1619: Synod of Dordt

1620: Pilgrims land in Plymouth

1628–1688: John Bunyan

1632–1704: John Locke

1639: First Baptist church established in America

1646: Westminster Confession

1663–1728: Cotton Mather

1664–1729: Jean Meslier

1692–1693: Salem Witch Trials

CHAPTER 21

The Protestant Reformers Concocted the Doctrine of Salvation by Grace through Faith

The Legendary Story

The Protestant teaching that we are saved by grace through faith apart from works—underscored by giants like Martin Luther—was a theological novelty, unheard-of in the history of the church before the Reformation. Previously, the church taught that salvation was merited through cooperation with God's grace. Works were absolutely essential. When Martin Luther (1483–1546) first articulated the doctrine of salvation by grace through faith, he promoted a view unheard of in history, reading his idiosyncratic view into the New Testament.

Introduction: Unraveling the Legend

The absence of salvation by grace through faith in the entire history of the church up to Luther is a startling claim, yet one that some continue to make. Consider the contention of Thomas R. Thompson, "The history of the doctrine [of] justification by faith alone is difficult to trace before the Reformation in the 1500's. A clear line of development of this doctrine from the Apostles to Martin Luther" does not exist.[1] Unfortunately, those who espouse this position

---

[1]   Thomas R. Thompson, "The History of Justification by Faith Alone up to the Reformation," Monergism website, accessed January 22, 2020, https://www.monergism.com/history-justification-faith-alone-reformation.

misunderstand the history of the church's teaching on salvation, as well as Luther's teaching on salvation.

Orthodox Christians have always believed that salvation has been by grace through faith. If this teaching did not exist before Luther, it raises major questions about the Holy Spirit's presence in the church throughout history. Did he abandon believers and leave the church teaching a false gospel? That would seem to contradict the assurances of Jesus that the Spirit would always be with us (John 14:16). While the church has seen her share of members offering incorrect teaching about salvation, the Holy Spirit has been remarkably faithful to preserve the truth that salvation has always been by grace through faith.

Headwaters: The Early Church

The early church knew and interacted with the New Testament, including Paul's teaching of the "by grace through faith" doctrine in places such as Eph 2:8–9 and Rom 4:3–5.

Consider the first century bishop of the church at Rome, Clement (c. 35–99), who wrote, "And so we, having been called through his will in Christ Jesus, are not justified through ourselves or through our own wisdom or understanding or piety, or works that we have done in holiness of heart, but through faith, by which the Almighty God justified all who have existed from the beginning; to whom be the glory for ever and ever. Amen."[2] Clement taught this about as clearly as one could hope—God makes believers right with him through faith and not as a result of works. And note that he explicitly rules out anything else cooperating with or contributing to this justification—rendering a very early articulation of the doctrine of justification by faith alone.

In the second century, the bishop of the church in Smyrna, Polycarp (c. 69–155), who in his younger years had been a disciple of the apostle John, wrote, "Though you have not seen him, you believe in him with an inexpressible and glorious joy (which many desire to experience), knowing that by grace you have been saved, not because of works, but by the will of God through Jesus Christ."[3] Polycarp's teaching is clear: we are not saved by works, but by grace, which comes to us not by our own will, but by the will of God.

Jumping ahead to the fourth century, Athanasius (290–374), the bishop of the church at Alexandria, Egypt, commented on the source of salvation

---

[2]   *1 Clement* 32.4 (Holmes, 87).
[3]   Polycarp, *Philippians* 1.3 (Holmes, 281).

not just in the current age, but in the Old Testament as well. He wrote, "The Patriarch Abraham received the crown, not because he suffered death, but because he was faithful unto God; and the other Saints, of whom Paul speaks . . . were not made perfect by the shedding of their blood, but by faith they were justified; and to this day they are the objects of our admiration, as being ready even to suffer death for piety towards the Lord."[4] Once again, a church father makes explicit that salvation comes not as a result of a great work, but rather that these doers of great deeds were saved by faith.

The doctrine of "justification by faith *alone*" (*sola fide*), seen very early in the writings of figures like Clement and Polycarp, was evident in the writings of other church fathers reflecting on Paul's writings. Thus, the fourth-century writer Marius Victorinus, in his commentary on Galatians, wrote, "Faith itself alone grants justification and sanctification. Thus any flesh whatsoever—Jews or those from the Gentiles—is justified on the basis of faith, not works or observance of the Jewish Law."[5]

Midstream: Augustine and Pelagius

Moving downstream from the early Christians, the fifth century finds the church's doctrine of salvation reaching a new level of maturity in the work of Augustine (354–430), bishop of the North African church at Hippo. In his basic statement of Christian doctrine, called the *Enchiridion (Handbook)* or *Faith, Hope, and Charity*, he argued, "The will owes its freedom in no degree to itself, but solely to the grace of God which comes by faith in Jesus Christ; so that the very will, through which we accept all the other gifts of God which lead us on to His eternal gift, is itself prepared of the Lord, as the Scripture says."[6] Augustine believed that because human beings were sinful from birth, only salvation frees a person to follow after God by the power of the Holy Spirit who indwells every believer. Therefore, salvation had to be a result of grace, since human beings would not otherwise seek after or follow God due to sin.

Pelagius (c. 360–418), a contemporary of Augustine, had other ideas about the means of salvation. He taught that human beings were free to choose

---

[4] Athanasius, *To the Bishops of Egypt* 21 (NPNF 2.4:234).

[5] Victorinus, *Commentary on Galatians* 2:15–16. Translation from Stephen Andrew Cooper, *Marius Victorinus' Commentary on Galatians*, Oxford Early Christian Studies (Oxford, UK: Oxford University Press, 2005), 282.

[6] Augustine, *Enchiridion* 106 (NPNF 1.3: 271).

God from birth, meaning grace was neither necessary nor sufficient for salvation. Salvation was based, for Pelagius, on human choice or work rather than upon grace.

Around the same time, another monk named John Cassian (c. 360–435) taught something of a middle ground between Augustine and Pelagius— that people were born in a weakened or diseased state due to their sin in Adam. Cassian felt, therefore, that human beings had some inherent ability to respond to God, even as he recognized human weakness due to sin and the need for the assistance of grace. The result was that Cassian called people to cooperate with the gracious work of God in their lives. For Cassian, God's grace was part of salvation, but so were our good efforts.[7]

In the midst of this dispute over sin and grace, the church united against Pelagius's ideas at the regional Council of Carthage (418), and then later at the ecumenical (church-wide) Council of Ephesus (431). However, they did not fully side with all of Augustine's theology, nor did they side with Cassian's mediating position.

River's End: The Medieval Church

The medieval church drifted from the Augustinian teaching on grace, as other tributaries deviated from that mainstream and gained influence in their own right. In the centuries immediately following Augustine, the church seemed to follow his views of humanity's depravity and need for grace, as evidenced by the Second Council of Orange (AD 529). At this council, the ideas of Pelagius were condemned explicitly, especially the notion that human souls remain free and unimpaired by sin. It also rejected Cassian's notion that humans have some natural capacity to cooperate with God's grace. However, the council did not follow Augustine completely. They backed away from some of the implications of his teaching that God might predestine some people to salvation. This decision charted a course of "semi-Augustinianism" in the early medieval church—people were largely with Augustine on these issues, though not on every point.

Cassian's view continued as a strong tributary alongside the river of salvation by grace alone, especially in the Eastern Orthodox view of salvation. And in the West, Thomas Aquinas (1225–1274), the premier theologian of

---

7   See Michael J. Svigel, "Humanity and Sin in Retrospect," in Nathan D. Holsteen and Michael J. Svigel, eds., *Exploring Christian Theology*, vol. 2, *Creation, Fall, and Salvation* (Minneapolis: Bethany House, 2015), 55–56.

the Middle Ages, argued for a doctrine of salvation that begins with the grace of God—an Augustinian view for sure—but then incorporated human cooperation with God throughout the process. Later theologians such as Gabriel Biel (1420–1495) shifted more decidedly in the direction of Pelagius, arguing for a view of salvation in which human cooperation precedes God's work of grace. Such thinking remained a minority view as the church largely followed Aquinas. This drift toward Pelagianism came as a result of the Roman Catholic Church's neglect of the Second Council of Orange (529). As Alister McGrath notes, "The canons of Orange II appear to have been unknown from the tenth century to the middle of the sixteenth. The theologians of the medieval period thus did not have access to this definitive statement of an Augustinian doctrine of justification, and appear to have been unaware of its existence."[8]

Enter Martin Luther (1483–1546) and the Protestant Reformers, steeped in the renewed study of Scripture, the early church, and especially Augustine. Luther brought a measure of clarity to the issues surrounding the medieval ideas of grace, arguing that God's grace was more than sufficient for salvation. One scholar writes that although the Roman Catholic "system of divine grace and human cooperation was itself the result of God's gratuitous love, within that system no grace could be dispensed from the treasury without some good cause . . . an act of love on our part. Luther's idea that God's grace is given freely . . . was foreign to this idea."[9] The distinction here was stark, coming down to a single question: Does God give grace freely, or does he give only in accordance with our actions? Therefore, while many in the church had emphasized salvation by grace through faith, Luther's immediate opponents had muddied the issue considerably.

Therefore, Luther's teaching of justification by grace through faith—apart from works that merit salvation or cooperate with God's grace—is not an idiosyncratic novelty. Rather, it is best viewed as a reassertion of the doctrine of salvation that originated in the apostolic period, was affirmed in the ancient church, and was emphasized by Augustinian theology until it was watered down in the late medieval era.

---

[8]   Alister E. McGrath, *Iustitia Dei: A History of the Christian Doctrine of Justification*, 3rd ed. (Cambridge: Cambridge University Press, 2005), 97–98.

[9]   David Bagchi, "Luther's Catholic Opponents," in *The Reformation World*, ed. Andrew Pettegree (London: Routledge, 2000),105. The mention of a "treasury" in the quotation refers to a treasury of merits, the medieval belief that Christ's cross generated an infinite amount of merit, but that merit is only dispensed as believers act in accordance with love.

MINI MYTHS

"The Reformers Summed Up Their Theology with Five Solas"

It is often repeated that the Reformers summed up their theology with the "Five Solas"— *Sola Scriptura, Sola gratia, Sola fide, Solus Christus*, and *Soli Deo gloria*. However, this convenient packaging of the five pillars of Protestant theology didn't occur until the twentieth century. This doesn't mean that the Reformers didn't hold the views these *Solas* summarize. Early on, they argued that salvation is by *grace alone* through *faith alone* in *Christ alone*, based on *Scripture alone* as the final authority in matters necessary for salvation. And they believed all things were to be done to the glory of *God alone*. But such a tidy packaging of the "Five Solas" was at least 400 years in the making.[10]

Application

Salvation by grace through faith has always been the view of orthodox Christians. One reason some Protestants and evangelicals foster suspicion of church history centers on this very issue—assuming that the fifteen centuries before Luther were characterized by so-called Christians who believed God would save them by their works. Instead, this chapter has shown that the Holy Spirit has preserved salvation by grace through faith throughout the history of the church, even as Luther clarified the issue.

Christians should also see a warning embedded in history of soteriology. The temptation is strong to insert oneself into the process of salvation, in order that the believer receives some measure of credit for our part in salvation. The tendency of fallen humanity often leans in the direction of overestimating our abilities while underestimating the work God has done on our behalf. Luther's teaching on salvation by grace through faith rightly clarified the teaching of Christians throughout the history of the church, placing God at the center of the saving act while leaving human beings as the recipients of God's lavish gift.

---

[10]   See Kevin J. Vanhoozer, *Biblical Authority after Babel: Retrieving the* Solas *in the Spirit of Mere Protestant Christianity* (Grand Rapids: Brazos, 2016), 26–27.

Resources

Cho, Dongsun. "Ambrosiaster on Justification by Faith Alone in His Commentaries on the Pauline Epistles," *Westminster Theological Journal* 74 (2012): 277–90.

———. "Justification in Marius Victorinus' Pauline Commentaries: Sola Fide, Solo Christo, and Sola Gratia Dei." *Journal for Baptist Theology* 11, no. 1 (Spring 2014): 3–25.

McGrath, Alister E. *Iustitia Dei: A History of the Christian Doctrine of Justification.* 3rd ed. Cambridge: Cambridge University Press, 2005.

Williams, Daniel H. "Justification by Faith: A Patristic Doctrine." *Journal of Ecclesiastical History* 57, no. 4 (October 2006): 649–67.

CHAPTER 22

—

The Reformers Believed the Bible Was
the Only Source for Theology

The Legendary Story

Through the principle of *sola scriptura* (Scripture alone), the Reformers properly cast off the encumbrances of tradition and provided the church with a
solid foundation upon which to build the faith. Essentially, the Reformers have
shown us that Scripture alone is the only proper source for building a truly
Christian theology. All other sources may be set aside, fraught as they are with
error and deception. With Scripture as the Christian's sole source, descendants
of the Reformation can have confidence in their church's doctrine.

Introduction: Unraveling the Legend

The Reformation has left the world with a number of important truths, especially regarding salvation and the Bible. Christians have long appreciated the
"five *solas*"[1] of the Reformation: *sola gratia* (grace alone), *sola fide* (faith alone),
sola Scriptura (Scripture alone), *soli Deo gloria* (to the glory of God alone),
and *solus Christus* (Christ alone). *Sola scriptura* remains the most misunderstood among the five solas, as some Protestant Christians have held a view
that presents a false choice: either embrace Scripture as God's authoritative,

---

[1]   While the content of the five "solas" appear in the writings of the Reformers at different points,
Johann Baptiste Metz's book *The Church and the World* (1965) marks the first time all five "solas" were
grouped together.

sufficient Word or deny its authority and sufficiency by using other sources of truth. In reality, the Reformers' idea of *sola scriptura* was developed to deal with the issue of competing so-called "infallible" doctrinal authorities in the church. *Sola scriptura* never meant choosing Scripture as the only source of theology. Rather, they saw Scripture as the primary source of theology, more authoritative than church traditions and individual interpretations. After a brief look at some historical context, this chapter will define *sola scriptura* and consider implications of the doctrine.

Abundant Authorities

At the time of the Reformation, people in the Roman Catholic Church made theological claims based on a number of competing authorities. To describe any church's approach to authority, there are two related questions: (1) What sources of information factor into an authoritative decision, and (2) who makes the decision about biblical interpretation and doctrine?

In answer to the first, medieval Catholics invoked two primary sources: sacred Scripture and apostolic tradition. Historically, the Catholic argument has been that doctrinal development requires attention to both Scripture and tradition. However, in the centuries leading up to the Reformation, the Roman Catholic Church moved from the ancient practice of developing tradition from direct applications and implications of Scripture to the practice of speaking dogmatically on issues outside of Scripture. One medieval Catholic, Gabriel Biel (1420–1495), represented this shift, making a case "for investing the unwritten traditions with the same apostolic authority as the Scriptures."[2] Doctrines and practices that had once been deemed secondary because Scripture was silent about them had now been declared primary. This trend contributed to the Reformation reaction against Roman Catholics and tradition.

While Scripture and tradition function as sources for theology, neither operates outside of the answer to the second question above: Who makes the decisions about interpretation and doctrine? For medieval Catholics, this was usually articulated in terms of "the church." But who exactly in the church should make such decisions? On this point, they disagreed.

Most Catholics at the time of the Reformation would have argued that the pope was the final authority. The argument for papal power was based on Matt

---

[2]   Heiko A. Oberman, *The Dawn of the Reformation* (Edinburgh: T&T Clark, 1986), 281.

16:18–19, that Peter (and his descendants, as it was interpreted) would receive "the keys of the kingdom of heaven." With the broad powers of government at their disposal, the popes functioned essentially as princes, "holding the place on earth not of mere man, but of God . . . whence he rules and judges all . . . he has no superior . . . he is set over all and he can be judged by no one."[3] Here, the pope's authority is drawn so broadly that it would extend over every aspect of church and life, including the interpretation of Scripture. Views like this make it much easier to appreciate the heart of the conflict between the Reformers and the medieval Catholics.

In the century or so before the Reformation, many Catholics advocated for another line of authority in what was called the conciliar movement. These Catholics thought too much power had been invested in the papal office, so to blunt the power of a single individual, they proposed that the final authority in matters of faith and practice should rest in church councils. Any pope would, of course, participate in such councils, but only the consensus of the council would determine doctrinal issues.

One other avenue for defining authority involved elevating personal experience. Some medieval Catholics were mystics, who looked inward to their own, personal experiences with God to make decisions and determine beliefs. These mystics believed in the power of their experiences to direct their spiritual lives. Despite the presence of mystics and the conciliar movement, the church broadly embraced the papal office as the final decision maker in matters of faith and practice.

A Misunderstood Meaning

Protestant Christians have misunderstood *sola scriptura* more regularly than any of the other "solas." For instance, sociologist of religion (and former Protestant) Christian Smith defined the *sola scriptura* of his youth as "the Bible alone and no other human tradition as authority."[4] This type of misunderstanding developed in connection to another popular error: that the Roman Catholic Church made decisions of doctrine and practice based purely on tradition and not on Scripture. These are both radical views, and while a subset of Protestants holds a view much like the one Smith describes in his quotation above, this meaning

---

3   Thirteenth-century legal commentator Gulielmus Durandus, as quoted in Brian Tierney, *Religion, Law, and the Growth of Constitutional Thought* (Cambridge: Cambridge University Press, 1982), 14.

4   Christian Smith, *How to Go from Being a Good Evangelical to a Committed Catholic in Ninety-Five Difficult Steps* (Eugene, OR: Wipf and Stock, 2011), 83.

does not reflect the way *sola scriptura* functioned for the Reformers, or even how it functions for most Protestants today.[5]

What did the Reformers teach about the place of Scripture in deciding matters of faith and practice? Christian Smith's quotation above is *almost* correct, lacking only a single word to properly reflect the Reformation ideal. However, that single word makes a big difference in meaning. *Sola scriptura* actually means that the Bible alone, and no other human tradition, functions as the *final* authority in matters of faith and practice. As theologian Timothy George has said, "The principle of *sola scriptura* was intended to safeguard the authority of Scripture from that servile dependence upon the church that in fact made Scripture inferior to the church. Scripture is the *norma normans* (the determining norm) . . . for all decisions of faith and life."[6]

In the Reformation era, Martin Luther made this plain in his reported remarks at the Diet of Worms:

Unless I am convinced by the testimony of the Scriptures, or by evident reason (for I put my faith neither in Pope nor Councils alone, since it is established that they have erred again and again and contradicted one another), I am bound by the scriptural evidence adduced by me, and my conscience is captive to the Word of God. I cannot, I will not recant anything, for it is neither safe nor right to act against one's conscience.[7]

For Luther, Scripture served as the final authority, distinct from other possible authorities, such as a pope or a church council.

John Calvin (1509–1564), who helped lead the Reformation from the church at Geneva, Switzerland, wrote that "there is this difference between the apostles and their successors, they [the apostles] were sure and authentic amanuenses of the Holy Spirit; and, therefore, their writings are to be regarded as the oracles of God, whereas others have no other office than to teach what is delivered and sealed in the holy Scriptures."[8] Calvin made a clear distinc-

---

[5]   Many Christians in the Restoration movement (Churches of Christ, Christian Church/Churches of Christ, Christian Church [Disciples of Christ]) hold to a view that affirms Scripture as the only authority for faith and practice. See chapter 25 for more on that group.

[6]   Timothy George, *The Theology of the Reformers*, rev. ed. (Nashville: B&H Academic, 2013), 81–82.

[7]   Quoted in James Atkinson, *The Trial of Luther* (New York: Stein and Day, 1971), 161–62.

[8]   Calvin, *Institutes* 4.8.9 (John Calvin, *Institutes of the Christian Religion*, vol. 3, trans. Henry Beveridge [Edinburgh: The Calvin Translation Society, 1845], 166).

tion between the writers/writings of Scripture and those who have followed the apostles to lead the church in succeeding generations. Those who came later have merely taught the Scriptures, rather than carrying special authority themselves. This distinction granted supreme authority to the Scriptures, over and above those who teach the Scriptures.

MINI MYTHS

"Luther's Dramatic Nailing of the Ninety-Five Theses Started the Reformation"

Luther wrote the Ninety-Five Theses in 1517 to challenge the theology and practice of the sale of indulgences, and he mailed them to the archbishop of Mainz on October 31, 1517. This set off a chain reaction leading to the Protestant Reformation. Whether he also nailed them to the castle church door in Wittenberg is debatable. So how did that story become the iconic event of the Reformation? Think about it. The image of Martin Luther, hammer in hand, striking a blow against the church with a list of protests? That's the stuff of legend! No artist ever would have thought of painting a young German monk calmly sealing a document and handing it off to a courier.[9]

Scripture *and* Tradition?

Appreciating Scripture as the final authority in matters of Christian faith and practice allowed tradition to assume a secondary place among Reformation-minded Protestants. Repeatedly, Reformers such as Martin Luther and John Calvin cited earlier Christians positively, revealing an appreciation for tradition. Protestant theology was marked, therefore, by an interaction not just with Scripture, but with Christian tradition as well.

---

[9] See Volker Leppin and Timothy J. Wengert, "Sources for and Against the Posting of the *Ninety-Five Theses*," *Lutheran Quarterly* 29 (2015): 373–98.

John Calvin offered a beautiful example of this early in his *Institutes of the Christian Religion*, noting the weightiness of the church's overarching acceptance of Scripture through history:

> The consent of the Church is not without its weight. For it is not to be accounted of no consequence, that, from the first publication of Scripture, so many ages have uniformly concurred in yielding obedience to it, and that, notwithstanding of the many extraordinary attempts which Satan and the whole world have made to oppress and overthrow it, or completely efface it from the memory of men, it has flourished like the palm tree and continued invincible.[10]

Calvin regarded Scripture so highly in part because of Christians doing the same in the centuries before him. Tradition mattered to Calvin.

Application

When the Reformers distinguished themselves from their Catholic forebears, they wanted to show their commitment to the Bible above all other sources of theology. However, those same Reformers made use of a multiplicity of sources in their theology. The Reformation, therefore, reveals to believers today a model for doing theology that emphasizes the importance of the Bible, while continuing to consider other sources of theology. One of the early Christian apologists, Justin Martyr, articulated the importance of utilizing multiple sources in theology when he said, "Whatever things were rightly said among all men, are the property of us Christians."[11] Whether a pagan philosopher does the speaking or a Christian pastor, if the content of the words is true, believers should affirm the idea. Many times in recent decades, believers have been hesitant to embrace the words of those outside the church, fearing some sort of compromise. But as Justin notes, and as the Reformers would agree, believers should be able to glean the truth wherever it is in God's creation—in history, science, philosophy, the arts, experience, and yes, ultimately the Bible.

Sola scriptura also continues to be immensely significant because it points believers toward keeping the Bible at the center of Christian theology. In a world that needs faithful words about God and his redemptive work, the

---

[10]   Calvin, *Institutes* 1.8.12, in John Calvin, *Institutes of the Christian Religion*, vol. 1, trans. Henry Beveridge (Edinburgh: The Calvin Translation Society, 1845), 108.

[11]   Justin Martyr, *2 Apology* 13 (ANF 1:193).

Scriptures continue to bear that witness. If believers today decided to minimize the importance of Scripture as God's revealed Word, the church would end up in dire straits. May the witness of the Reformation remind today's church that Scripture stands as the determining norm of both our thoughts and our deeds.

Finally, Protestants need to heed a warning: singular focus on the Bible may result in neglect of the means by which that Bible is interpreted. Too often in Protestantism, that task has fallen simply to the individual, leading to all manner of strange interpretations and heretical detours. Protestants should appreciate the importance of tradition—community past and present—as a guide to interpretation and doctrinal development.

Resources

Adair, John. "Why the Five Solas Matter Today." *DTS Magazine* 3, no. 3 (fall 2017).

Barrett, Matthew. *God's Word Alone: The Authority of Scripture*. Grand Rapids: Zondervan, 2016.

George, Timothy. *The Theology of the Reformers*. Rev. ed. Nashville: B&H Academic, 2013. (Note especially the chapter on Luther.)

———

CHAPTER 23

The Reformers Were Trying to Restore the Church of the New Testament Era

The Legendary Story

The Reformers tried to restore their churches to the pattern of the New Testament church, winding the clock back almost 1,500 years to an era before doctrinal deviation. By restoring the church to the doctrinal purity reflected in the New Testament, they could move forward with confidence in their theology, worship, church order, and ministry. However, some of the Reformers were more successful than others at this program of rigorous reform. Many only made it so far back before they gave up, succumbing to the pressures of political realities or their own prejudices. Yet others were able to reform their churches to the ideal conditions that align more closely with the New Testament church, just as God always intended.

Introduction: Unraveling the Legend

None of the major Protestant Reformers tried to restore the first-century church of the New Testament. To do so would have been to neglect the beneficial contributions of the pastors and teachers of especially the early church as well as the treasures of wisdom and insight passed down from generations of faithful Christians through the centuries. Rather, Reformers hoped to restore the New Testament's central focus on the gospel of Jesus Christ as well as the early church's maturely articulated theology reflected in the creeds of the early councils. However, certain "radical" movements in the Reformation did try to roll things back to the primitive church of the first century, claiming that their churches followed a New Testament–only pattern of ministry. The reality, though, is that not only was it impossible to reestablish the first-century church, but it was not really desirable to do so.

Sola **What?**

As we saw in the last chapter, the Protestant concept of *sola scriptura*—"Scripture alone"—has been frequently misunderstood. We often hear people say that Reformers like Martin Luther (1483–1546) stood on the Word of God alone, rejecting popes, tradition, church fathers, councils, creeds, and anything else "not Bible" as sources for theology. However, this would be a gross exaggeration of the meaning behind *sola Scriptura*.

In reality, *sola Scriptura* originally meant that only Scripture carries direct divine authority in itself—that is, its words alone have absolute apostolic and prophetic authority, as "inspired by God" (2 Tim 3:16). Therefore, it is the sole final authority and inerrant source of truth in all it affirms. It is, to use another Latin phrase, the *norma normans non normata*, or "norming norm which cannot be normed." There is no written or oral source that can correct the plain teaching of Scripture. No pope, no council, no scientific theory, no historian, no feeling, no opinion can stand over Scripture to correct its affirmations. If Scripture and church tradition clash, Scripture wins. If the Bible says one thing, but a pope says another, the pope is wrong.

Yet when it came to actually studying theology and doing ministry constructively, the Reformers understood they were heirs of a wealth of wisdom and insights of godly pastors and teachers that had gone before them. Though Scripture was their sole *final authority* in matters of faith and practice, they drew on positive contributions of others in the past—especially the church fathers, councils, and creeds—as they articulated doctrine and carried out public worship. Church historian Jaroslav Pelikan notes, "Despite their protestations of 'sola Scriptura,' the Reformers showed that the 'Scriptura' has never been 'sola.'"[1]

---

[1] Jaroslav Pelikan, *The Christian Tradition: A History of the Development of Doctrine*, vol. 4, *Reformation of Church and Dogma (1300–1700)* (Chicago: University of Chicago Press, 1984), vii.

Depending on Tradition

Though Reformers clearly believed Scripture alone was the final authority in matters of faith and practice, they still depended on church fathers, councils, and creeds for their insights into doctrinal and practical matters. The Lutheran *Augsburg Confession* (1530) asserts, "The churches, with common consent among us, do teach that the decree of the Nicene Synod concerning the unity of the divine essence and of the three persons is true, and without doubt to be believed."[2]

Later, when defending their view that true faith brings forth good works, the authors note, "The same also do the ancient writers of the Church teach; for Ambrose [of Milan, 339–297] saith. . . ."[3] And on the matter of free will, the same confession cites Augustine [354–430]: "These things are in as many words affirmed by St. Augustine."[4]

Similarly, the Swiss Reformed *Second Helvetic Confession* (1566) states,

> We do not despise the interpretations of the holy Greek and Latin fathers, nor reject their disputations and treatises as far as they agree with the Scriptures; but we do modestly dissent from them when they are found to set down things different from, or altogether contrary to, the Scriptures. . . .
>
> We freely profess, whatsoever things are defined out of the Holy Scriptures, and comprehended in the creeds, and in the decrees of those four first and most excellent councils—held at Nicaea, Constantinople, Ephesus, and Chalcedon—together with blessed Athanasius's creed and all other creeds like to these, touching the mystery of the incarnation of our Lord Jesus Christ; and we condemn all things contrary to the same.[5]

---

[2]   *Augsburg Confession*, 1, in Philip Schaff, ed., *The Creeds of Christendom*, vol. 3, *The Evangelical Protestant Creeds, with Translations*, 4th ed., rev. (New York: Harper & Brothers, 1905), 7.
[3]   *Augsburg Confession*, 6, in Schaff, 3:11.
[4]   *Augsburg Confession*, 18, in Schaff, 3:18.
[5]   *Second Helvetic Confession*, 2, 11, in Schaff 3:833, 854.

For most mainline Reformers, the question was not *whether* we also use tradition alongside Scripture in doing ministry in the modern world.[6] The question was *to what extent* do we use tradition? This led to two lines of thinking within Protestantism regarding the function of Scripture.

"Regs" vs. "Norms"

Even in the early days of the Reformation, Protestants differed on how to reform their public worship. All agreed that the Roman Catholic Church had gone to excesses and taken unwarranted liberties. And all agreed that returning to the New Testament period with its living and active eyewitnesses of Jesus, its Spirit-empowered prophets, and its reliance on only a handful of New Testament writings without a completed Bible was impossible. They all valued the contributions of the creeds and confessions of the early church and the mature theologies of Fathers like Athanasius, Ambrose, and Augustine.

However, Protestant thinkers disagreed on matters related to worship and church order. They tended to argue from one of two perspectives regarding the respective roles of Scripture and tradition: either the *regulative principle* or the *normative principle*. This same ideological division prevails today. Those who adhered to the regulative principle urged that whatever is not expressly commanded in Scripture is to be prohibited in worship and church order. On the other hand, those who held to the normative principle argued that whatever is not prohibited by Scripture is permissible in worship and church order. Thus, when dealing with forms of worship and organization, the regulative principle would only accept those that could be clearly supported through biblical evidence. Those who held to the normative principle would allow for the incorporation of developed church traditions as long as they didn't break any biblical commands.

For example, some proponents of the regulative principle rejected artwork and images in their churches, vestments for their clergy, and the use of incense in worship because these things are not mentioned in the New Testament. On the other hand, followers of the normative principle allowed artwork (as long as it was not venerated), vestments, and incense because nothing in the New Testament expressly forbids their use.

---

6   See Peter Fraenkel, *Testimonia Patrum: The Function of Patristic Arguments in the Theology of Philip Melanchthon* (Geneva: Droz, 1961); Timothy George, *Theology of the Reformers*, rev. ed. (Nashville: B&H Academic, 2013), 132-33. Anthony N. S. Lane, *John Calvin: Student of the Church Fathers* (Edinburgh: T&T Clark, 1999); Pelikan, *The Christian Tradition*, 4:176–77.

Neither side wanted to recreate the first-century New Testament church per se. They acknowledged that such a pursuit was futile. However, the issue of how New Testament teachings related to church ministry was one of constant debate, as it still is today.

The Radicals

We would be remiss if we didn't mention a movement in the Reformation that took a more radical approach, jettisoning entirely the history of Christian witness from the second century forward. The erstwhile companion of Martin Luther, Andreas Karlstadt (1486–1541), was one such radical who threw out the proverbial "baby with the bathwater." Snyder notes, "Karlstadt was willing to allow *no* human tradition to remain, and called rather for a reform of the church only according to what had been commanded in Scripture. . . . Karlstadt purged the sanctuary of images and radically undid the sacramental view."[7]

Some (though not all) groups known as the "Anabaptists" or "Radical Reformation" bought into the narrative that the entire church apostatized after the New Testament (see chapters 2 and 14). Thus, their own movement, based solely and squarely on Scripture, was a restoration of the true church, indistinguishable in mission and ministry from that of the first-century. One radical, Sebastian Franck (1499–1543), claimed, "I believe that the outward church of Christ through the invasive and all-corrupting Antichrist, ascended into heaven immediately after the death of the Apostles, and is still hidden only in Spirit and in truth. Yes, for 1400 years there has been no gathered church or congregation with their sacraments."[8]

Obviously, in such a radical view, the only solution would be to go straight back to the New Testament as the only source for informing the practice of the ordinances, ordering church, and doing ministry. However, this radical biblicism, which ignored the insights of all other Christians throughout history, resulted in not one "restored" New Testament church, but countless competing churches all claiming to be *the* restored church while all differing with each other in what that was supposed to look like. Ripping the New Testament from the matrix of its historical context, these radical Reformers tended to interpret

---

[7]   C. Arnold Snyder, *Anabaptist History and Theology*, rev. student ed. (Kitchener, ON: Pandora, 1997), 49.

[8]   Sebastian Franck, *Letter (1531)*, in Karl Rembert, *Die "Wiedertäufer" im Herzogtum Jülich: Studien zur Geschichte der Reformation, besonders am Niederrhein* (Berlin: Gaertners, 1899), 219. Translation from German by Michael J. Svigel.

the Bible from the perspective of their own contexts, convictions, presuppositions, and prejudices. The result was almost always idiosyncratic doctrines and
practices, and sometimes even disastrous deviations from orthodox theology.[9]

Application

The goal of the major Protestants was to reform the church of their day in
light of the absolute authority of Scripture, with the wise input of early church
fathers, and within the boundaries of classic orthodoxy articulated in the ecumenical creeds. Their goal was not to restore the New Testament church exactly
as it was in the first century; and neither should it be our goal. Rather, in light
of the inerrant Word of God, we should read widely and wisely, seeking positive
lessons to embrace and negative examples to avoid.

Think about what a restoration of the New Testament church would look
like: we'd have to get rid of most of our New Testament books; they didn't
have them. We'd have to conjure infallible apostles and prophets as God's
own mouthpieces to run our churches. We'd have to make sure Christianity
was an illegal religion so we could have the same persecution they had. In
other words, their situation was radically different from our own. Instead
of this primitivist approach, we should follow the examples of the mainline
Reformers and some Anabaptists, depending on Holy Scripture as the *norming norm which cannot be normed*, but drawing on the wisdom and insights
of believers in every generation whose words were sweet and lives fruitful. To
focus solely on the "apostles and prophets" in Scripture while neglecting the
contributions of the "evangelists, pastors, and teachers" throughout history
and today (see Eph 4:11) would be like the Corinthians' accepting the foundational teachings of Paul but neglecting the edifying teaching of Apollos
(1 Cor 3:6–7). All of these Spirit-gifted teachers are necessary for the building
up of the body of Christ and protection from error.

Resources

Pelikan, Jaroslav. *The Christian Tradition: A History of the Development of Doctrine*, vol. 4,
    Reformation of Church and Dogma (1300–1700). Chicago: University of Chicago Press,
    1984.
Snyder, C. Arnold. *Anabaptist History and Theology*, rev. student ed. Kitchener, ON: Pandora,
    1997.

---

   [9]   See Snyder, *Anabaptist History and Theology*.

CHAPTER 24

The Reformers Removed the Apocrypha from the Bible

The Legendary Story

Until the time of the Reformation, the Catholic Church had a stable canon of Scripture reaching back into ancient times. This Bible included what are sometimes called the Old Testament Apocrypha—Tobit, Judith, 1 and 2 Maccabees, Wisdom of Solomon, Wisdom of Sirach (Ecclesiasticus), and Baruch—as well as additions to the books of Esther and Daniel. However, during the sixteenth century, at the time of the Reformation, Protestants removed these authoritative writings from the Old Testament because they disagreed with their doctrine. Both the Roman Catholic Church and the Eastern Orthodox Churches retain these writings and preserve the original canon of inspired, authoritative Scriptures.

Introduction: Unraveling the Legend

The true history of the Apocrypha—or "deuterocanonical" books—is more complicated than simply saying "Roman Catholics added them to the Bible in the sixteenth century" or "Protestants removed them from the Bible in the sixteenth century." Rather, the church's relationship with the Apocrypha has been off-again/on-again, with various church leaders throughout history (1) accepting them fully as inspired Scripture; (2) valuing them as edifying but uninspired writings; or (3) setting them aside as secondary sources of historical or spiritual interest. In the sixteenth century, the Roman Catholic Church officially decreed the Apocrypha to be inspired Scripture (category 1), while Protestants tended to regard them as falling in categories 2 or 3. Thus, what was once a range of various opinions on the status and authority of the Apocrypha throughout church history became fixed and inflexible in the official dogmas of Roman Catholics and Protestant churches after the sixteenth century.

A Crash Course on the Old Testament Canon

The first thing to note is that the books known as the "Apocrypha" are additions to the Old Testament writings, not the New Testament. All historical traditions of Christianity since the fourth century have agreed on the content of the New Testament canon (see chapter 6). Second, neither the Old nor the New Testament canon was ever officially decreed by an ecumenical council—that is, a worldwide council regarded as authoritative by all churches. As discussed in chapter 6, only local synods (regional councils with localized authority) produced descriptive lists of the books in their Old and New Testaments, sometimes including several of the apocryphal books. Third, the Protestant Reformers never regarded the Apocrypha as utterly useless; rather, they regarded them as merely uninspired writings originating from the Jewish community. They provide helpful historical information and contain inspiring stories. Thus, they can and should be read, but they should not be read and preached from in church as inspired, inerrant Scripture.

Roger Beckwith succinctly summarizes the divergent positions of the Protestants and Roman Catholics in the wake of the Reformation:

> The Reformers followed the lead of Jerome and drew a sharp distinction between the Apocrypha of the Greek and Latin Bibles (which some of them kept in use just as edifying reading) and the books of the Hebrew Bible (which they all agreed were alone inspired and authoritative). The Council of Trent, on the other hand, in 1546 promulgated a list of inspired books of the Hebrew Bible and the Apocrypha, and anathematized those who did not accept it. To Trent's challenge the Reformers were able to make an equally bold reply, by echoing Augustine's claim that Jesus himself endorsed the Jewish canon, and pointing out that the Jewish canon was the canon of the Hebrew Bible, which did not include the Apocrypha.[1]

---

[1]   Roger T. Beckwith, *The Old Testament Canon of the New Testament Church and Its Background in Early Judaism* (Eugene, OR: Wipf and Stock, 2008), 2.

This brief quote from Beckwith hints at a rich and interesting history behind the divergent views: Jerome, Greek and Latin Bibles, Hebrew Bible, and Augustine. Clearly, then, we need to dig a little deeper to uncover the historical reasons Protestants relegated the Apocrypha to a different shelf, separate from the "inspired and authoritative" writings.

Apocrypha in the Patristic Period

In the patristic period (c. 100–500), as J. N. D. Kelly notes, the Christian Old Testament "always included, though with varying degrees of recognition, the so-called Apocrypha, or deutero-canonical books."[2] At first blush this may appear to confirm the claim that Protestants evicted the Apocrypha from their comfortable home in the canon. However, Kelly explains that the reason Christians included these books was because after the first century, Christians around the world were mostly Greek-speaking Gentiles who knew no Hebrew and thus used as their Old Testament Scriptures the Greek translation known as the Septuagint. The Septuagint translation included not only the books regarded as inspired by the Jews but also books that Jews regarded as "religiously edifying," though not inspired.[3] These are what we call today the Apocrypha.

Thus, when Gentile Christians received the Hebrew religious writings in the only form they could read—the Greek translation—they also received those writings that the Jews would have regarded as secondary sources. However, some church fathers in this period were well informed regarding the history of the Septuagint's translation and its relationship to the Hebrew Old Testament. Around the year 170, the bishop Melito of Sardis (c. 110–180) wrote to a fellow Christian, Onesimus, regarding the number and order of the Old Testament books. He reported that he had traveled east "and came to the place where these things were preached and done" and there "learned accurately the books of the Old Testament."[4] The canon reported by Melito matches the Protestant Old Testament in content, with one exception—it lacks the book of Esther.[5] Melito's well-researched Old Testament canon did not include the Apocrypha.

Another example of the patristic view of the Apocrypha is found in the *Catechetical Lectures* of Cyril of Jerusalem (c. 313–386). His list of Old

---

2   J. N. D. Kelly, *Early Christian Doctrines*, 5th rev. ed. (New York: HarperOne, 1978), 53.

3   Kelly, 53.

4   These words of Melito of Sardis come to us in quotations from Eusebius, *Church History* 4.26.14 (NPNF 2.1.206).

5   See F. F. Bruce, *The Canon of Scripture* (Downers Grove, IL: InterVarsity Press, 1988), 70–71.

Testament books matches that of Protestants with the exception of the exclusion of Esther and the inclusion of the apocryphal Baruch, which is included as part of Jeremiah along with Lamentations. The rest of the Apocrypha are not included.[6] These representative perspectives of Melito and Cyril are not minority reports among the Eastern church fathers. Likewise, the view among prominent fathers such as Athanasius of Alexandria (290–374) and Gregory of Nazianzus (330–390) "was that the deutero-canonical books should be relegated to a subordinate position outside the canon proper."[7]

It seems, though, the farther away churches were from the Holy Land and the original canon preserved by the Jews, the more likely church leaders were to embrace the Apocrypha less critically. The Western churches, which eventually coalesced into what we call the Roman Catholic Church under the papacy, tended to regard the Apocrypha as canonical Scripture. However, Jerome (c. 347–420), who was responsible for the Latin Bible translation known as the Vulgate, spent considerable time in the Holy Land to learn Hebrew in service of his translation efforts. Consequently, he came to the same conclusions as many Eastern fathers, that "books not in the Hebrew canon should be designated as apocryphal."[8]

Apocrypha in the Medieval Period

Jerome's contemporary, the great Augustine of Hippo (354–430), dissented from his colleague. He affirmed the miraculous origins of the Greek Septuagint translation and embraced the Apocrypha included in that collection. F. F. Bruce notes, "Augustine's ruling supplied a powerful precedent for the western church from his own day to the Reformation and beyond."[9] In following Augustine, the Roman Catholic Church often unwittingly deviated from the original Jewish canon. Many Roman Catholics apparently were unaware of the hesitancy of many early fathers regarding the Apocrypha.

Throughout the medieval period, then, many in the Roman Catholic Church regarded the Apocrypha as authoritative Scripture, as did, with less dogmatism, the Eastern Orthodox churches (though East and West differed on which additional books should be included). This general acceptance grew,

---

6   Cyril of Jerusalem, *Catechetical Lectures* 4.35–36.
7   Kelly, *Early Christian Doctrines*, 54–55.
8   Carol A. Newsom, "Introduction to the Apocrypha/Deuterocanonical Books," in *The New Oxford Annotated Apocrypha: New Revised Standard Version*, 5th ed., ed. Michael D. Coogan, and others (Oxford: Oxford University Press, 2018), 5.
9   Bruce, *Canon of Scripture*, 97.

without the support of an ecumenical council and without early, widespread, and consistent testimony of the early church fathers. Furthermore, Westcott observes that "a continuous succession of the more learned fathers in the West maintained the distinctive authority of the Hebrew Canon [without the Apocrypha] up to the period of the Reformation."[10] Those rejecting the Apocrypha included Pope Gregory the Great (540–604), the Venerable Bede (673–735), Hugh of St. Victor (1096–1141), William of Ockham (1288–1348), Cardinal Thomas Cajetan (1469–1534), and numerous others who "repeat with approval the decision of Jerome, and draw a clear line between the Canonical and Apocryphal books."[11]

Apocrypha in the Reformation and Counter-Reformation

The question of the Old Testament canon came to a head during the Reformation. Because the issue was not completely settled in any universal and binding sense, various church leaders and scholars had until that point sided with either Augustine in accepting the apocryphal writings or with Jerome in relegating them to secondary status. Martin Luther (1483–1546), along with most of the Reformers, sided with Jerome for historical and theological reasons,[12] though Luther's German translation of the Bible as well as several other Protestant translations included the books in a separated category clearly marked as "Apocrypha."[13]

In direct response to the reforms of theology and practice made by Protestants, the Roman Catholic Church's "Counter-Reformation" at the Council of Trent (1545–1563) established the Apocrypha as part of the Old Testament canon. The council actually decreed the Latin *translation* to be the final source of appeal in matters of scriptural fidelity—discounting appeal to the original Hebrew and Greek texts. Not surprisingly, Trent sided with Augustine rather than Jerome in the matter of the Apocrypha. Westcott notes, "This hasty and peremptory decree" was "unlike in its form to any catalogue before published."[14]

That decree, on April 8, 1546, stated, "Following, then, the examples of the orthodox fathers, it receives and venerates with a feeling of piety and

---

[10] Brooke Foss Westcott, "Canon of Scripture, The," in *Dr. William Smith's Dictionary of the Bible*, vol. 1, rev. and ed. H. B. Hackett and Ezra Abbot (New York: Hurd and Houghton, 1877), 363.

[11] Westcott, 363.

[12] Euan Cameron, *The European Reformation*, 2nd ed. (Oxford: Oxford University Press, 2012), 165.

[13] Bruce, *Canon of Scripture*, 102–4.

[14] Westcott, "Canon," 363.

reverence all the books both of the Old and New Testaments."[15] Then, "lest a doubt might arise in the mind of someone as to which are the books received by this council," the decree lists the Old and New Testament books, including Tobias, Judith, Ecclesiasticus ("Wisdom of Sirach"), Baruch, and 1 and 2 Maccabees. It concludes, "If anyone does not accept as sacred and canonical the aforesaid books in their entirely and with all their parts, as they have been accustomed to be read in the Catholic Church and as they are contained in the old Latin Vulgate edition, and knowingly and deliberately rejects the aforesaid traditions, let him be anathema." One wonders whether men like Athanasius, Jerome, Gregory the Great, and the Venerable Bede—who did not receive the Apocrypha as "sacred and canonical"—would have been anathematized if they had lived during the Council of Trent.

Conclusion

In light of the actual history of the Apocrypha, it would be a gross exaggeration to say the Reformers removed the Apocrypha from the Bible while the Roman Catholic Church maintained the original Scriptures handed down from the beginning. The place of the Apocrypha in the household of canonical Scripture had always been that of distant relatives at best or uninvited houseguests at worst. Despite some who called them "brothers and sisters," the Apocrypha were not, in any case, undisputed members of the family of inspired writings. Most Reformers clarified this fact by putting them up, so to speak, in the above-garage apartment rather than treating them like equal siblings of the universally acknowledged books of the Bible.

In response, the Roman Catholic Council of Trent in 1546 doubled down on its tenuous claim by adopting the houseguests into the family of canonized Scripture. This act was historically revolutionary and deviated from the soft reception the Apocrypha had enjoyed in the early church. Then, in response to this response, more rigorous "puritan" elements—and eventually evangelical Protestants in the modern age—evicted the Apocrypha even from the category of "non-canonical but inspirational" or "helpful" writings. This extremely negative approach to the Apocrypha itself is a radical departure from the generally positive reception of the Apocrypha even among those who did not accept the writings as Holy Scripture.

---

[15] H. J. Schroeder, *The Canons and Decrees of the Council of Trent* (Rockford, IL: Tan Books and Publishers, 1978).

Application

Though most of the Apocrypha contain helpful insights on historical events or harmless inspirational poetry or stories of bold faith and piety, in a few instances they could be used to defend doctrines that find no other footing in canonical Scripture. For example, Roman Catholic theologians have defended the doctrines of purgatory and prayers for the dead from 2 Maccabees 12:46, which says, "It is therefore a holy and wholesome thought to pray for the dead, that they may be loosed from sins" (Douay-Rheims 1899 Translation). Of course, the entire theology of purgatory couldn't be constructed from this one verse, but it certainly helped it along.

Because Holy Scripture functions as the final authority in all matters of faith and practice, it is vital that no "Bible wannabes" are incorporated into the canon. This is why Protestants must understand not only the proper content of the Old Testament canon but also the reasons why the apocryphal books are regarded as secondary sources—fine to read, but not reliable for supporting doctrine and practice.

Resources

Beckwith, Roger T. *The Old Testament Canon of the New Testament Church and Its Background in Early Judaism*. Eugene, OR: Wipf and Stock, 2008.

Bruce, F. F. *The Canon of Scripture*. Downers Grove, IL: InterVarsity Press, 1988.

Newsom, Carol A. "Introduction to the Apocrypha/Deuterocanonical Books." In *The New Oxford Annotated Apocrypha: New Revised Standard Version*. 5th ed., edited by Michael D. Coogan et al. Oxford: Oxford University Press, 2018.

CHAPTER 25

Protestants Don't Accept the Church Councils and Creeds

The Legendary Story

The Protestant Reformation set the church free from the shackles of man-made religion. Among the works and rituals that supposedly paved the way to salvation in the Roman Catholic Church, that so-called church sought to extend its authority over the lives of faithful believers by means of church councils and creeds. These insidious measures sought to blunt the force of biblical authority by mixing it with (or placing it in service to) human authority.

The creeds and councils of Christian history became the centerpiece for debates and divisions among those who claimed Christ. Satan used these man-made words to compromise the unity of Christians. Instead, Protestants accept only a single standard of authority—the Bible. This uncompromised vision is the best way forward for the Christian church, gathering as one around inspired Scripture. In light of this, true believers have no creed but the Bible.

Introduction: Unraveling the Legend

Protestants have historically been concerned with elevating the place of Scripture in the life of the church. Some Protestants have decided that declaring Scripture authoritative means they cannot place any credence in the church councils and historic creedal statements. However, just as someone can declare oranges her favorite fruit and still enjoy eating apples, so, too, can a Christian declare the

Bible as the ultimate standard of authority and still appreciate the contribution of traditional statements such as creeds.[1]

From the era of the early church, Christians considered creeds and councils authoritative—but not more so than Scripture. Reformers regularly showed their appreciation for tradition—including early church creeds and councils. And while there have been post-Reformation groups affirming phrases such as "no creed but the Bible," some reflection shows this idea to be a logical impossibility.

Were Creeds and Councils Authoritative in the Early Church?

Evangelicals have often misunderstood the function of creeds and the councils that produced them, seeing them in competition with Scripture, or worse, as carrying ultimate authority over Scripture. In reality, creeds and councils had a far different function in the early church. Historian D. H. Williams notes that "creedal statements were not proposed as antitheses to Scripture or as alternative norms of the faith. They were meant as fitting representations of biblical truth, drawn from scriptural precepts and designed by scriptural language as much as possible."[2] Williams helps clarify the intent and use of creeds in the early church—they were a means to explain difficult theological and interpretive issues or summarize the basic content of the Christian faith.

One classic example of a council developing a creedal statement occurred in the town of Nicaea in AD 325. Those in attendance at this ecumenical (worldwide church) council had come to discuss teachings related to the person of Jesus Christ. One churchman, Arius (260–336), had been teaching that God the Son was created and, therefore, Jesus was less than fully God. As the Christian leaders in attendance at this council gathered to discuss this teaching, they decided Arius and his teaching were outside the bounds of Christian orthodoxy. Therefore, they studied the Scriptures and used the results to craft the Nicene Creed, in part to articulate clearly and properly the relationship between God the Father and God the Son. The Nicene Creed affirms that Father and Son share the same divine essence, in order to protect the notion that Jesus, God the Son become human, is himself fully God.

This conclusion has informed orthodox Christian doctrine ever since, not

---

[1]   See chapter 22 for a discussion of a related subject: the meaning of the Reformation doctrine of *sola scriptura* (Scripture alone).

[2]   D. H. Williams, *Retrieving the Tradition and Renewing Evangelicalism* (Grand Rapids: Eerdmans, 1999), 170.

just in Roman Catholic and Eastern Orthodox churches, but in Protestant churches as well. All orthodox Protestants, whether they recite creeds or not, benefit from and draw upon the insights of the Nicene Creed. They just might be doing it unconsciously. As Williams notes, "For all the emphasis that evangelicals have placed on the Bible and the Bible alone as the only ground of faith, their tacit but universal acceptance of the Nicene and post-Nicene Christ is not derived from the Bible alone. We must recognize that the Bible alone has never functioned as the sole means by which Christians are informed about their faith. It was never meant to."[3]

In the early church, the councils and creeds clearly did carry authority. But how much? The early church did not argue anyone should elevate the creedal or conciliar tradition above Scripture. Rather, as was evident at Nicaea, those creeds and councils were seen as faithful explanations of God's Word, reflecting the universal consensus of the church from the first century onward.

MINI MYTHS

"The Tradition of Icons Goes Back to the First Century"

Many churches today venerate icons of significant biblical figures or Christian saints. The final ecumenical council at Nicaea in AD 787 affirmed the use of icons in Christian worship. Occasionally, some in this camp will argue that the practice of venerating icons goes back to the earliest Christian communities in the first century. But historians have been unable to establish such veneration much earlier than the third or fourth century. An early reference to the practice comes from Eusebius of Caesarea (263–339), who, writing in the fourth century, referred to a longtime practice of Christian sculpture and image making.[4]

---

[3] Williams, 29.

[4] See Andre Grabar, *Christian Iconography: A Study of Its Origins.* (Princeton, NJ: Princeton University Press, 1968); David Mark Hionides, "Images in the Early Church: A Survey of the First Three Centuries" (ThM thesis, Dallas Theological Seminary, 2010).

Churches and Creedal Authority

When the Reformation occurred in the sixteenth century, every single leader that would have called himself a Reformer had a background with Christian tradition. In fact, though some have painted the Reformation as a reaction against tradition, it was really an embrace of the true and lasting Tradition. Once more, Williams clarifies the issue: "The Reformation was not about Scripture versus tradition but about reclaiming the ancient Tradition against distortions of that Tradition, or what eventually became a conflict of Tradition versus traditions. To put this another way, the insight which we received from the Protestant Reformation is that every church's 'traditions' are subordinate to Holy Scripture and under the judgment of the Tradition, Christ being the Lord of both."[5] Therefore, believers today should recognize that Protestants never offered a blanket rejection of traditional elements in the church, but only rejected those bits that conflicted with the biblical witness.

This appreciation for Tradition—those elements of Christian doctrine that properly reflected the teaching of Scripture and had been embraced throughout the history of the church—came out in the writings of the Reformers and their followers, particularly as they wrote their own confessional statements. Indeed, these statements were most often fashioned at something like councils, gatherings of like-minded individuals and churches invested in Lutheran or Reformed or Anabaptist doctrinal positions. In the production of such statements, the Reformers followed very closely their forebears in the Roman Catholic Church. If they had been so virulently anti-creedal, would they have fashioned such statements themselves?

Many of these statements refer to earlier creeds and councils, approving the work of their spiritual forefathers. Take, for instance, the early Lutheran Augsburg Confession, which includes the following statement: "We unanimously hold and teach, in accordance with the decree of the Council of Nicaea."[6] Another early Protestant confession, the Second Helvetic Confession of 1566 associated with the Reformation movement started by Ulrich Zwingli (1484–1531), made explicit a debt to the early councils and creeds, saying, "We sincerely believe and loudly confess all that has been determined out of the Holy Scriptures concerning the mystery of the incarnation of our Lord Jesus Christ, and is contained in the creeds and decrees of the first four œcumenical Councils held in Niceæ,

---

5 Williams, *Retrieving*, 176.
6 John H. Leith, ed., *Creeds of the Churches: A Reader in Christian Doctrine from the Bible to the Present*, 3rd ed. (Louisville: John Knox, 1982), 67.

Constantinople, Ephesus, and Chalcedon, in the Creed of St. Athanasius, and all similar creeds."[7] Clearly, the Protestants shared theological positions with their Catholic forebears, enough to affirm the very creeds that sat at the heart of Christian doctrine throughout church history. The Protestant objections were not around the content of these creeds, but rather around other traditions of doctrine and practice that had developed throughout the medieval era.

No Creed but Christ?

So, where does the myth of this chapter come from, if not from the Protestant movement at large? In the early nineteenth century, 300 years after the Protestant Reformation, a strand of American Christianity developed that sought a return to the first-century church of Acts. "Restoration movement" is an umbrella term used to describe several different types of churches of this kind, such as those founded by men like Barton Stone (1772–1844) and Alexander Campbell (1788–1866).[8] The use of the term *Restoration* is meant to distinguish this American movement from the Reformation—these Restoration churches were not trying to reform the Catholic Church or even protest it (as the name Protestant presumes). Rather, they were seeking to restore the church to what it once was under the leadership of the apostles, to bring it back to its simple and direct origins.

Part of the movement's ethos is its anti-creedal stance. Restorationists believe they have stripped away all the overstated opinions, confusing conundrums, and divisive dictates that have hindered the basic mission of the church—to preach Christ to the ends of the earth. This means Restorationists have no place for church councils or creedal statements. The Christian Restorationist Association has noted, "As to our creed . . . we believe in Jesus Christ the Son of God, as Lord and as Savior. Our book of doctrine, or list of beliefs, is simply the Word of God. Thus, as one man has expressed it, 'We have no creed but Christ, no book but the Bible, no name but the name Christian.'"[9] This last quote is a staple of restoration movements and expresses well the anti-creedal position. Indeed, similar statements find their

---

[7]   Philip Schaff, *The Creeds of Christendom, with a History and Critical Notes: The History of Creeds* (New York: Harper & Brothers, 1878), 1:404.

[8]   *Restoration* is a term used to describe three main branches of churches: Churches of Christ, the Christian Church/Churches of Christ, and the Christian Church (Disciples of Christ).

[9]   Robert Mallett, "What Do You Mean, Restoration Movement?," website of the Christian Restoration Association, accessed January 22, 2020, https://thecra.org/home/what-is-the-restoration-movement.

way into broader evangelical churches—especially in Baptist and nondenominational churches.

However, to believe that there is "no creed but Christ," or its corollary, "no creed but the Bible," offers its own challenges. Even the Restorationists believe *something* about Christ. As they state in their own literature, "We believe in Jesus Christ the Son of God, as Lord and as Savior." A statement like that is not inspired Scripture, but is itself a creed. Creeds are authoritative statements "of the main articles of the Christian faith to which believers are expected to assent."[10] That the Restoration movement has only one main article doesn't deny that article's creedal status.

Application

The false choice between Scripture and creed leads believers into two errors. First, it forces believers to affirm that their interpretations of Scripture are equivalent to the statements of faith they make. Believers everywhere—even in the Restoration movement—operate under the rubric of statements of faith derived from Scripture. For example, when Baptist churches affirm believer's baptism by immersion or some Churches of Christ affirm a believer's baptism that saves, both are making statements of their faith as a result of *interpreting* Scripture. To suggest that believers have no creed but the Bible leads Christians into the dangerous waters of making human interpretations equivalent to the inspired Word of God—the very thing these groups suggest they are trying to avoid.

Second, the false choice forces believers to deny the historical roots of their beliefs. Orthodox Christians of every stripe affirm that Jesus Christ is the God-man, fully God and fully human. However, no modern group derived this view from the simple and straightforward exercise of quoting a Bible verse. Every modern group that holds this view leans on the early church councils of Nicaea and Chalcedon, both of which formulated an orthodox Christian understanding of the person of Jesus. Many in the "no creed" camp assume that recognizing historical development of doctrine compromises the authority of Scripture. Instead, recognizing our historical rootedness should deepen our appreciation for the way God has revealed himself through Scripture, and the way his Spirit continues to illuminate his people as we interpret it.

---

[10]   Sinclair B. Ferguson and J. I. Packer, *New Dictionary of Theology* (Downers Grove, IL: InterVarsity Press, 2000), 179.

Resources

Bray, Gerald. "Scripture and Tradition in Reformation Thought." *Evangelical Review of Theology* 19, no. 2 (April 1995): 157–66.

Leith, John H., ed. *Creeds of the Churches: A Reader in Christian Doctrine from the Bible to the Present.* 3rd ed. Louisville: WJK, 1982.

Williams, D. H. *Retrieving the Tradition and Renewing Evangelicalism.* Grand Rapids: Eerdmans, 1999.

CHAPTER 26

The Anabaptists Were the Predecessors
of Modern Baptists

The Legendary Story

Baptist churches all over the world are the direct heirs of the Anabaptists of the Reformation. Those heroes in the sixteenth century took a stand not only against the pope and the Roman Catholic Church but also against the mainline Reformers like Luther (1483–1546), Zwingli (1484–1531), and Calvin (1509–1553). And they paid dearly for it. The issue that set them apart—and for which they suffered persecution and execution—was the matter of believer's baptism. Instead of accepting infant baptism, Anabaptists stuck with the Bible and baptized only believers upon a profession of faith. As persecution intensified, those Anabaptists made their way around the world, preaching the true gospel, baptizing believers, and establishing independent congregations.

Introduction: Unraveling the Legend

Scholars and pastors have spilled much ink on the relationship between the Anabaptists—who lived on the European continent—and the Baptists, who grew to prominence in England. Simply stated: Modern-day Baptists are not direct descendants of Reformation-era Anabaptists. The history shows that the two groups developed independently of one another, even as they held certain concerns and theological views in common.

Anabaptists Aren't Baptists?

A brief introduction to Anabaptists and Baptists is in order. The Anabaptists were the original post-Reformation group to practice believer's baptism on the main continent of Europe. "Anabaptists" (meaning: re-baptizers) was a name given by outsiders (Catholics and other Protestants) to this group of people in the late sixteenth and early seventeenth centuries, because they practiced adult believers's baptism. Early Swiss Anabaptists such as Conrad Grebel (1498–1526), Felix Manz (1498–1527), and George Blaurock (1491–1529) had originally been followers of Ulrich Zwingli. But as they rejected infant baptism, they were themselves rejected by Zwingli and the ruling council in Zurich. Some religious groups today, such as Mennonites, organized under Menno Simons (1496–1561), and the Hutterites, founded by Jacob Hutter (1500–1536), descend from those original European Anabaptists.

Baptists, on the other hand, were English. However, they, too, got their start on the European continent, having emigrated to the Netherlands in search of religious freedom. This origin on the European continent has raised legitimate questions about the relationship between Anabaptists and Baptists and has led to a popular misconception that Baptists are direct heirs of the original Anabaptist communities.

Finally, a proper discussion of this question requires a clear view of what characterizes a "modern Baptist." In addition to basic trinitarian Christian orthodoxy, modern Baptists tend to be characterized by the teaching of God's truthful and authoritative Word, a special care and concern for evangelism and missions, and a commitment to local church autonomy. However, the most distinctive feature of Baptist life has historically been believer's baptism by immersion.

But how do Baptists and Anabaptists relate to one another historically? Some have argued that the first Baptists branched off from the Anabaptists, suggesting that "Anabaptism influenced several nonconformist sects in England and the New World, especially the early Baptists."[1] Or did Baptists originate from some other source?

---

[1]   David Plant, "Anabaptists & Baptists," BCW Project, accessed January 22, 2020, http://bcw-project.org/church-and-state/sects-and-factions/anabaptists-and-baptists.

Smyth's Separatist Congregation

One of the earliest Baptist leaders, John Smyth (c. 1570–1612), trained as an Anglican priest and even served in the Church of England for a short period. He had always been a Puritan among the Anglicans. Puritans were English Protestants who wanted to heighten the level of spiritual commitment in themselves and in their communities and to cleanse the Anglican Church of the last trappings of Roman Catholic rites and traditions. Smyth decided that he had to leave the Anglican Church over its spiritual laxity, so he started a Separatist congregation in England. Two years of persecution from the English government prompted Smyth's congregation to flee to the Netherlands, where they found religious freedom.

Up to this point in his career, Smyth had remained a staunch Calvinist, which wasn't really surprising. Puritans typically adopted Calvinistic theology. Smyth's Separatist congregation in England was oriented around church discipline, which is not an issue that typically distinguishes modern Baptists from other Christian denominations. However, Smyth's desire to separate from the larger Church of England suggests a feature that would become a defining one for Baptists—complete autonomy for each local congregation.

A Discovery among the Dutch

Once Smyth and his congregation arrived in the Netherlands, they found a land true to its reputation. The Englishmen were finally free of religious persecution. Into this more open society the Separatists plunged, though Smyth was anything but settled theologically. While he had severed his religious connections with a denominational group (not to mention the government), Smyth continued to reflect on the theology and practices of his congregation.

As Smyth studied the Scriptures, he found himself captivated and convinced by the idea of believer's baptism. Everywhere Smyth found baptism in the Bible, he found believer's baptism alone, a position for which he argued in his book *The Character of the Beast* (1609). He seems to have conceived this argument before any interaction with earlier Anabaptist views, as Smyth himself indicated "that the Mennonites were insignificant in his decision to accept believer's baptism."[2]

---

[2]   Jason K. Lee, *The Theology of John Smyth: Puritan, Separatist, Baptist, Mennonite* (Macon, GA: Mercer University Press, 2003), 85.

By early 1609, Smyth decided to have his own congregation of Separatists adopt the practice of believer's baptism, making them the first congregation of Baptists in the world. Smyth's logic went something like this: (1) the Separatists rejected the Anglican Church. (2) Therefore, the Separatists rejected their own Anglican infant baptisms. (3) As a result, they needed to receive true, adult believer's baptism. Smyth wrote in the preface to his *Character of the Beast*, "They that do Seperate from England as from a false Chu. must of necessity Seperate from the baptisme of England, & account the baptisme of England false, & so account the baptisme of infants false baptisme: Therefor the Separation must either goe back to England, or go forward to true baptisme."[3] Smyth's solution meant that he baptized himself, before baptizing the rest of his congregation. In his mind, he had to baptize himself because there was no other true baptism (meaning believer's baptism) in the world.

Soon after establishing this Baptist congregation, Smyth was introduced to the teachings of Dutch Anabaptists (Mennonites), who provided a theological contrast to Smyth's Calvinism. When Smyth's friend and fellow congregant Thomas Helwys (c. 1575–1616) decided to split from Smyth, the issues were largely theological. Helwys criticized Smyth for his Christology as well as his view of church and state.[4] One strain of faulty Anabaptist Christology, called Melchiorite Christology—named after Melchior Hoffman (1495–1543)—tended to deny the full humanity of Christ, while Anabaptist views on the church's relationship to the state tended to warn Christians against serving in any official state function.

Of course, the Dutch Mennonites also happened to practice believer's baptism. Since they practiced what Smyth considered to be true baptism, Smyth decided to dissolve his Baptist congregation and join the Mennonites by receiving their baptism. Many of his congregation followed him, though some objected, having no wish to become Mennonites themselves. This objecting party, led by Thomas Helwys, made their way back to England in 1612 and established the roots of the English Baptist churches we know today. Smyth died that same year.

On the question of modern Baptist origins, the history here is clear: disenchanted Mennonites (Anabaptists) did not start the Baptist denominations we know today, such as the Southern Baptists, the General Association

---

[3]　John Smyth, *The Works of John Smyth*, with notes and biography by W. T. Whitley, vol. 2 (Cambridge: Cambridge University Press, 1915), 567.

[4]　James R. Coggins, "The Theological Positions of John Smyth," *Baptist Quarterly* 30, no. 6 (1984): 258.

of Regular Baptists, the Conservative Baptists, or any of the other Baptist denominations. Rather, disenchanted Anglicans founded the first Baptist congregations. Sometime after establishing their churches, the Baptists were introduced more directly to the Anabaptist communities. Thus, the relationship between Anabaptists and Baptists is not one of forefathers and descendants; rather, the relationship is simply that both groups independently arrived at similar conclusions about believer's baptism and adjusted their practices accordingly.

An Immersive Experience

One other point on this history bears mentioning. Smyth's congregation, and then that of Helwys in England, were established as Baptist precisely because they practiced adult, believer's baptism. This singular, distinctive feature is what set this community apart from all others at the time.

However, one significant difference exists between those first Baptist congregations and virtually all modern Baptists: the mode of baptism. When modern Baptists teach on baptism, they make much not just of believer's baptism, but also that for believer's baptism to be valid, it must occur *by immersion*. The argument usually involves defining the Greek word for baptism in the New Testament, which means "to put or go under water."[5]

However, those first Baptist congregations of Smyth and Helwys did not baptize by immersion. They baptized in the same way their Mennonite neighbors baptized: by pouring water over the head of the new believer. Generally, this involved the "baptizee" kneeling before the congregation while the pastor ladled water over his or her head. Baptizing pastors usually invoked the imagery of pouring from passages such as Acts 2:17, where the Spirit was poured out on believers, or Titus 3:6, which mentions the Spirit being poured out on believers through Jesus Christ.

The Baptist practice of baptism by pouring lasted throughout the first generation of Baptist churches in England. In 1640, a Baptist named Richard Blunt began to wonder whether the Bible taught baptism by immersion. His argument centered on two biblical texts (Col 2:12 and Rom 6:4), which linked baptism with the death, burial, and resurrection of Jesus. After discovering a small group of Dutch Mennonites that practiced baptism by immersion, Blunt

---

[5]   William Arndt et al., *A Greek-English Lexicon of the New Testament and Other Early Christian Literature* (Chicago: University of Chicago Press, 2000), 164.

learned from them and brought the practice to his Baptist church. This appears to be the first instance of Baptists baptizing by immersion.[6]

Clearly, the Anabaptists were the first group after the Reformation to recover believer's baptism. Yet they seem to, at most, have been passive witnesses to the formation of Baptist churches. Modern Baptists, characterized as they are by believer's baptism *by immersion*, were not direct descendants of Anabaptists, but a separate tradition in England that developed in a fashion largely independent from the Anabaptists on the European continent.

Thereafter, Baptist churches began to appear in the British colonies in the seventeenth and eighteenth centuries. Though most of these had their direct roots in the English Baptist movement, some infant-baptizing congregations "became" Baptists simply by changing their practice of baptism from infant to believer's baptism. Today, Baptist churches most likely trace their historical origins not in the Anabaptists of the European Reformation but to either the English Baptists of Smyth and Helwys or later dissenting congregations in England and the New World.

Application

The early years of John Smyth instruct in at least one important way. Smyth had declared that no church possessed the true baptism—by which he meant believer's baptism—the result being that he baptized himself. However, even Smyth felt discomfort over this decision, and when made aware of Mennonites who practiced believer's baptism, Smyth went to them and asked them to baptize him properly. Baptism has always been, in the Christian church, a gift to receive rather than a task to be accomplished. Smyth understood this, and so submitted himself to others in order to receive the gift. In turn, Smyth's followers and the Baptist tradition as a whole have always maintained the need for people to be baptized by someone else. Believers are not mere individuals before God, but adopted children, brought into a family full of others. Baptism recognizes that communal reality by involving more than just the individual being baptized.

Second, recognizing the distinction between Anabaptists and the origins of Baptist churches helps believers today understand the distinctive role of the mode of baptism in Baptist churches. Anabaptists almost always baptized by

---

[6]   Anthony L. Chute, Nathan A. Finn, Michael A. G. Haykin, *The Baptist Story: From English Sect to Global Movement* (Nashville: B&H Academic, 2015), 22–23.

pouring. And while early Baptists followed that practice, within a generation, the movement was known for emphasizing immersion as the only proper mode for baptism. This emphasis has continued into the present day and stands as one of the most significant distinctives of modern Baptists. While the mode of baptism has remained a distinguishing characteristic among Baptists, history shows that the first generation of Baptists prioritized believer's baptism over a particular way of performing that baptism.

Resources

Chute, Anthony L., Nathan A. Finn, and Michael A. G. Haykin. *The Baptist Story: From English Sect to Global Movement*. Nashville: B&H Academic, 2015.

Coggins, James R. "The Theological Positions of John Smyth." *Baptist Quarterly* 30, no. 6 (1984).

Lee, Jason K. *The Theology of John Smyth: Puritan, Separatist, Baptist, Mennonite*. Macon, GA: Mercer University Press, 2003.

CHAPTER 27

John Calvin Summarized His Theology in "Five Points"

The Legendary Story

"Calvinism" is a system of doctrine stemming from the Reformer John Calvin (1509–1564), who summarized his theology in five easy-to-remember points in the acronym "TULIP":

Total Depravity,
Unconditional Election,
Limited Atonement,
Irresistible Grace, and
Perseverance of the Saints.

These five points set Calvin apart from many others in church history, distinguished him from his fellow Reformers, and has generally defined the Reformed or Calvinist tradition ever since. These five points represent the heart and heartbeat of John Calvin's theology.

Introduction: Unraveling the Legend

Though Calvin (and many others throughout church history) likely held these five doctrines, the "five points of Calvinism" ("TULIP") as a summary of Calvinism didn't originate with Calvin himself. Rather, they were first formulated at the Synod of Dort (1618–1619) by theologians of the Dutch Reformed

Church in response to five detractions by the followers of Jacob (James) Arminius (1560–1609). However, as the points that have distinguished Calvinist theology from Arminian theology since the seventeenth century, the five points have become a shorthand for pointing out distinct features of Calvinism.

Catching Calvin in the Street

If you were to catch John Calvin as he walked through the streets of Geneva, Switzerland, around the year 1560, and if you were to get him to summarize his theology in five points, he almost certainly would not have rattled off the "five points of Calvinism." Most likely, though, Calvin wouldn't even have attempted to sum up his theology in such a manner. He would probably tell you to read the latest (massive) edition of his *Institutes of the Christian Religion* instead. On the other hand, if you were to ask Calvin if he held to the doctrines of total depravity, unconditional election, limited atonement, irresistible grace, and perseverance of the saints, he would almost certainly nod in affirmation: "*Oui*, just like Saint Augustine, Augustinian theologians throughout history, and my fellow Augustinian Reformers today."

What do these particular points mean?

The Five Points Explained

Before we examine the historical origins of TULIP, let's take a moment to understand what it signifies. Much more could be said about these points, including the arguments and variations among detractors. However, a basic overview will help establish the context of the debates in the seventeenth century.

Total Depravity—According to Augustinian, Lutheran, and Calvinist theology, because of the fall, every aspect of humanity—including the human mind, emotions, and will—is *totally depraved*, lost and unable to respond to God's offer of salvation without his quickening Spirit giving the ability to believe (Rom 3:9–10; 8:7–8).

Unconditional Election—If all human beings throughout history are lost and stand condemned before God, God must act first to save anybody. Thus, God chooses some to be saved (Acts 13:48; Romans 9; Eph 1:3–6). God's election to salvation is *unconditional*, not based on anything people have done or will do.

Limited Atonement—Next, the doctrine of limited atonement does not teach that Christ's blood is insufficient to pay for all sins, but that in the purpose of God's election, the saving benefits of Christ's atonement are *limited* only to the elect (see Eph 5:25–27). Many Calvinists today would prefer to replace the term *limited atonement* with *particular atonement.*

Irresistible Grace—Because God chose who will be saved, all the elect will come to believe through the preaching of the word and faith. No non-elect will accidentally believe or even believe in vain. God's grace for the elect is *irresistible* (John 6:44; 10:27; Acts 2:39; Rom 8:29–30), because faith is itself a result of the regenerating grace of the Spirit.

Perseverance of the Saints—Finally, those whom God elected, called, and saved by grace through faith can never lose their salvation. True saints will persevere in faith and the fruit of genuine saving faith until the end. They are saved eternally (John 10:27–29; Rom 8:29–39; Eph 2:8–10).

The Road to Dort

We have little doubt that John Calvin held to the five points described above (though we acknowledge legitimate debate about whether Calvin clearly and consistently affirmed the doctrine of limited atonement).[1] These five points were not new to Calvin but were present in some form in Augustine's doctrine of salvation from the fifth century on. And with these Augustinian doctrines of sin and grace came detractors and critics: "As had some of Augustine's contemporaries, more theologians of the later medieval period (c. 1000–1500) backed away from his clear and decisive emphasis on God's sovereign grace, preferring a soteriological model that incorporated much more human responsibility."[2]

When figures like Luther (1483–1546), Zwingli (1484–1531), Calvin, and their associates in the sixteenth century reasserted many of Augustine's distinctives, it was only a matter of time before alternative voices began to assert themselves. Dissent from the consolidated Calvinist theology of the Dutch Reformed Church arose among the followers of Jacob (James) Arminius. A year after the Amsterdam theology professor's death, the supporters of Arminius's theology issued a *Remonstrance* (or "Protest") affirming five positive doctrines against what they perceived as the excesses of confessional Reformed theology:

---

[1]   For a chronicle of the debate, see Roger R. Nicole, "John Calvin's View of the Extent of the Atonement," *Westminster Theological Journal* 47, no 2 (Fall 1985): 197–225. Hans Boersma notes that Calvin "never addresses the question directly" and "is not always consistent on the point." "Calvin and the Extent of the Atonement," *Evangelical Quarterly* 64, no. 4 (1992): 354, 355.

[2]   Glenn R. Kreider and Michael J. Svigel, "Salvation in Retrospect," in Nathan D. Holsteen and Michael J. Svigel, eds., *Exploring Christian Theology*, vol. 2, *Creation, Fall, and Salvation* (Minneapolis: Bethany House, 2015), 176.

Article I modified election from the Calvinist "unconditional" to an Arminian "conditional" election—"that God . . . before the foundation of the world, hath determined, out of the fallen, sinful race of men, to save in Christ, for Christ's sake, and through Christ, those who, through the grace of the Holy Ghost, shall believe on this his Son Jesus, and shall persevere in this faith and obedience of faith, through this grace, even to the end."[3]

Article II then affirmed that Christ's death was for all, not only for the elect—"Jesus Christ, the Savior of the world, died for all men and for every man, so that he has obtained for them all, by his death on the cross, redemption, and the forgiveness of sins; yet that no one actually enjoys this forgiveness of sins, except the believer."

Article III reaffirms the classic Augustinian doctrine of total depravity, emphasizing that "man has not saving grace of himself, nor of the energy of his free-will, inasmuch as he, in the state of apostasy and sin, can of and by himself neither think, will, nor do anything that is truly good (such as having faith eminently is); but that it is needful that he be born again of God in Christ, through his Holy Spirit, and renewed in understanding, inclination, or will, and all his powers, in order that he may rightly understand, think, will, and effect what is truly good."

Article IV insists that the depraved sinner is made capable of belief through a "prevenient" (or "assisting") grace as "the beginning, continuance, and accomplishment of all good," without which it is impossible for people to be saved. However, such grace "is not irresistible." People may, by the enabling grace of God, choose to cooperate with God's grace or not.

Finally, Article V affirms that the truly saved have the power to "win the victory . . . through the assisting grace of the Holy Ghost." As long as they desire Christ's help through the Spirit to resist temptation and actively participate in their battle against "Satan, sin, the world, and

---

[3]   The English texts of the Five Articles of the Remonstrants are drawn from Hendrik Cornelis Rogge, "Remonstrants," in *The New Schaff-Herzog Religious Encyclopedia*, vol. 9, *Petri–Reuchlin*, ed. Samuel Macauley Jackson and George William Gilmore (repr., Grand Rapids: Baker, 1953), 482.

their own flesh," then Christ "keeps them from falling." However, the Remonstrants leave open the possibility that a truly saved person can actually lose his or her salvation, "again returning to this present evil world" and "becoming devoid of grace."

In direct response to these five protests against the official Calvinist confession of the Dutch Reformed Church (the Belgic Confession) and the Heidelberg Catechism, a series of meetings was held from November 1618 to May 1619 at the Dutch city of Dortrecht (also called "Dort" or "Dordt"). This Synod of Dort eventually rejected each of the five Remonstrances, essentially reaffirming with greater clarity what are today called the "Five Points of Calvinism." John Hannah sums up the outcome succinctly: "In the synod's response to the Five Remonstrances, they combined assertions three and four together, considering them inseparables, presenting their reply in the form of four articles. Calvinists rearranged them over time to five and centuries later created the acrostic, TULIP, a teaching device to articulate their antithesis to Remonstrant Party claims."[4]

Application

In the space between the five points of Arminianism and the five points of Calvinism, several intermediate positions exist. Some see in Calvin himself some ambiguity regarding the doctrine of limited atonement. Moderate "four-point" Calvinists today find space there to affirm that Christ's death was *sufficient* for all, but *applied* only to the elect. Modified Arminians today may hold to a grace-enabled free will to believe but eternal security after receiving salvation. Others may regret the reduction of Calvinism to merely the "five points," preferring to understand even these only in the context of a broader system of Reformed theology. Still others dodge the matter of the "five points" completely, preferring to regard themselves as Augustinian or Lutheran in their perspectives on the issues.

In light of the history of Calvinism and Arminianism, it seems we have done a disservice to the various perspectives by reducing Calvin's grandiose theology to the "five points" and then using them as a means of either including fellow believers "in our tribe" or building impenetrable walls between "us

---

[4]   John D. Hannah, *Invitation to Church History: World*, Invitation to Theological Studies (Grand Rapids: Kregel, 2018), 330–31.

and them." As we dig deeper into the significance and history of these "five points," it becomes clear that they were never reflective of all Protestantism or even all those who were heirs of Luther, Zwingli, and Calvin himself.

Resources

Allen, R. Michael. *Reformed Theology*. Doing Theology. London: Bloomsbury, T&T Clark, 2010.
Horton, Michael. *For Calvinism*. Grand Rapids: Zondervan, 2011.
Spencer, Duane Edward. *TULIP: The Five Points of Calvinism in the Light of Scripture*. 2nd ed. Grand Rapids: Baker, 1979.

CHAPTER 28

Jacob Arminius Denied Depravity and Taught That Christians Could Lose Their Salvation

The Legendary Story

Arminians follow the teaching of Jacob (or "James") Arminius (1560–1609), who rejected the view of total depravity taught by John Calvin (1509–1564). Arminius believed we had some innate capacity to cooperate with God's grace, to "meet him halfway," to choose to be saved by our own free will. Consequently, because we can choose to be saved, we might also one day choose not to be saved—to sin and rebel against God to such a degree that we lose our salvation. Arminius rejected eternal security, taking a step backward from the Reformation toward Roman Catholic works-salvation.

Introduction: Unraveling the Legend

Just as in the tradition of Calvinism, we see a diversity of opinions among the followers of Jacob Arminius down to our own day. While it may be true that many who identify themselves as "Arminians" today emphasize their belief in free will to accept God's salvation, Arminius and his immediate followers agreed with the doctrine of total depravity in the sense that *left to ourselves*, in our natural state, without God's grace, we lack freedom of the will. Likewise, Arminius himself denied that he said truly regenerate Christians could lose their salvation, though both he and his followers regarded the matter to be unclear in Scripture, requiring further study rather than dogmatic declarations.

"I *Thought* I Was an Arminian . . ."

I (Mike) have a little trick I play on my theology students. I admit, I take a little delight in its subtle and harmless cruelty because it can be a profound teaching moment. I've never hidden my Calvinistic theology, so when I teach about Reformation soteriology (the doctrine of salvation), it's pretty obvious that as I quote from Calvin, I do so rather positively. At the seminary where we teach, though, Calvinism isn't required by our official doctrinal statement, so students in our classes range from five-point Calvinists to full-blown free-will Baptists! Yet the trick I play easily exposes some ignorance among the students regarding their own positions.

Here's what I do: I project several quotes regarding divine sovereignty and free will by John Calvin, complete with his portrait staring at them. Of course, the Arminians in the classroom, who have usually self-identified by now, find Calvin's reasoning unconvincing. Then I project this quotation beside Calvin's picture:

> In his *lapsed and sinful state*, man is not capable, of and by himself, either to think, to will, or to do that which is really good; but it is necessary for him to be regenerated and renewed in his intellect, affections or will, and in all his powers, by God in Christ through the Holy Spirit, that he may be qualified rightly to understand, esteem, consider, will, and perform whatever is truly good. When he is made a partaker of this regeneration or renovation, I consider that, since he is delivered from sin, he is capable of thinking, willing and doing that which is good, but yet *not without the continued aids of Divine Grace*.

At that point I address the Arminians (or at least non-Calvinists) in the room: "What's your reaction to this? Where do you see problems?" Inevitably, they begin picking apart the quotation, usually insisting that if only the regenerate aided by divine grace can think, will, or do any good, then God's commands to believe and obey are vacuous. It destroys the fundamental principle of free will, without which there could be no real relationship with God. What basis would God have to reward the righteous or punish the wicked?

Then, after allowing those students to tear apart the quotation, I press my clicker, replacing the image of Calvin with an image of Arminius and revealing the true source of the quotation: Arminius's own defense of his position on depravity and free will.[1] At that point many of my self-proclaimed Arminian students realize they disagree with Arminius himself on the role of grace and free will. They realize, in fact, that they are not quite Arminian at all, but a step away from Arminianism in the direction of "natural" free will, an ability to believe and to live apart from divine grace. A step, in fact, closer to John Cassian (360–435) than to Arminianism (see chapter 21 on these views).

Arminius's Depravity

The truth is, Jacob Arminius himself—and the great majority of his informed disciples through the generations—fully embraced the doctrine of total depravity. One description puts the doctrine this way: "The doctrine of sin associated with Augustinian, Calvinist, and Arminian theology [is] that because of the fall, humans are spiritually dead—essentially and unchangeably bad apart from divine grace. Their guilt before God is *total.* Total depravity doesn't mean everyone is as evil as they could possibly be, but that everyone absolutely needs the grace of God to even understand the gospel and choose to accept it."[2]

This view of total depravity was shared by Lutherans, Calvinists, and Arminians alike in the wake of the Reformation. Arminian theologian Roger Olson notes that "the original Arminianism of Arminius, Wesley and their evangelical heirs . . . emphatically do[es] not deny total depravity . . . or the absolute necessity of supernatural grace for even the first exercise of a good will toward God."[3] He continues, "Arminians together with Calvinists affirm total depravity because of the fall of humanity in Adam and its inherited consequence of a corrupted nature in bondage to sin."[4]

Clearly, Arminius and classic Arminianism embrace the same doctrine of total depravity as Calvinists. On the other hand, many who claim to be heirs of Arminius's theology have taken significant steps away from this position, denying that the natural free will of a fallen sinner is in bondage, and rather affirming that even fallen human begins have free will sufficient to believe

---

[1] The block quote above comes from Jacob Arminius, *A Declaration of the Sentiments of Arminius, on Predestination, Divine Providence, the Freedom of the Will, the Grace of God, the Divinity of the Son of God, and the Justification of Man before God,* in James Arminius, *The Works of James Arminius,* vol. 1, trans. James Nichols (Auburn: Derby, Miller and Orton, 1853), 252–53.

[2] Nathan D. Holsteen and Michael J. Svigel, eds., *Exploring Christian Theology,* vol. 2, *Creation, Fall, and Salvation* (Minneapolis: Bethany House, 2015), 258.

[3] Roger E. Olson, *Arminian Theology: Myths and Realities* (Downers Grove, IL: IVP Academic, 2006), 17.

[4] Olson, 56.

by their own power. Yet that position of a natural free will would be utterly unacceptable to Arminius and his immediate followers, who taught that grace is absolutely necessary for anybody to believe and obey God.

The issue that separates Calvinists and Arminians is not total depravity and the need for grace. Their disagreement revolves around how such grace comes to people. In Calvinist theology, God elects certain people from among the pool of lost sinners then grants to those elect the effectual grace of regeneration to believe and be saved. This is effectual in that those given such regenerating grace actually respond in faith, which is an irresistible gift. The result is that all of the elect will be saved and preserved in this state (see chapter 27).

In Arminian theology, God grants to all lost, depraved sinners not effectual saving grace, but *enabling grace*—provided for in the death of Christ—so all people are given, by grace, a choice to accept or reject God's revelation. Left to themselves, humans are totally depraved. But by God's general, prevenient, enabling grace, all helpless sinners have a limited capacity to receive the good news of Jesus Christ by faith. The "free will" to believe or reject is not something humans have by nature. It is something given to them by grace. Thus, in Arminian theology, there is no salvation apart from divine grace.

Arminius's Security

The Arminian doctrine of "prevenient" or "enabling" grace granted to all fallen humans affects three other elements of the "five points of Calvinism": the doctrine of predestination, the extent of the atonement, and whether saving grace can be resisted. If all totally depraved humans are, by grace, given enough gracious ability to understand and believe the gospel, then the offer of saving grace is open to all people. The decision becomes that of the graciously enabled sinner to accept or reject. In this case, predestination may involve God's predetermined election of Christ and those who, through faith, are incorporated into Christ, sharing his destiny. Or it could involve God foreseeing those who will, by their restored free will, accept the gospel and be saved. This would not be unconditional, but conditional, election, conditioned upon a person exercising faith by God's grace. Naturally, then, saving grace offered through the preaching of the gospel would not be irresistible. Nor would the benefits of Christ's atoning work be limited exclusively to the elect. In fact, for all humans to receive the general prevenient grace that enables them to believe, the effects of Christ's death are received—to a certain degree—by all people. Unlimited atonement is necessary to apply this prevenient grace to all, though it does not save all people. They must, by exercising their restored ability to believe, be reconciled to God through personal faith.

But what about "eternal security"? Doesn't it naturally follow that if a person chooses to believe, he or she could one day choose to disbelieve? Didn't Arminius teach that a truly saved person could lose his or her salvation through free choice, neglect, or sin? Actually, Arminius himself stated:

> I never taught that a *true believer can either totally or finally fall away from the faith, and perish*; yet I will not conceal, that there are passages of Scripture which seem to me to wear this aspect; and those answers to them which I have been permitted to see, are not of such a kind as to approve themselves on all points to my understanding. On the other hand, certain passages are produced for the contrary doctrine [of unconditional perseverance] which are worthy of much consideration.[5]

Even Arminius's disciples, in their Five Remonstrances against Dutch Calvinist theology (see chapter 27), indicated an unsettled opinion on whether a truly regenerate person could ultimately fall away.[6] In the unfolding history of Arminianism, then, we do find some who have affirmed at least three views: (1) that through negligence or impudence, a truly regenerate person could lose salvation; (2) that Scripture is not entirely clear, so we must not take a dogmatic position on this, being careful to simply live lives of faith, obedience, and fear of the Lord; or (3) that Scripture does, in fact, teach that once a person has accepted God's gift of salvation by the power of enabling grace, that person is sealed forever and can never lose salvation. Technically, the second position would fall under what we might call "classic Arminianism." The first view, that one can lose his or her salvation, has become rather typical of most self-identifying Arminians over the centuries. And the third view tends to be that of a "moderate" or "modified" Arminianism.

In any case, though many people claiming the name "Arminian" today affirm natural free will and insist that true believers can lose their salvation, Jacob Arminius himself did not teach these things. There are clear and irreconcilable differences between Calvinism and Arminianism, but these issues are not the main focus of disagreement. The real disagreement is over the nature

---

5   Arminius, *A Declaration of the Sentiments of Arminius* 5 (Arminius, *Works*, 1:254).
6   Hendrik Cornelis Rogge, "Remonstrants," in *The New Schaff-Herzog Religious Encyclopedia*, vol. 9, *Petri—Reuchlin*, ed. Samuel Macauley Jackson and George William Gilmore (repr., Grand Rapids: Baker, 1953), 482.

of grace—is it effectual and irresistible, given only to the elect (Calvinism), or is it enabling and resistible, giving all people the ability to believe by grace?

Application

Both Arminians and Calvinists (and those holding certain mediating positions in between) teach a vital, fundamental truth of Protestant orthodoxy: that we are all, left to ourselves, helpless sinners in need of grace. Apart from God's gracious intervention, we will—every one of us—be utterly lost. Classic Arminianism has taught that even the ability to accept or reject the offer of the gospel is itself a result of God's enabling grace, not something we have in our own human capacity. Thus, when we are saved, we are saved by grace alone, through faith alone, in Christ alone.

It would be a gross exaggeration to say that all Arminians believe we have natural, innate free will, in and of ourselves, to believe and obey. If we believe, it is by the enabling grace of God. If we obey, it is by his sanctifying grace. If we persevere, it is by his sustaining grace. As more in sympathy with the Calvinist perspective on these matters, we hold or teach the distinctive doctrines of classic Calvinism. But with a proper understanding of the Arminian position, we (1) call self-styled Arminians who actually reject true Arminianism back to the healthier articulation of their position; and (2) acknowledge that classic Arminian theology is not a denial of salvation by grace through faith, but an allowable variation, along with Calvinism, within the spectrum of orthodox, Protestant evangelicalism.

Resources

Olson, Roger E. *Arminian Theology: Myths and Realities*. Downers Grove, IL: IVP Academic, 2006.

Pinson, J. Matthew. "Jacob Arminius: Reformed and Always Reforming." In *Grace for All: The Arminian Dynamics of Salvation*, edited by Clark H. Pinnock and John D. Wager. Eugene, OR: Wipf and Stock, 2015.

Stanglin, Keith D., and Thomas H. McCall. *Jacob Arminius: Theologian of Grace*. Oxford: Oxford University Press, 2012.

CHAPTER 29

The King James Version Was the First Authorized Protestant Translation

The Legendary Story

In a world filled with competing claims and confusing concepts, God's people need a sure repository for the truth. By God's providence, the text of the King James Bible has been produced and preserved in English for just such a purpose. Brought about as a result of a decree by King James I in 1604, a group of translators worked from Greek and Hebrew manuscripts to complete the first such authorized translation of the Bible.

Since its completion, this translation of the Bible has been called the Authorized Version, recognizing its status as the premier translation of the Bible in English. Indeed, the Authorized or King James Version was the seventh of seven key English translations, revealing its purity, as predicted in Psalm 12:6 ("The words of the Lord are pure words . . . purified seven times").[1] God has, therefore, seen fit to position the King James Version as *the* continuing witness to the inspired words he has given to the world.

Introduction: Unraveling the Legend

Since 1611, an interesting movement has developed around the King James Version of the Bible. Adherents of this movement use the King James as a test

---

[1] Dr. Laurence M. Vance, "The AV 1611: Purified Seven Times," Biblebelievers.com, accessed January 22, 2020, https://www.biblebelievers.com/Vance5.html.

of orthodoxy—those who use and affirm the translation of the King James are "in," while those who question the King James Version or use some other English translation are "out." This "King James Only" movement is itself diverse, with people on a spectrum from mere preference for the King James to those who believe it is the first authorized English version, or even the only inspired English translation of Scripture.[2]

However, a look at the history leaves suspect many of the claims made by the "King James Only" movement—most notably, the King James Bible was not the first authorized version, but the third. This chapter will highlight key features in the history of English Bible translation as well as within the King James Version itself and interact with several of the most significant "King James Only" arguments.

Translating the Word with New (and Old) Words

Advocates for a King James Only position often speak of the 1611 version as England's Authorized Version of the Bible. In their view, this notion gives the King James pride of place among all other "lesser" English translations. A closer look at the history of English translations, as well as of the King James itself, presents a murkier picture.

First of all, the King James Bible was not the first English translation of the whole Bible. That honor goes to the Bible produced in Middle English by John Wycliffe (1325–1384) and his team of translators in the late fourteenth century, more than 200 years before the King James translation appeared.

Nor was the King James Bible the first translation of the Bible into modern English, a feat accomplished primarily by William Tyndale (1494–1536) in the 1520s and '30s. However, Tyndale had long been on the run from English authorities, leaving England altogether in the 1520s and eventually settling in Antwerp, Belgium. In 1535 a young English lawyer named Henry Phillips betrayed Tyndale to the authorities, and after imprisonment and trial over the next eighteen months, Tyndale was strangled and burned at the stake. Tyndale's assistant, Myles Coverdale (1488–1569), took Tyndale's existing published work—the Pentateuch and the New Testament—and completed a copy of the Bible in 1535 while Tyndale sat imprisoned in a Belgian castle.[3]

Only two years later the Matthew Bible was published, which incorpo-

---

[2]   James R. White, *The King James Only Controversy* (Minneapolis: Bethany House, 2009), 23–30.
[3]   Before he died, Tyndale also translated many of the historical books and prophets, but they remained unpublished.

rated into Coverdale's Bible nearly all of Tyndale's unpublished Old Testament. The Coverdale and Matthew Bibles set a pattern of publishing translations that served as "drafts" for what would become the King James Bible, the translators of each new English version referring to older English versions. Along the way, Coverdale made another pass at translation at the behest of Henry VIII, called the Great Bible (1539), while Queen Elizabeth commissioned a new translation for the churches called the Bishops Bible (1568). Both of these Bibles carried the official authorization of the English crown, making them the first two "authorized" Bibles in English.[4]

The King James Bible of 1611 was at least the ninth English Bible translation, most of which had been completed in the century prior. Three of those English translations were "authorized" by the British crown, including the King James Bible. Any argument for the primacy of the King James Bible based on its authorization by the King of England fails on historical merits, not to mention theological ones.[5]

What's in a Name?

The English Bible translation of 1611 has popularly been called the Authorized Version and/or the King James Bible. Neither phrase appeared on the original title page of the Bible, which said, "The Holy Bible, containing the Old Testament and the New: newly translated out of the original tongues, and with the former translations diligently compared and revised by his Majesty's special commandment. Appointed to be read in churches."[6]

The title page clearly refers to the king's command to translate the Bible, which came out of the Hampton Court Conference in 1604. As a result of that meeting and a demand from Puritans to have a Bible in the language of the people, King James appointed about fifty translators to begin work on what would become the translation of 1611—what we call the King James Bible.[7] But if the translators did not use "King James Bible" or "Authorized Version" on the title page, from where, then, did those titles come?

---

[4]   Other translations of the Bible into English before the King James include the Geneva Bible (1560) and the Catholic Douay-Rheims Bible (1582).

[5]   Arguing for the primacy of a translation based on a secular king's authorization is theologically dubious. Inspired Scripture is God's Word, not the king's word.

[6]   David Norton, *The King James Bible: A Short History from Tyndale to Today* (Cambridge: Cambridge University Press, 2011), 119.

[7]   Puritans were also dissatisfied with Elizabeth's Bishops Bible. The Puritans were all dissatisfied Anglicans, so this makes a great deal of sense.

The first recorded use of "Authorized" as a title appears to be from Ambrose Ussher in 1620, who described the King James Bible as "the authorized bible" in a preface to his own partial translation of the Old and New Testaments.[8] Interestingly, Ussher invoked this "authorized" phrase to describe the 1611 King James Bible as a lesser work than his own translation. In his view, the King James needed a revision. "Authorized Version" did not appear regularly in print as a title for more than 200 years, as the *Oxford English Dictionary* traces it back only to 1874.[9]

In a similar fashion, the language of "King James Version" or "King James Bible" didn't appear until the early nineteenth century as a descriptive reference.[10] The first printed use of "King James Version" as a title originates from a letter written by a Catholic from Mississippi in the 1850s.[11] Interestingly, both "Authorized Version" and "King James Version" first saw the printed page via those seeking alternatives to the King James Bible.

The development of these titles over more than 200 years underlines the King James Version's high standing among English readers. Beyond the King's initial appointment of translators, however, no evidence exists that James ever gave his official approval to the translation published in 1611. Indeed, when the Bible was published, the translators themselves wrote the king a dedication in which they asked him to approve their work: "Humbly craving of your most Sacred Majesty, that since things of this quality have ever been subject to the censures of ill meaning and discontented persons, *it may receive approbation and patronage from so learned and judicious a Prince as your Highness is*."[12] Such factors underline the fact that the King James Version, while an important literary work and a fine example of the biblical text in English, bears no more authority—earthly or divine—than a whole host of other English translations.

---

[8] Ambrose Ussher, "Ambrose Ussher's English Version of the Bible: Extract from 'Epistle Dedicatorie' to James I," in *Fourth Report of the Royal Commission on Historical Manuscripts* (London: Eyre and Spottswood, 1874), 598.

[9] *Oxford English Dictionary* 1:572c, as cited in Jack Lewis, "The King James Bible Editions: Their Character and Revision History," in David G. Burke, ed., *Translation that Openeth the Window: Reflections on the History and Legacy of the King James Bible* (Atlanta: Society of Biblical Literature, 2009), 90.

[10] William Smith, *The Reasonableness of Setting Forth the Most Worthy Praise of Almighty God* (New York: T. and J. Swords, 1814), 209.

[11] James L. Chapman, *Americanism versus Romanism* (Nashville: n.p., 1856), 270.

[12] "1611 King James Bible Introduction," King James Bible Online, accessed March 23, 2019, https://www.kingjamesbibleonline.org/1611-Bible/1611-King-James-Bible-Introduction.php, emphasis added. Spelling updated for readability.

The King James Version Today

As is evident from the original title page of the 1611 translation, and from a "translators' preface" published with it, the committee that translated the King James Bible saw their work as another in a long line of valuable Bible translations, rather than as a fundamentally unique, God-breathed set of writings. However, many today of the King James Only camp disagree with this assessment.

For instance, one author suggests that "the 1611 KJV is the first authorized version of the Bible translated for [*sic*] the original Hebrew, Koine Greek and Aramaic. This translation did not use other English versions to translate from."[13] While all of the qualifiers (date, authorized, original languages) give the illusion of truth, the reality is that the title page makes explicit reference to correcting and revising earlier English translations. The translators wrote a preface to the King James Version that makes the same point: "We never thought from the beginning, that we should need to make a new Translation, nor yet to make of a bad one a good one . . . but to make a good one better, or out of many good ones, one principal good one."[14] In fact, scholars have helped to clarify the major influence of Tyndale's work on the King James Version. One scholar notes, "Some ninety per cent of the New Testament in that version [KJV] is Tyndale's."[15]

Furthermore, advocates for the 1611 translation alone make another grave error: virtually no one today actually reads the 1611 translation, but rather an updated and revised text from 1769.[16] More than 150 years after its publication, the King James Version had been printed and reprinted many times, with corrections and new errors incorporated each time. In the effort to produce a standard text, the 1769 edition corrected these typographical errors and offered a clear standard for other printers to work from. Further, the Apocrypha—

---

[13]   Tony Mariot, "Which Bible Translation Is Older or Closest to the 1711 Version: KJV or KJVA?," Quora, accessed January 22, 2020, https://www.quora.com/Which-Bible-translation-is-older-or-closest-to-the-1711-version-KJV-or-KJVA.

[14]   As cited in James R. White, *The King James Only Controversy* (Minneapolis: Bethany House, 2009), 119.

[15]   Donald Coggan, "Spirit, Bible and Preaching Today with Special Reference to William Tyndale," in W. P. Stephens, ed., *The Bible, the Reformation and the Church: Essays in Honour of James Atkinson* (Sheffield: Sheffield Academic Press, 1995), 82. Another estimate puts the percentage of overlap more conservatively at above 75 percent. See John Nielson and Royal Skousen, "How Much of the King James Bible Is William Tyndale's?" *Reformation* 3 (1998): 49–74.

[16]   Jack P. Lewis, *The English Bible from KJV to NIV: A History and Evaluation* (Grand Rapids: Baker, 1984), 39.

which had been included in the 1611 translation but often left out in intervening years—was excluded from this revision.[17]

Application

The King James Version of the Bible is a fine translation. Its phraseology has made its way into the English vernacular, such as "in the twinkling of an eye" (1 Cor 15:52) or "out of the mouth of babes" (Ps 8:2). A huge majority of English speakers from 1611 into the twenty-first century have used it as a primary Bible. This version has major cultural credibility in the English-speaking world today.

However, what the King James Version accomplished in 1611—bringing God's Word to the people—is precisely why new translations need to be produced over time as language and culture shifts. As God continually comes near to his creation, so do Christians need to work to bring his Word near to people in language they can understand.

Take heed: focusing on a single translation alone as God's Word can have negative effects, leading people to question the Christian doctrine of inspiration—that the Bible is God's word to humanity. Some King James Only advocates believe that without a "true" text in our possession, one that lacks textual variants, we cannot have a reliable Bible. This position is similar to Muslim assertions about the Koran, which is thought to be divine revelation only in its original Arabic text. Many Bible readers have made the King James Bible the standard by which all translations can be judged. Thus, when confronted with typographical errors or textual variants in the original 1611 text, some King James Only advocates might go to the other extreme—from "the King James Version is the only inspired word" to "there is no inspired word of God at all." Such a shift would be tragic, because Christians should consider inspired the Bibles we hold in our hands today. Bibles today are not inspired because they are all the same, but because God has always communicated with us in and through human translations, and because we have access to a long, wide, and reliable tradition of Bible manuscripts that help us understand the true nature of the text with a very high degree of precision.

---

[17] The Apocrypha had actually been removed some 100 years earlier, in an edition from 1666. KJV readers today read a "non-apocryphal" version of the text.

Resources

Burke, David G., ed. *Translation That Openeth the Window: Reflections on the History and Legacy of the King James Bible.* Atlanta: Society of Biblical Literature, 2009.

Lane, Tony. "The Crown of English Bibles." In "How We Got Our Bible, Canon to King James," issue 43, *Christian History* magazine, 1994.

Norton, David. *The King James Bible: A Short History from Tyndale to Today.* Cambridge: Cambridge University Press, 2011.

White, James R. *The King James Only Controversy.* Minneapolis: Bethany House, 2009.

CHAPTER 30

The Pilgrims Fled Religious Oppression to Establish a Society of Religious Freedom

The Legendary Story

Every Thanksgiving Americans not only thank God for his abundant provisions; they also commemorate a great moment in the history of religious freedom. The Pilgrims fled England because of religious intolerance and persecution, risking life and limb to cross the treacherous Atlantic to establish a colony of religious liberty. Finally, they could worship in freedom of conscience, unlike the intolerant, stifling religious oppression of the state church in their native England. In fact, the principle of religious liberty brought by the Pilgrims eventually made its way into the First Amendment of the Constitution, guaranteeing freedom of religion for all.

Introduction: Unraveling the Legend

The truth is, the original "Pilgrims" and the "Puritans" who followed them, as separatist nonconformists, wanted to be liberated from the doctrines and practices of the Church of England, but this didn't mean they were enthusiastic about broad religious toleration for others. In fact, it was just as much their own religious intolerance of the Anglican Church that led them first to leave England for Holland, then from Holland to New England. Later, when the growing number of Puritan immigrants founded the Massachusetts Bay Colony and absorbed the Pilgrims' Plymouth Colony, they established their own state church that was intolerant of deviations from their strict Congregational

Reformed ideals, forcing those who genuinely believed in religious liberty to depart and establish colonies elsewhere.

Flight for Freedom?

One online resource states, "Above all, the Pilgrims wanted to be free. . . . So the Pilgrims left England, in search of a safe place to practice their religion."[1] This straightforward characterization of the motivation behind what eventually became the *Mayflower* voyage to New England, though accurate on the surface, sometimes leads people to believe that the Pilgrims' idea of religious freedom was the same as ours. That is, they were seeking a tolerant society in which freedom of religion was the norm and the government didn't dictate which religion was acceptable and which church a person had to join.

Often coupled with this characterization is the notion that the waves of British colonists who followed in their wake to plant communities in the New World were also motivated by such ideals of liberty—especially religious liberty. Having experienced intolerance, repression, and persecution in the Old World, they longed for a life of tolerance, free expression, and freedom from prosecution for matters of conscience. Historian Garry Wills notes, "We were taught as children that Pilgrims and Puritans fled to the New World to escape religious repression under the British monarch and find tolerance for their views."[2] However, the truth behind his urban legend is much more complicated.

Pilgrims and Puritans

Puritans in England were so named because they wanted to complete the Reformation by purifying the Church of England of what they saw as the last stains of Roman Catholic beliefs and practices, including the institutional church's liturgy and hierarchy. They held to the "regulative" principle regarding the role of Scripture in church practice—that is, only those things explicitly commanded in or warranted by Scripture were permitted in worship. In contrast, the Church of England adhered to the "normative" principle, believing that the church had the freedom to incorporate practices from tradition as long as they were not forbidden by Scripture. Because of their inability to accept the

---

[1]   David White, "The Pilgrims: Voyage for Freedom," part 1, "The Need for Freedom," available online at http://www.socialstudiesforkids.com/articles/ushistory/pilgrims1.htm, accessed April 5, 2019.

[2]   Garry Wills, *Head and Heart: A History of Christianity in America* (New York: Penguin, 2007), 18.

official church's "middle way," the Puritans either strived to change the official state church or decided to abandon it to form their own separate groups.

From this conflict in England, the Pilgrims of yore emerged. They sought a new homeland where they could exercise their purified religion without the interference of the king. Then, after the landing of the *Mayflower* in the New World and the establishment of Plymouth Colony in 1620, wave after wave of English Puritans continued to make the same journey across the Atlantic to establish additional colonies based on the same kinds of ideals. Janice Knight notes, "The colonists intended to plant pure churches in what they saw as a vacant land; they dreamed of establishing a New Jerusalem in the wilderness."[3] With a few notable exceptions, however, most Puritans did not hold to the idea of a separation of church and state. They took for granted the position that the church should be a partner of the state, that they should "cooperate with godly magistrates to promote the total reformation of society."[4]

Their utopian dream of establishing a pure church and ideal Christian society, however, quickly dissolved when the New England Puritans experienced a rude awakening. Just as the Puritans themselves had dissented from the government-sponsored state church in England, members of their own government-sponsored state church in New England also dissented on doctrinal and practical matters.

Dissenting from Dissenters

"Puritan New England" is sometimes perceived as a unified political and religious society composed of men and women united in their dissent against the strictures of the Church of England. However, Puritanism was hardly monolithic, even in its movement from England to America: "The records of New England's first three decades reveal an unsettling amount of debate, controversy, and even violent confrontation."[5] From the beginning of the emigration to the New World, men and women dissented from the dissenters, demanding freedom of conscience in religion matters, just as their leaders in the colonies had demanded from the king years earlier.

For example, from 1636 to 1638, the Massachusetts Bay Colony was

---

[3]   Janice Knight, *Orthodoxies in Massachusetts: Rereading American Puritanism* (Cambridge, MA: Harvard University Press, 1994), 14.

[4]   Mark A. Noll, *A History of Christianity in the United States and Canada* (Grand Rapids: Eerdmans, 1992), 33.

[5]   Knight, *Orthodoxies in Massachusetts*, 5.

shaken by the teachings of the "Antinomians." To the strict Puritans in power, the so-called Antinomians, such as Anne Hutchinson (1591–1643), Reverend John Wheelwright (1592–1679), and, to a lesser degree, the minister of the church of Boston, John Cotton (1585–1652), seemed to be teaching a form of Christian liberty and free grace that threw off all lawfulness and moral norms. On the other hand, the "Antinomians" regarded established Puritans like John Winthrop (1588–1649) to be holding something like a works-based salvation and strict legalism. While Cotton himself established a middle ground and retained his place in Boston,[6] Wheelwright and Hutchinson were found guilty of a number of crimes and exiled from the colony.

Another dissenter from the Massachusetts Bay Colony's repressive form of Puritan orthodoxy was Roger Williams (c. 1603–1683). Williams arrived in Massachusetts in 1631 among the earliest waves of Puritan emigrants from England. He eventually settled in Plymouth, where the Pilgrims had first established themselves about a decade earlier. However, it soon became obvious that Williams's opinions on the relationship between church and state were at odds with the Puritan dream of establishing a Christian society. He "saw no future in a Christian faith compromised by attempts to rule in the world."[7]

When Williams moved from Plymouth to become a minister in Salem in 1633, his views of true toleration and real religious liberty didn't sit well with the New England establishment. In 1635, he was banished from Massachusetts and made his way south, where he founded the city of Providence and the colony of Rhode Island. In contrast to the compacts and laws of Plymouth and Massachusetts, Roger Williams's Providence compact explicitly limited the government's authority, permitting it to enact laws "only in civil things."[8] Religious tolerance was retained in Rhode Island, and Williams spent the rest of his life criticizing the intolerance and oppressiveness of the Massachusetts Puritans and their fading dreams of a Christian state.

Thus, the facts are clear. Most Pilgrims and Puritans did not place a high priority on religious liberty—unless it was their own. By the 1660s, the intolerance and persecution of the Puritans in Massachusetts had become so extreme that it led not only to arrests, trials, and exiles, but also to torture and executions. In some cases, it would have been better if the dissenters had gone back to England than to remain in New England. The infamy of the early Puritans' intolerance of religious dissent within their boundaries was so

---

6   Knight, 71.
7   Noll, *A History of Christianity in the United States and Canada*, 59.
8   John Franklin Jameson, *The Arrival of the Pilgrims* (Providence, RI: Brown University, 1920), 30.

acute that King Charles II himself had to order the governors of the colony to stop executing people for their religious views. Historian Garry Wills notes, "Here we see the King championing tolerance and the colonists engaged in repression."[9] At least 460 public executions occurred between 1623 and 1825 for a variety of capital crimes.[10]

MINI MYTHS

"An Apple Tree Ate Roger Williams"

Roger Williams (1603–1683) was not only the founder of Rhode Island; he also established the first Baptist church in the New World. When he died, he was buried near an apple tree. Nearly 200 years later, when his body was exhumed to move it to a monument constructed in his honor, they found only a few bits of bone, some mushy earth, and a root of the nearby apple tree that had eaten his body. It grew down his spine, split at his legs, and bent at his feet. Unsure of what to do with the "Roger Williams Root," the Rhode Island Historical Society displays it in the John Brown House Museum behind a glass case. Almost everything in this story is true, except there's just no way to know whether the shape of that root was just a coincidence or it actually fed the apple tree by consuming nutrients from Roger Williams's remains. If true, at the resurrection of the dead Roger Williams will be in for a "root awakening."[11]

Application

Over and over again, Christian "purists" have tried to cleanse both the church and society of deviant doctrines and practices. Before the American Revolutionary War (1776–1783) and the forming of the United States

---

9   Garry Wills, *Head and Heart*, 18
10   Scott D. Seay, *Hanging between Heaven and Earth: Capital Crime, Execution Preaching, and Theology in Early New England* (DeKalb: Northern Illinois University Press, 2009), 14.
11   See Michael Kammen, *Digging Up the Dead: A History of Notable American Reburials* (Chicago: University of Chicago Press, 2010), 174–77.

forced men and women of radically differing theological and philosophical backgrounds to unite despite their differences, Puritan New England tried to enforce unity and community by uniformity and conformity. They hoped to establish a near-utopian Christian society with right religion, strong moral instruction, and God-honoring laws.

However, their puritanical pursuit led to many missteps and disasters. In many ways, the Puritans failed to apply the words of Jesus: "Whatever you want others to do for you, do also the same for them" (Matt 7:12). They should have done for others what the king failed to do for them—grant religious toleration. It wasn't as though such ideals of toleration were unheard of in the seventeenth century. Many philosophers and theologians had advanced those notions and actually put them into practice in parts of the Old and New World.

The Puritans' failed experiment at enforcing a Christian society in New England, with close cooperation between church and state, should serve as a cautionary tale for us. We should resist modern attempts of Christians using the state to advance their doctrines and morals, or the state enlisting the church to advance its political and social agendas. And in our own Christian circles, we should strive for unity on the essential truths of the faith while allowing for diversity of opinions on less central matters on which true Christians have never agreed.

Resources

Bremer, Francis J. *The Puritan Experiment: New England Society from Bradford to Edwards*. Rev. ed. Hanover, NH: University Press of New England, 1995.

Fiske, John. *The Beginnings of New England, or The Puritan Theocracy in Its Relations to Civil and Religious Liberty*. Cambridge, MA: Riverside, 1898.

Knight, Janice. *Orthodoxies in Massachusetts: Rereading American Puritanism*. Cambridge, MA: Harvard University Press, 1994.

PART IV

—

Urban Legends
of the Modern Age
(1700–Present)

Modern Age Time Line
(Some of the dates below are approximate)

1700–1800: Rise of liberal theology in Europe

1703–1758: Jonathan Edwards

1703–1791: John Wesley

1706–1790: Benjamin Franklin

1711–1776: David Hume

1713–1784: Denis Diderot

1714–1770: George Whitefield

1718–1747: David Brainerd

1722–1803: Samuel Adams

1723–1739: Baron d'Holbach

1724–1804: Immanuel Kant

1727–1795: Ezra Stiles

1730s–1740s: First Great Awakening

1735–1826: John Adams

1737–1809: Thomas Paine

1740–1821: Elias Boudinot

1743–1826: Thomas Jefferson

1745–1829: John Jay

1755–1835: John Marshall

1761–1834: William Carey

1768–1834: Friedrich Schleiermacher

1772–1844: Barton Stone

1776–1783: American Revolution

1782–1834: Robert Morrison

1788–1866: Alexander Campbell

1791: Methodist denomination born

1792–1875: Charles Finney

1800–1882: John Nelson Darby

1801–1890: John Henry Newman

1805–1844: Joseph Smith

1807–1880: William Adams

1809–1882: Charles Darwin

1813–1873: David Livingstone

1813–1887: Henry Ward Beecher

1820–1893: James Robinson Graves

1821–1881: Fyodor Dostoevsky

1827–1915: Ellen White

1837–1920: Abraham Kuyper

1843–1921: C. I. Scofield

1844–1913: James Orr

1846–1922: Wilhelm Herrmann

1851–1921: B. B. Warfield

1851–1930: Adolf von Harnack

1861–1865: American Civil War

1869–1870: First Vatican Council

1877–1960: Walter Bauer

1884–1972: Harry Truman

1884–1976: Rudolf Bultmann

1886–1968: Karl Barth

1895–1987: Cornelius Van Til

1909: *Scofield Reference Bible*

1910–1915: *The Fundamentals*

1914–1918: World War I

1918–2018: Billy Graham

1921–2011: John Stott

1925–2016: Charles C. Ryrie

1930–2007: D. James Kennedy

1931–2016: Thomas Oden

1937: World Council of Churches

1939–1945: World War II

1962–1965: Second Vatican Council

CHAPTER 31

Modern Scholars Were the First to Notice "Problem Passages" in the Bible

The Legendary Story

Until the modern era, scholars and theologians—not to mention laypeople—were mostly unaware of the great problem passages, internal contradictions, absurd claims, historical errors, scientific blunders, and outright absurdities of the Bible and the Christian faith. However, with the dawn of the Enlightenment in the eighteenth century and the rise of a more rational, objective, scientific approach to religion, scholars were finally able to see how riddled with problems the Bible really was. This new discovery of problems led to an awakening of reason and a rejection of old-fashioned superstition.

Introduction: Unraveling the Legend

Christianity has always had its critics—from the first-century Jewish rabbis who tried to disprove the preaching of the apostles to the sophisticated philosophers who tried to pick apart the Scriptures. These critics pointed to apparent contradictions in Scripture as well as the alleged absurdity of the doctrines of the Christian faith. Against the critics, however, Christian apologists and theologians responded with well-reasoned defenses of the faith as well as detailed explanations of the "problem passages" in the Bible. The modern era, from about 1700 onward, did see a new willingness to adapt Christianity to the claims of critics, but it saw very little new in the criticisms themselves.

Suffering from *Duja Vé*

Many Christians today think, speak, and behave as if the challenges they face in the modern era have never been faced by anybody else in the history of the world. The heresies are more destructive, the morals more depraved, the persecutions more severe, and the attacks on Christianity more acute. In some places, this may be the case. However, most of the time those who sound these alarms are just suffering from a case of what some have jokingly labeled *duja vé*. What's that? Well, you have probably heard of *déjà vu*—the strange feeling that "this has happened before." On the other hand, the tongue-in-cheek term *duja vé* is just the opposite: the nagging sense that "none of this has ever happened before."

The fact of the matter is that most challenges to the Christian faith in the modern era are not new. From atheism to pantheism, from materialism to evolution, from cults to false religions, from apostasy to persecution—the principle of Eccl 1:9–10 holds true: "What has been is what will be, and what has been done is what will be done; there is nothing new under the sun. Can one say about anything, 'Look, this is new'? It has already existed in the ages before us." Of course, many things *appear* new. Or, like a used car handed down, they may be "new to me." But most of the time Christians who think they or others have discovered an entirely new interpretation of Scripture, doctrine, or practice (whether positive or negative) are usually just victims of historical ignorance. Almost always, somebody somewhere has read Scripture that way, believed similar doctrines, or done similar things.

When it comes to the revolt against orthodox theology in the modern era, the situation is basically the same. As the story is often told, throughout church history Christians were simply unaware of the countless problems in the Bible. Only with the advent of science and serious historical studies—as well as closer, more scholarly attention to the text of Scripture—were modern scholars able to see things clearly. The result was the advent of biblical criticism and ultimately theological liberalism.

The problem is, this is simply not true. What changed in the modern era was not so much a discovery of such apparent difficulties in Scripture. Scholars throughout church history have been aware of such challenges, and critics from every era attempted to turn them against the Christian faith. What was new in the modern era was that such criticisms against the Bible and the doctrines of the faith were embraced not merely by critics of Christianity, but by a "new kind of Christian" who wanted to remain in the church and retain the name "Christian," but deny the foundational authorities and essential doctrines of the historic Christian faith.

"Critics" before the Age of Criticism

John Barton notes, "It could not be said that criticism began with the Enlightenment, since difficulties in the text have been noted since very ancient times. Origen, Augustine, and some medieval Jewish writers would qualify as critics."[1] Questions regarding problem passages in the biblical text "were asked in the ancient world and are not the product of modern skepticism."[2]

The term "critical reading" can be used in different ways, though. The early church had its share of hostile critics—people who simply didn't agree with Christianity, didn't like Christians, and therefore ridiculed Christian sources. One such critic of Christianity was a second-century Greek philosopher named Celsus (c. 120–180). Around the year 175, he wrote a work entitled *On the True Doctrine* as an attempt at refuting Christianity. Origen of Alexandria (c. 184–253), around the year 248, provided a point-by-point refutation of his criticisms. At one point he wrote:

> Celsus, indeed, did not see that it was an inconsistency for the same persons both to be deceived regarding Jesus . . . and to invent fictions about Him, knowing manifestly that these statements were false. Of a truth, therefore, they were not guilty of inventing untruths, but such were their real impressions, and they recorded them truly; or else they were guilty of falsifying the histories, and did not entertain these views, and were not deceived when they acknowledged Him to be God.[3]

Not long afterwards, the philosopher Porphyry of Tyre (c. 234–304) wrote his own series of critical essays against Christianity, consisting of fifteen books. Though this body of work is mostly lost to us today, several Christians replied to his criticisms in the generations following the publication. Robert Berchman notes, "Porphyry used historical and literary criticism" in an attempt to "demolish claims of the divine origin and prophetic value of the Bible."[4] Throughout this writing, Porphyry pointed out what he

---

[1]   John Barton, *The Nature of Biblical Criticism* (Louisville: WJK, 2007), 3
[2]   Barton, 10.
[3]   Origen, *Against Celsus* 2.26 (ANF 4:443).
[4]   See Robert M. Berchman, *Porphyry Against the Christians*, Studies in Platonism, Neoplatonism, and the Platonic Tradition (Leiden, NL: Brill, 2005), 9.

thought were unresolvable contradictions in Christian Scripture, irrational and absurd beliefs in Christian doctrine, and unacceptable explanations of these "problem passages" by apologists of Christianity such as Origen.

Many church fathers wrote treatises in response to these and other attacks on the integrity and reliability of the Christian Scriptures and the reasonableness of the Christian faith. Augustine of Hippo (354–430), for instance, interacted with the views of critics who ridiculed such things as the extremely long lives of the patriarchs in the Old Testament and apparent discrepancies in chronology.[5] Others wrote harmonies of the Gospels, explained passages of Scripture that seemed contradictory or absurd, and provided alternate allegorical or spiritual interpretations of passages that, if taken too literally, resulted in embarrassing theological or philosophical problems.

Not only were critics of Christianity aware of "problem passages" in the Bible, but so were believers, who saw these not as obstacles to faith but as opportunities to dig deeper and trust God to reveal the solutions. The words of Irenaeus of Lyons (c. 120–200) are pertinent here: "If, however, we cannot discover explanations of all those things in Scripture which are made the subject of investigation, yet let us not on that account seek after any other God besides Him who really exists. . . . We should leave things of that nature to God who created us, being most properly assured that the Scriptures are indeed perfect, since they were spoken by the Word of God and His Spirit."[6] And around the year 300, Lactantius (250–325) wrote against another critic of Scripture, Hierocles, "In these writings he endeavored so to prove the falsehood of sacred Scripture, as though it was altogether contradictory to itself; for he expounded some chapters which seemed to be at variance with themselves . . . What rashness was it, therefore, to dare to destroy that which no one explained to him!"[7]

So, modern scholars were not the first to question the date, authorship, integrity, historicity, and truthfulness of Scripture or the reasonability of Christian doctrine. These kinds of challenges had been going on for well over 1,000 years before the dawning of the "Enlightenment." John Barton notes:

> It is not the rationalism of the Enlightenment, or the materialism of the nineteenth century, or the supposed skepticism of modern German theology, that have discovered the inconsistencies and histori-

---

[5]   Augustine, *City of God* 15.9–14 (NPNF 1.2:291–95).
[6]   Irenaeus, *Against Heresies* 2.28.2 (ANF 1:399).
[7]   Lactantius, *Divine Institutes* 5.2 (ANF 7:138).

cal difficulties in the biblical text. . . . Careful readers have always noticed such things. It is not a particularly modern achievement to have spotted discrepancies, puzzles, and apparently tall stories in the Bible.[8]

The New "Modern Christian"

So, if modern critical scholars of the eighteenth and nineteenth centuries weren't the first to discover, as it were, the "new world" of Bible problems, what was so unique about the modern age? Simply put, in the ancient, medieval, and Reformation periods, critics of the Bible and of classic Christian orthodoxy were either unbelievers attacking from the outside or apostates who defected from the faith. Until the modern era, all Christians accepted the inspiration and authority of Scripture and the truthfulness of Christianity (see chapter 33). Christian scholars saw it as their task to explain apparent contradictions or "problem passages" in Scripture, to harmonize the truths of Scripture with truths from reason and experience, and to defend the integrity of the classic Christian faith. It seems everybody knew that if you rejected the authority and truthfulness of Scripture, you were rejecting Christianity itself.

Not so in the modern era. From about 1700 on, a new kind of "modern Christian" emerged—one who accepted the presuppositions of critical scholarship, rejected the integrity and truthfulness of the Bible, and deviated completely from classic Christian doctrines, *while still claiming to be a genuine Christian.* Such individuals retained their teaching positions in seminaries and their preaching posts in pulpits. Unlike ancient critics of Christianity, these "modern Christians" didn't seem to realize that when you completely reject the foundations of Christian orthodoxy, you cease to be a Christian.[9]

Bingham notes, "Nineteenth-century Protestant liberals opted for severe modification of the traditional faith. They viewed themselves as the saviors of a defunct, out-of-date Christianity. They would make Christianity palatable to a mindset that could no longer accept traditional orthodoxy."[10] So instead of the traditional approach to explaining "problem passages" in the Bible or the classic method of reconciling apparent contradictions between faith and

---

[8]   Barton, *The Nature of Biblical Criticism*, 11.
[9]   Jaroslav Pelikan, *The Christian Tradition: A History of the Development of Doctrine*, vol. 5, *Christian Doctrine and Modern Culture (since 1700)* (Chicago: University of Chicago Press, 1989), viii.
[10]   D. Jeffrey Bingham, *Pocket History of the Church* (Downers Grove, IL: InterVarsity Press, 2002), 149.

reason, "modern Christians" saw it as their task to reinterpret Christianity itself, capitulating to the prevailing modern philosophy and science. Giving voice to this modern critical approach to Christianity, Henry Ward Beecher (1813–1887) proclaimed, "If ministers do not make their theological systems conform to the facts as they are, if they do not recognize what men are studying, the time will not be far distant when the pulpit will be like a voice crying in the wilderness."[11]

To sum up: modern scholars were not the first to recognize "problem passages" in the Bible or to acknowledge apparent contradictions between Christian truth claims and the "facts" of philosophy, science, reason, or experience. However, unlike in the premodern era, scholars who still claimed to be Christians no longer upheld the priority of God's revelation and the essential truths of the Christian faith. Instead, they attempted to "save" Christianity by fully accepting the criticisms of the enemies of Christianity and revising Christian theology accordingly.

Application

The approach of Christians to criticisms of the Bible and of Christian doctrine and practice has remained the same for almost 2,000 years. Christians have never buried their heads in the sand, ignoring the claims of critics. Instead, believers with extensive training in biblical studies, theology, history, and philosophy have always sought to engage these critics and respond to their claims reasonably and thoroughly. Yet they did so from the standpoint of faith, not of neutrality. Just as the critics attack Christianity from a perspective of unbelief and skepticism, Christians respond to the critics from a vantage point of belief and confidence in the truthfulness of Scripture and the fundamental doctrines of the faith.

The Bible hasn't changed in 2,000 years, nor have the church's essential doctrines. Thus, the attacks on Scripture and theology have remained rather constant as well. Christians today should arm themselves with a thorough understanding of Bible and theology while at the same time familiarizing themselves not only with criticisms of the faith but also classic responses by qualified contenders for the faith "that was delivered to the saints once for all" (Jude 3).

---

[11] Henry Ward Beecher, *Yale Lectures on Preaching* (New York: Fords, Howard, and Hulbert, 1881), 88.

Resources

Arndt, William, Robert G. Hoerber, and Walter R. Roehrs. *Bible Difficulties and Seeming Contradictions*. St. Louis: Concordia, 1987.

Barton, John. *The Nature of Biblical Criticism*. Louisville: WJK, 2007.

Geisler, Norman L., and Thomas A. Howe. *When Critics Ask: A Popular Handbook on Bible Difficulties*. Wheaton, IL: Victor, 1992. Republished as *The Big Book of Bible Difficulties*. Grand Rapids: Baker, 2008.

CHAPTER 32

The United States Was Originally
a Christian Nation

The Legendary Story

The Founding Fathers of the United States were strong Bible-believing Christians who believed they were establishing "one nation under God." These Christian men sought to found a government on distinctly Christian principles, creating a nation that was primarily shaped by the Christian religion. The founders received this ideal of a Christian nation from the earliest British settlers in North America—Pilgrims and Puritans. Throughout American history the nation's leaders have made explicit statements reflecting dependence on God, the Scriptures, and Christianity in general. Such a heritage requires defense and preservation. However, over the past half century or more, the United States government has become increasingly secular and godless. The decline of this nation from its distinctly Christian founding principles is the single greatest tragedy in American history.

Introduction: Unraveling the Legend

The myth of America as a Christian nation has persisted throughout much of American history. There is no doubt that Americans, for the better part of 250 years, have made claims along these lines. Such comments have been made regularly by American judges, legislators, and presidents. In a private letter, John Marshall (1755–1835), the fourth chief justice of the United States Supreme Court, said that in America, "Christianity and religion are identified. It would be strange, indeed, if with such a people our institutions did not presuppose Christianity and did not often refer to it and exhibit relations with it."[1] The United States Senate issued a proclamation that said that the gospel of Jesus Christ is "the vital and conservative element in our system [of government],"[2] while President Harry Truman (1884–1972) called the United States "a Christian nation."[3] A look at history also finds clergy making the same types of statements. For example, minister and former president of Union Theological Seminary William Adams (1807–1880) once wrote, "We as individuals, and as a nation, are identified with that kingdom of God among men, which is righteousness, and peace, and joy in the Holy Ghost."[4] However, the fact that numerous people have stated it does not make it so. The term "Christian" carries with it particular beliefs and ethics, neither of which were enshrined into the founding American documents. A look at the beliefs of the most significant and well-known founders, as well as their specific vision for the country, reveals another, more pertinent influence than Christianity—the Enlightenment.

The Faith of the Founders

Not many of the Founding Fathers were strong or even orthodox Christians. With a few notable exceptions, they were primarily deists, Unitarians, or theistic rationalists who believed more in a "God of nature" and natural religion than the triune God revealed in the Bible.[5] This section will focus on some of the most significant and well-known of those early founders: Benjamin Franklin (1706–1790), John Adams (1735–1826), and Thomas Jefferson (1743–1826).[6]

Though raised by Puritans, Benjamin Franklin did not hold to traditional

---

[1]   John Marshall, *The Papers of John Marshall*, ed. Charles Hobson (Chapel Hill: University of North Carolina Press, 2006), 12:278.

[2]   *Journal of the Senate of the United States of America, Being the Third Session of the Thirty-Seventh Congress* (Washington, DC: Government Printing Office, 1863), 379.

[3]   Harry S. Truman, "Exchange of Messages with Pope Pius XII," American Presidency Project, August 28, 1947.

[4]   William Adams, "The War for Independence and the War for Secession," *American Presbyterian and Theological Review* 13 (1866), 92.

[5]   The term "theistic rationalist" comes from Gregg L. Frazier, *The Religious Beliefs of America's Founders* (Lawrence, KS: University Press of Kansas, 2012).

[6]   While it would be ideal to also deal with George Washington, he was famously opaque about his personal religious beliefs, even refusing to take communion in any church once the Revolution began. Washington seems to have kept his religious views private to encourage religious freedom in the new country.

Christian beliefs during his adult life. In his autobiography, he described once having listened to some lectures against deism, then writing that "the arguments of the Deists, which were quoted to be refuted, appeared to me much stronger than the refutations; in short, I soon became a thorough Deist."[7]

In the year of his death, Franklin wrote a letter to Ezra Stiles (1727–1795), a minister and then president of Yale College. In this letter, Franklin most famously expressed his religious views. After professing beliefs in God as Creator, that God governs the world via his providence, and that people will be treated justly in the next world based on their conduct in this life, Franklin opined on Jesus himself:

> As to Jesus of Nazareth, my opinion of whom you particularly desire, I think his system of morals and his religion, as he left them to us, the best the world ever saw or is like to see; but I apprehend it has received various corrupting changes, and I have, with most of the present dissenters in England, some doubts as to his divinity; though it is a question I do not dogmatize upon, having never studied it, and think it needless to busy myself with it now, when I expect soon an opportunity of knowing the truth with less trouble.[8]

Franklin's deism, as well as his appreciation for Jesus as an ethical teacher, did not dissuade him from demurring on the question of Christ's deity. These qualities anticipate much of nineteenth-century Protestant liberal theology, which elevated ethics while ignoring or discarding specific dogmatic beliefs about the person and work of Jesus.

John Adams, an early American lawyer who helped to write the Declaration of Independence and served as the new nation's second president, garnered a reputation for being fiercely independent. This quality extended into many areas of his life, including on the subject of religion, as people identified Adams throughout his years in numerous ways: a Puritan, a deist, a Christian, and a humanist.[9]

Adams had a more substantial belief about God's miraculous interaction

---

[7] Benjamin Franklin, *The Works of Benjamin Franklin, Including the Private as Well as the Official and Scientific Correspondence, Together with the Unmutilated and Correct Version of the Autobiography*, comp. and ed. John Bigelow (New York: G. P. Putnam's Sons, 1904). The Federal Edition in 12 volumes, vol. 1, *Autobiography, Letters and Misc. Writings 1725–1734*, accessed April 11, 2019, https://oll.libertyfund.org/titles/2452#Franklin_1438-01_38.

[8] Franklin, *The Works of Benjamin Franklin*. The Federal Edition, vol. 12, *Letters and Misc. Writings 1788–1790, Supplement, Indexes*, accessed April 11, 2019. https://oll.libertyfund.org/titles/2661#Franklin_1438-12_65.

[9] Norman Cousins, *In God We Trust* (New York: Harper and Brothers, 1958), 75.

with the world than many of his contemporaries, writing, "The great and Almighty author of nature, who at first established those rules which regulate the world, can as easily suspend those laws whenever his providence sees sufficient reason for such suspension. This can be no objection, then, to the miracles of Jesus Christ."[10] However, Adams's independence also leaves him outside any kind of traditional Christian belief. He identified himself in a letter to his son as a lifelong Unitarian, before making this striking and unorthodox claim about Jesus: "An incarnate God!!! An eternal, Self-existent, omnipotent omnipresent omniscient Author of this Stupendous Universe, Suffering on a Cross!!! My Soul Starts with horror, at the Idea, and it has Stupified the Christian World. It has been the Source of almost all the Corruptions of Christianity."[11]

Finally, Thomas Jefferson positioned himself outside any hint of orthodox Christianity, despite his positively invoking terms such as "Christian" and "Jesus." For instance, after denouncing trinitarian belief (and its ancient defender Athanasius), Jefferson wrote in his letter to Dr. Benjamin Waterhouse that

> had the doctrines of Jesus been preached always as pure as they came from his lips, the whole civilized world would now have been Christian. I rejoice that in this blessed country of free inquiry and belief, which has surrendered its creed and conscience to neither kings nor priests, the genuine doctrine of one only God is reviving, and I trust that there is not a young man now living in the United States who will not die an Unitarian.[12]

Due to his anti-trinitarianism, Jefferson most closely aligned with Unitarianism during his life. Even more striking, perhaps, is a perusal of Jefferson's Bible, a harmony of the four Gospels. The final three verses read as follows: "Now in the place where he was crucified there was a garden; and in the garden a new sepulchre, wherein was never man yet laid. There laid they Jesus, And rolled a great stone to the door of the sepulchre, and departed."[13] Jefferson

---

[10]   John Adams, *The Works of John Adams, Second President of the United States: with a Life of the Author, Notes and Illustrations, by his Grandson Charles Francis Adams* (Boston: Little, Brown, 1856), vol. 2, accessed April 11, 2019. https://oll.libertyfund.org/titles/2100#Adams_1431-02_37.

[11]   "From John Adams to John Quincy Adams, 28 March 1816," Founders Online, National Archives, https://founders.archives.gov/documents/Adams/99-03-02-3058, accessed January 18, 2019.

[12]   Thomas Jefferson, *The Works of Thomas Jefferson*, Federal ed. (New York: G. P. Putnam's Sons, 1904–5), vol. 12, https://oll.libertyfund.org/titles/808#Jefferson_0054-12_262.

[13]   Thomas Jefferson, *The Jefferson Bible: The Life and Morals of Jesus Christ* (Radford, VA: A & D, 2009), 97.

excluded the central event in Christianity, the resurrection, from his Bible, as a result of his rejection of the miraculous.

The Vision of the Founders

The most significant founders believed the United States should be an enlightened moral and religious nation that tolerated a diversity of beliefs and practices. Their ideal was radically different from that of Pilgrims and Puritans of the early colonial period, who had sought to establish a new Jerusalem or a "city on a hill," and therefore come much closer to the union of church and state that they had run from in England (see chapter 30).

In contrast to those early settlers, the Declaration of Independence (written by Thomas Jefferson) refers to "the Laws of Nature and of Nature's God" as the basis upon which the American colonies would attain separate and equal status from England. This idea of "Nature's God" sounds pious enough on its own. However, the term is another feature of key founders' rationalistic understanding of theism.

John Adams used the phrase in a letter that gives some perspective to its use in the Declaration. In a letter to Thomas Jefferson, Adams wrote, "The human understanding is a revelation from its Maker, which can never be disputed or doubted. . . . We can never be so certain of any prophecy, or the fulfillment of any prophecy, or of any miracle, or the design of any miracle, as we are from the revelation of nature, that is Nature's God, that two and two are equal to four."[14] Here Adams contrasted the supernatural experiences of prophecy and miracles with the phrase "Nature's God"—any "revelation" that comes from nature or the human understanding. Adams, like many of the other founders, believed he could understand this revelation purely based on human reason, without need of any supernatural revelation such as Scripture.

This type of belief grounds the very rights that come from the Creator—life, liberty, and the pursuit of happiness. Their observation of the world around them, and especially the damaging ways church and state had functioned together in centuries past, led them to enshrine religious toleration alongside these fundamental rights.

One of the key background figures for the founders was seventeenth-century British philosopher John Locke (1632–1704), who argued in his *A*

---

[14] Adams, *The Works of John Adams*, vol. 10, https://oll.libertyfund.org/titles/2127#Adams_1431 -10_261.

Letter Concerning Toleration that above all other things, people should "distinguish exactly the Business of Civil Government from that of Religion."[15] This leaves a commonwealth "constituted only for the procuring, preserving, and advancing of their own Civil Interests. Civil Interests I call Life, Liberty, Health, and Indolency of Body; and the Possession of outward things, such as Money, Lands, Houses, Furniture, and the like."[16] Locke's vision, rather than the Bible's, stood as the primary ground upon which the United States was founded.

Application

To be sure, American government and culture were never as antagonistic toward conservative Christian morality and faith as they are today. Most of the Founding Fathers would lament the current condition of the United States; they wanted a religious and moral people. But "religious" is not the same as Christian. Despite this lamentable shift away from religion today, it is just as problematic to reenvision the early years of the United States as a kind of Christian utopia.

One negative result of linking the term "Christian" with America is the association of America's checkered history with Christianity. The most obvious example of this problem involves the institution of slavery. How can Americans call this a Christian nation when we participated in slavery and even made space for it in the United States Constitution? The treatment of Native Americans should be considered as well. Whatever the particular issue, every time someone designates the US as a "Christian nation," it harms the cause of Christ, especially among those wronged by our nation.

Resources

Dreisbach, Daniel L., Mark D. Hall, and Jeffry H. Morrison. *The Founders on God and Government*. Lanham, MD: Rowman & Littlefield, 2004.

Fea, John. *Was America Founded as a Christian Nation?* Rev. ed. Louisville: WJK, 2016.

Gaustad, Edwin S. *The Faith of the Founders: Religion and the New Nation 1776–1826*. Waco, TX: Baylor University Press, 2004.

Lambert, Frank. *The Founding Fathers and the Place of Religion in America*. Princeton, NJ: Princeton University Press, 2003.

---

[15] John Locke, *A Letter Concerning Toleration and Other Writings*, ed. Mark Goldie (Indianapolis: Liberty Fund, 2010), 12.

[16] Locke, 12.

CHAPTER 33

Fundamentalists Were the First Christians to Believe in the Inerrancy of Scripture

The Legendary Story

The doctrine of the complete inerrancy of Scripture is a recent development birthed in the fundamentalist reaction against modernist liberal extremes in the nineteenth century. Before that, most church fathers and even Reformers held a more dynamic view of Scripture's truthfulness that allowed for errors by the human authors.

Introduction: Unraveling the Legend

Though many had a dynamic understanding of the interpretation of Scripture that allowed for allegorical and symbolic meanings intended by the divine Author, no church father, medieval theologian, or mainline Reformer ever attempted to correct the assertions of Scripture in any matter. They believed in what is today called the "complete inerrancy of Scripture" and its absolute doctrinal and practical authority.

The Error of Inerrancy?

One critic of modern fundamentalism notes, "In the effort to shore up the basic truths of Christian faith, a relatively novel doctrine of Scripture evolved, the doctrine of inerrancy."[1] Another suggests, "Fundamentalists have perceived the presence of . . . disharmonies [in Scripture], but have unfortunately sought to protect themselves and their churches from them by inventing a distortion: the concept of the inerrancy or infallibility of Scripture."[2] Another critique of the doctrine of inerrancy published in 1968 states that the doctrine "did not exist in either Europe or America before its formulation in the last half of the nineteenth century."[3] And in an extreme detraction, the doctrine of inerrancy has been called "the worst heresy that has ever afflicted the Church" and "an evil from which the Church must repent."[4]

Is inerrancy a novelty, a distortion, or a heresy—unheard-of in the history of the church until the nineteenth century? Was it contrived by wild-eyed fanatics to exorcise the specter of liberalism? Or concocted by stone-faced scholastics to protect their narrow orthodoxy from the disastrous effects of modernism? This notion that inerrancy is an embarrassing tattoo on the body of Christ rather than a natural feature of the Christian faith lingers in many circles. However, it's a myth. Throughout history, Scripture has been seen as the "norming norm" of theology, inspired by the Holy Spirit and thus true in all it affirms, never erring or leading astray in its assertions.

What Is Inerrancy?

How a person defines "inerrancy" will often determine their conclusion about whether (and when) anybody actually believed or taught it before the modern era. If we define inerrancy very narrowly as the belief that "because the Bible is God's Word it must be accurate in matters of science and history as well as in doctrine,"[5] we necessarily limit the doctrine to an era in which "science" and "history" are unique fields of inquiry with their own

---

[1] James Davison Hunter, "Fundamentalism in Its Global Contours," in Cohen, *The Fundamentalist Phenomenon: A View from Within; A Response from Without*, ed. Norman J. Cohen (Grand Rapids: Eerdmans, 1990), 68.

[2] Preston N. Williams, "Religion Challenge of Fundamentalism," in *The Fundamentalist Phenomenon*, 257.

[3] Ernest Sandeen, *The Origins of Fundamentalism: Toward a Historical Interpretation* (Philadelphia: Fortress, 1968), 14. Also see the classic critique of inerrancy and biblical authority in Jack B. Rogers and Donald K. McKim, *The Authority and Interpretation of the Bible: An Historical Approach* (Eugene, OR: Wipf and Stock, 1999).

[4] Rodger L. Cragun, *The Ultimate Heresy: . . . the Doctrine of Biblical Inerrancy* (Eugene, OR: Wipf and Stock, 2018), xviii.

[5] George M. Marsden, *Understanding Fundamentalism and Evangelicalism* (Grand Rapids: Eerdmans, 1991), 160.

methodologies. Thus, inerrancy as such would only make sense in a modern (and mostly Western) historical context—since, say, the seventeenth or eighteenth century.

If, however, we define inerrancy more generally as the "full truthfulness of inspired Scripture, emphasizing its inability to speak falsely in anything it affirms to be true,"[6] then it positions the discussion more positively: Scripture is true in what it affirms—and in the ways it affirms them. This view acknowledges that Scripture is not primarily a history book (though it contains historical accounts), nor is it primarily a science book (though its affirmations touch on matters of common interest to scientists). We understand "inerrancy" primarily in this latter sense: Scripture is completely true in all it affirms; it makes no errors in the propositions it presents as fact.

Now, it is a fact that the terms "inerrancy" and "inerrant" do not appear in the Bible. Nor do they appear in most of church history, whether in ecumenical creeds, declarations of church councils, or the writings of theologians throughout the patristic, medieval, and Protestant periods. Of course, the terms "inerrant" and "inerrancy" are English words and thus couldn't possibly be found on the lips of anybody until the modern era anyway. Yet the absence of these specific theological terms doesn't mean the concept of the complete truthfulness and trustworthiness of Scripture was a modern invention. If we let church fathers, medieval theologians, and Protestant Reformers express the truthfulness of Scripture in their own words, we will see that what they articulated fits with the normal definition of inerrancy: "an attribute of Scripture whereby everything that it affirms is true."[7]

Inerrancy Then and Now

The following quotations from early church fathers, medieval theologians, Protestant Reformers, and early modern pastors and teachers demonstrate that the doctrine of the complete truthfulness and trustworthiness of Scripture—indeed, its "inerrancy"—was consistently held by Christians until the modern era. None, of course, used the English word "inerrant." They were writing mostly in Greek and Latin and did not face nineteenth-century historical-critical attacks on the authority of Scripture. Yet it will be clear that

---

    [6]   Nathan D. Holsteen and Michael J. Svigel, eds., *Exploring Christian Theology*, vol. 1, *Revelation, Scripture, and the Triune God* (Bloomington, MN: Bethany House, 2014), 261.

    [7]   Gregg R. Allison, *The Baker Compact Dictionary of Theological Terms* (Grand Rapids: Baker, 2016), 114.

Christians from every tradition, East and West, regarded Holy Scripture as true in everything it affirms.

From the patristic period, we see an unambiguous embrace of the belief that Scripture is true in all it affirms, impervious to error or inaccuracy. Clement of Rome (c. 95): "You have searched the holy scriptures, which are true, which were given by the Holy Spirit; you know that nothing unrighteous or counterfeit is written in them."[8] Irenaeus of Lyons (c. 180): "The Scriptures are indeed perfect, since they were spoken by the Word of God and His Spirit."[9] Clement of Alexandria (c. 215): "He who believeth then the divine Scriptures with sure judgment, receives in the voice of God, who bestowed the Scriptures, a demonstration that cannot be impugned."[10] Tertullian of Carthage (c. 220): "The statements, however, of holy Scripture will never be discordant with truth."[11] Hippolytus of Rome (c. 235): "The Scripture deals falsely with us in nothing."[12] Gregory of Nazianzus (c. 380): "We, however, who extend the accuracy of the Spirit to the merest stroke and tittle, will never admit the impious assertion that even the smallest matters were dealt with haphazard by those who have recorded them."[13] Augustine of Hippo (c. 420): "I have learned to yield this respect and honour only to the canonical books of Scripture: of these alone do I most firmly believe that the authors were completely free from error. And if in these writings I am perplexed by anything which appears to me opposed to truth, I do not hesitate to suppose that either the MS [manuscript] is faulty, or the translator has not caught the meaning of what was said, or I myself have failed to understand it."[14]

Following the overwhelming patristic consensus on the complete truthfulness and trustworthiness of Scripture in all it affirms, the medieval theologians, Protestant Reformers, and modern evangelicals showed no signs of doubt about the inerrancy of Scripture. Anselm of Canterbury (c. 1077): "I am sure that, if I say anything which plainly opposes the Holy Scriptures, it is false; and if I am aware of it, I will no longer hold it."[15] Bernard of Clairvaux (c. 1150): "They are the words of the Lord, and it is not permitted to doubt or hesi-

---

8   *1 Clement* 45.2–3, in Michael W. Holmes, ed., *The Apostolic Fathers: Greek Texts and English Translations of Their Writings*, 3rd ed. (Grand Rapids: Baker, 2007), 105.
9   Irenaeus, *Against Heresies* 2.28.2 (ANF 1:399).
10   Clement of Alexandria, *Stromata* 2.2 (ANF 2:349).
11   Tertullian, *Treatise on the Soul* 22 (ANF 3:202).
12   Hippolytus, *Fragments on Susannah* 52 (ANF 5:193).
13   Gregory of Nazianzus, *Orations* 2.105 (NPNF 2.7:427).
14   Augustine, *Letter (to Jerome)* 82.3 (NPNF 1.1:350).
15   Anselm, *Cur Deus Homo* 1.18, in Deane, trans., *St. Anselm*, 220 (see chap. 12, n. 17).

tate."[16] John Calvin (1560): "We treat Scripture with the same reverence we do God, because it is from God alone, and unmixed with anything human."[17] Jacob Arminius (c. 1605): "If some things in those sacred books seem to be contradictions, they are easily reconciled by means of a right interpretation."[18] John Bunyan (1688): "Suffer thyself, by the authority of the word, to be persuaded that the scripture indeed is the word of God; the scriptures of truth, the words of the holy one; and that they therefore must be every one true, pure, and for ever settled in heaven."[19] John Wesley (1776): "If there be any mistakes in the Bible, there may as well be a thousand. If there be one falsehood in that book, it did not come from the God of truth."[20] Abraham Kuyper (1900): "Inspiration is the name of that all-comprehensive operation of the Holy Spirit whereby He has bestowed on the Church a complete and infallible Scripture."[21] Charles Ryrie (1999): "God superintended the human authors of the Bible so that they composed and recorded without error His message to mankind in the words of their original writings."[22]

Besides this sampling of explicit statements concerning the truthfulness and infallibility of Scripture spanning the history of the church, we would do well to observe how the countless pastors, teachers, theologians, and scholars throughout history actually used Scripture. Though they may at times have challenged translations and interpretations of Scripture, they never pitted Scripture against Scripture nor attempted to correct the truth claims of Scripture by appealing to some other authority. Rather, throughout history Christians regarded Scripture as the *norma normans non normata*—"the norming norm which cannot be normed." Fundamentalists in the nineteenth century may have coined a new term—*inerrancy*—in the midst of their battle against liberal Christians who, contrary to centuries of consistent teaching, began to assert that Scripture contains errors. But fundamentalists—and their

---

[16] Bernard of Clairvaux, *Sermon 84 on the Song of Songs* 7 in *Late Medieval Mysticism*, ed. Ray C. Petry, The Library of Christian Classics (Philadelphia: WJK, 1957), 78.

[17] John Calvin, "Commentary on Second Timothy 3:16–17," in *Calvin: Commentaries*, ed. and trans. Joseph Haroutunian and Louise Pettibone Smith, The Library of Christian Classics (Philadelphia: WJK, 1958), 85.

[18] James Arminius, "Oration III: The Certainty of Sacred Theology," in *The Works of James Arminius*, trans. James Nichols (London: Longman, Hurst, et al., 1825), 1:322.

[19] John Bunyan, "Of the Trinity and a Christian," *The Entire Works of John Bunyan*, ed. Henry Stebbing (London: James S. Virtue, 1860) 2:534.

[20] John Wesley, *Journal*, August 24, 1776, in John Wesley, *The Works of the Rev. John Wesley*, vol. 4, 3rd ed. (London: John Mason, 1829), 82.

[21] Abraham Kuyper, *The Work of the Holy Spirit*, trans. Henri de Vries (New York: Funk & Wagnalls, 1900), 76.

[22] Charles C. Ryrie, *Basic Theology* (Chicago: Moody, 1999), 81.

modern heirs, conservative evangelicals—did not invent the doctrine of the complete truthfulness and trustworthiness of Scripture.

Application

Conservative Christians today do not believe in the complete inerrancy of Scripture because they have proved that every one of its thousands of truth-claims measure up to some set of external standards. Rather, we believe the Bible to be the inspired, inerrant Word of God as a basic article of the Christian faith. In many early baptismal confessions and in the universal church's ecumenical creed, Christians have confessed that the Holy Spirit "spoke through the prophets," that is, that the words of prophetic Scriptures are the very words of God the Holy Spirit. As such, our pledge as baptized disciples of Christ is to take the torch of confidence in the inspiration and inerrancy of Scripture from the previous generation, keep it lit, and pass it on faithfully to the next—just as those before us did for nearly 2,000 years.

Resources

Carson, D. A., and John D. Woodbridge, eds. *Scripture and Truth*. Grand Rapids: Baker, 1992.

Geisler, Norman L., ed. *Inerrancy*. Grand Rapids: Zondervan, 1980.

Moorhead, Jonathan. "Inerrancy and Church History: Is Inerrancy a Modern Invention?" *Masters Seminary Journal* 27, no. 1 (spring 2016): 75–90.

Woodbridge, John D. *Biblical Authority: A Critique of the Rogers/McKim Proposal*. Grand Rapids: Zondervan, 1982.

CHAPTER 34

None of the American Founding Fathers Were Orthodox Christians

The Legendary Story

The Founding Fathers of the United States, influenced as they were by the philosophy of John Locke and the "religion" of the Enlightenment, were all outside the boundaries of true Christianity. These founders, while often invoking "God" and making references to religion and morality, actually represented rationalistic philosophy rather than orthodox Christianity. Indeed, the founders' main religious concern was not their own practice and beliefs, but rather others' right to worship freely. This makes a great deal of sense, given the founders' own faith that cannot be classified neatly among any kind of traditional Christian belief or practice.

Introduction: Unraveling the Legend

The narrative surrounding the Founding Fathers of the United States has become polarized in the popular imagination. On one side stand those who believe that nearly all the founders were orthodox Christians and that they established the nation in line with those beliefs.[1] The other side of the argument usually comes from those with an interest in seeing the United States distanced from religion. In this view, none of the founders were orthodox Christians. If the founders can be shown to lack orthodox Christian bona

---

[1] See chapter 32 for the debunking of that myth.

fides, America can press on with a secular vision of her future. As is often the case with historical study, the reality of the American Founding Fathers lies somewhere in between these extremes. This chapter will examine the orthodox beliefs of several founders. While most of these orthodox Christians were peripheral figures when it came to writing America's founding documents, they nonetheless had roles to play in the founding of the country.

No Christian Founders

In recent decades, the people of the United States have more openly embraced the nonreligious among them. Atheism and agnosticism are less of a cultural taboo than ever before. One result of greater visibility for nonreligious people is a preponderance of arguments that the Founding Fathers of the United States were not Christian whatsoever. For example, atheist Stephen Morris, in an opinion piece for the *Los Angeles Times*, argued that the "Founding Fathers as Christian" narrative is "not true," and that "the early presidents and patriots were generally deists or Unitarians, believing in some form of impersonal Providence but rejecting the divinity of Jesus and the relevance of the Bible."[2]

Orthodox Founders

One need not look hard to find orthodox Christians among the founders of the United States, even though many such believers took on secondary roles in comparison with those who penned our founding documents and filled key leadership positions in the earliest years of the nation.

Samuel Adams (1722–1803), second cousin to John Adams (1735–1826), had something of an extreme character, a quality that served him well as a leader of the revolutionary movement in New England. Adams led much of the organizing and encouraging of insurrection in the colonies. This clarity of purpose extended to his views on religion. No fan of Roman Catholics or Quakers, Adams instead clung closely to a conservative Christian orthodoxy that resembled that of his Puritan forefathers. In a letter to his daughter Hannah, Adams compliments her faith—which he believes was her own, rather than a mere affirmation of her parents' faith. He concludes by encouraging her to seek "the favor of Him who made and supports you—who will supply you with whatever his infinite wisdom sees best for you in this world, and above all, who has

---

[2] Stephen Morris, "America's Unchristian Beginnings," *Los Angeles Times*, August 3, 1995.

given us his Son to purchase for us the reward of eternal life."[3] A clear reference to the saving work of Jesus suggests he held to the core elements of Christian doctrine. Later in his life, while serving as governor of Massachusetts, he issued a Thanksgiving proclamation in which he hoped "that the peaceful and glorious reign of our Divine Redeemer may be known and enjoyed throughout the whole family of mankind."[4] Adams again referred to God's salvific work and expressed a desire that all people would know him as redeemer.

One of the most striking orthodox Christians among the founders was a delegate and president of the Continental Congress, Elias Boudinot (1740–1821). A congressman from New Jersey in the first three United States Congresses, Boudinot was also the first president of the American Bible Society. He wrote books on the First Great Awakening and Christ's return, as well as a book called *The Age of Revelation*, which was his response to *The Age of Reason* by Thomas Paine (1737–1809).

The authority of human reason over divine revelation constituted a central claim of the Enlightenment. Boudinot saw that clearly at the turn of the nineteenth century. Writing of the rationalist Paine and his followers, Boudinot argued that "these objectors find it difficult to submit to the faith of the gospel, because many things are above their reason." He noted the irony that rationalists exercised faith in everyday life, believing nothing sufficient to cast doubt upon "their unfeigned faith in their fellow men: but in revealed religion, nothing is to be believed, even on the veracity of God himself if they cannot fully comprehend and understand, every principle and mode of truth, proffered as an object of their faith."[5] Boudinot made clear that he meant to defend "the leading and essential facts of the Gospel," and to show Paine's "extreme ignorance of the divine Scriptures," which are "the power of God unto salvation."[6]

A final figure from the founding of America, John Jay (1745–1829), held conservative views both politically and theologically. At age twenty-nine, Jay served as the youngest delegate to the Continental Congress, where the founders wrote the United States Constitution. A lawyer, he also sat as the nation's first chief justice of the Supreme Court, though only for six years, since President Washington called on him to serve in an ambassadorial role

---

[3]　　Samuel Adams, *The Writings of Samuel Adams*, vol. 4, *1778–1802*, ed. Harry Alonzo Cushing (New York: G. P. Putnam's Sons, 1908), 200.

[4]　　Adams, 385.

[5]　　Elias Boudinot, *The Age of Revelation, or The Age of Reason Shewn to Be an Age of Infidelity* (Philadelphia: Asbury Dickins, 1801), vi–vii.

[6]　　Boudinot, xiii–xiv.

in Europe. Jay carried a reputation for sober thinking and cared deeply about the cause of religious freedom. During his time as governor of New York, his Christian faith informed his approach to politics, as "he avoided partisanship" and "remained as free from control as practicable from his Federalist party. When political adversaries had performed well, he tended to keep them in office. As governor he improved New York's prison system, outlawed the flogging of prisoners, reduced the number of executions, and secured the passage of a bill that gradually outlawed slavery in New York."[7]

On the subject of his personal beliefs, Jay affirmed the Calvinism of his mother's native Dutch Reformed Church, even as his family attended the Church of England, common in southern New York at the time. Later in life, Jay became vice president, and then president of the American Bible Society (ABS), which existed to give out free Bibles to any who would take them. In one of his annual addresses to the ABS, Jay said the Bible teaches "that our gracious Creator has provided for us a Redeemer, in whom all the nations of the earth should be blessed—that this Redeemer has made atonement 'for the sins of the whole world,' and thereby reconciling Divine justice with Divine mercy, has opened a way for our redemption and salvation." Such salvation, Jay said, comes "of the free gift and grace of God, not of our deserving, nor in our power to deserve."[8]

Application

Orthodox Christians were clearly among the founders of the United States. However, these figures were not primarily responsible for writing the nation's founding documents. Orthodox Christian founders help believers today to see the difference between a Christianity committed to Christ in both doctrine and practice and the "Christianity" often claimed by key founders (Adams, Jefferson, etc.) who sought to affirm a Christian ethic apart from Christian doctrine.

Christians should make careful study of such brothers and sisters from the past to get a better sense of how to interact politically today. These Christian founders sought to bolster freedom (and especially the free exercise of religion) rather than using their power to coerce Christian faith. Samuel Adams saw the

---

[7]   David L. Holmes, *The Faiths of the Founding Fathers* (Oxford: Oxford University Press, 2006), 157.

[8]   John Jay, *The Correspondence and Public Papers of John Jay*, ed. Henry P. Johnston, vol. 4, *1794–1826* (New York: G. P. Putnam's Sons, 1890–93), accessed April 13, 2019, https://oll.libertyfund.org /titles/2330#Jay_1530-04_1959.

English breach of Christian morality as a justification for American revolt. John Jay assiduously avoided partisanship and sought to help the cause of prisoners in his state. While arguing forcefully against deistic and rationalistic views, Elias Boudinot engaged in public service quietly as a congressman supportive of President George Washington and then as director of the US Mint. These founders looked beyond blind allegiance to political parties toward the higher value of union with their fellow Americans. In this divisive age of the twenty-first century, we have much to learn from these faithful men.

Resources

Cousins, Norman. *In God We Trust: The Religious Beliefs and Ideas of the American Founding Fathers*. New York: Harper & Brothers, 1958.

Frazier, Gregg L. *The Religious Beliefs of America's Founders*. Lawrence, KS: University Press of Kansas, 2012.

Holmes, David L. *The Faiths of the Founding Fathers*. Oxford: Oxford University Press, 2006.

—

CHAPTER 35

Christians Took Genesis 1 Literally until Darwin's Theory of Evolution

The Legendary Story

The publication of *On the Origin of Species* in 1859 by Charles Darwin (1809–1882) put tremendous pressure on the traditional, literal interpretation of Genesis 1. For 1,800 years Christians had agreed that the Bible set forth a straightforward historical narrative of creation *ex nihilo* in six twenty-four-hour periods, perhaps 6,000 or 7,000 years ago, as described in Genesis 1. However, the scientific community insisted the universe had to be billions of years old because evolution required long periods of time to occur. To stay relevant and keep up with the times, modern, liberal Bible scholars were the first to reject the literal interpretation of Genesis 1 and replace it with an allegorical reading to accommodate evolution. Faithful Bible scholars stayed true to the clear teaching of a young Earth and six-day creation.

Introduction: Unraveling the Legend

From the earliest days of the church, Christians have offered a variety of interpretations of Genesis 1. This often included "historical" readings of the text as a literal six-day creation, but it also included "theological" readings. Sometimes the same interpreter would read Genesis 1 as having both a historical meaning as well as spiritual, typological, or even prophetic meanings. Those who read Genesis 1 less literally sometimes did so to accommodate external philosophical influences; sometimes they did so because of words and phrases they saw in the text itself. In any case, it is an exaggeration to say that the interpretation of Genesis 1 as a literal, six-day creation was the sole or even dominant view for most of church history.

Conscripting the Past for the Present

In case you haven't noticed, Christians today disagree over how to best interpret Genesis 1. On the one hand, many promote a "plain, literal" reading, asserting that the text is crystal clear and any attempts at denying that God created the heavens and the earth in six twenty-four-hour days between 6,000 and 10,000 years ago simply don't believe the Bible.[1] On the other hand, some insist that Genesis 1 involves a gap of unknown time between verses 1 and 2, with some tragic catastrophe (perhaps the fall of Satan?) occurring between 1:1 and 1:2, resulting in the chaos described in verse 2.[2] Others suggest Gen 1:1 is more of a heading or prologue than an event, previewing what is about to be described in verses 2 and following.[3] The action really begins in verse 2 with a formless and empty earth. This interpretation takes no stand on exactly when the physical universe was created out of nothing. Still others opt for less literal, historical readings and instead regard the text as something like a polemical poem or song, sometimes prompted by the rhythm and repetition of the chapter as well as parallels and contrasts with other ancient Near East creation accounts.[4] Perhaps, some say, each day in Genesis 1 represents a period of time, not a twenty-four-hour day.[5] And a few have even pondered whether the seven days of Genesis 1 are just a seven-day series of symbolic visions Moses had on Mount Sinai.

Many Christians are dissatisfied with such a diversity of opinions on something so central to the Christian faith as creation. Instead of tolerating different interpretations, they wage campaigns to convince believers that their interpre-

---

[1]   This view is found among supporters of "young earth creationism," the classic defense of which is found in Henry M. Morris, *Scientific Creationism*, 2nd ed. (Green Forest, AR: Master Books, 1985). A more recent defense of this view is from James B. Jordan, *Creation in Six Days: A Defense of the Traditional Reading of Genesis One* (Moscow, ID: Canon Press, 1999).

[2]   This view was popularized by the *Scofield Reference Bible* note on Gen 1:1, first published in 1909.

[3]   Bruce K. Waltke and Charles Yu, *An Old Testament Theology: An Exegetical, Canonical, and Thematic Approach* (Grand Rapids: Zondervan, 2007), 179–81.

[4]   See, for example, John H. Walton, *The Lost World of Genesis One: Ancient Cosmology and the Origins Debate* (Downers Grove, IL: InterVarsity, Press, 2009).

[5]   Hugh Ross, *A Matter of Days: Resolving a Creation Controversy* (Colorado Springs: NavPress, 2004).

tation is truer to the text and more faithful to sound theology than other views. In these skirmishes, sometimes the various factions turn to church history to establish precedence for their particular view—conscripting the church fathers, medieval theologians, or Protestant scholars to their side. If it could be shown that the great minds of the past consistently read Genesis 1 in a particular way, perhaps that would argue in favor of one view against another—or at least show that a certain view is not outside the bounds of orthodoxy.

The result has often been a superficial, selective, and anachronistic reading of the history of Genesis 1 interpretation. What's needed is a more balanced historical understanding of what the church—even before the scientific consensus of evolution—held in common regarding the doctrine of creation, and what competing interpretations they held in tension.

Without controversy, all orthodox Christians throughout history have confessed belief in "God, the Father Almighty, maker of heaven and earth and of all things visible and invisible" and in "the Lord Jesus Christ . . . by whom all things were made," and in the Holy Spirit, "the Lord and Giver-of-Life."[6] However, contrary to many who insist that a literal, six-day creation interpretation is the "traditional" or "classic" Christian view, we must admit that within the bounds of a confession that all things came from the Father, through the Son, and by the Spirit, there is no universally accepted, dogmatically defined interpretation of Genesis 1.

A Few Examples

We couldn't begin to catalogue the numerous interpretations of Genesis 1 from the pre-Christian Jewish exegetes to the modern era. To demonstrate that a plain, literal reading of Genesis 1 was not the only option for Christians throughout history, we only need a few examples. All of these will be drawn from pre-nineteenth-century orthodox writings by Bible-believing Christians, showing that well before Darwin's theory of evolution was published, believers were divided on whether creation occurred in six twenty-four-hour periods.

Up front, though, we need to affirm that many interpreters did, in fact, understand Genesis 1 as referring to six literal, twenty-four-hour days and the event of creation occurring about 6,000 years ago. For example, Theophilus of Antioch (120–185), based on a reconstruction of chronological indicators

---

6   Creed of Constantinople (381) (NPNF 2.14:163).

in the Old Testament, concluded that "the years from the creation of the world amount to a total of 5,698 years."[7] And Clement of Alexandria (c. 150–215) noted that "the period in which Creation was consummated" was "seven days."[8] The Venerable Bede (672–735) asserted that each day of Genesis 1 was "without doubt a day of twenty-four hours."[9] Such statements are quite common, demonstrating that something like a "young earth creationism" in six literal days was a prominent if not at times dominant view in church history.

However, as early as the late first or early second century, we see an interpretation of the days in Genesis 1 move in a more allegorical direction. The so-called *Epistle of Barnabas* applies the six days of creation not to the original formation of heaven and earth in the past, but to the history of humanity leading to the second coming of Christ: "Observe, children, what 'he finished in six days' means. It means this: that in six thousand years the Lord will bring everything to an end, for with him a day signifies a thousand years."[10] Similarly, over a century and a half later, Cyprian of Carthage (c. 200–258) claimed the "first seven days in the divine arrangement" signify 7,000 years.[11]

Sometimes allegorical interpretations were added to literal readings. Theophilus of Antioch, who was seen to have affirmed a young earth above, also wrote, "Of this six days' work no man can give a worthy explanation and description of all its parts, not though he had ten thousand tongues and ten thousand mouths; nay, though he were to live ten thousand years, sojourning in this life, not even so could he utter anything worthy of these things, on account of the exceeding greatness and riches of the wisdom of God which there is in the six days' work above narrated."[12] Throughout his exposition, then, Theophilus draws spiritual analogies and less-than-obvious conclusions based on his theological interpretation of the six days. Thus, the "light" of the first day is none other than the glorious presence of God the Son. The great

---

[7]   Theophilus of Antioch, *To Aucolycus* 3.28 (ANF 2:120).

[8]   Clement of Alexandria, *Stromata* 4.25 (ANF 2:438).

[9]   Bede, *On Genesis* 1.9 (Gen 1:5b), in Calvin B. Kendall, trans., *On Genesis, Bede,* Translated Texts for Historians (Liverpool: Liverpool University Press, 2008), 48:75.

[10] *Barnabas* 15.4 (Homes, 427–28).

[11] Cyprian of Carthage, *Exhortation to Martyrdom* 11 (ANF 5:503).

[12] Theophilus of Antioch, *To Autolycus* 2.12 (ANF 2:99).

variety and beauty of created things is a foreshadowing of "the resurrection of all men which is to be."[13] And then, the creation of the heavenly lights on the fourth day "contain a pattern and type of a great mystery. For the sun is a type of God, and the moon of man . . . In like manner also the three days which were before the luminaries, are types of the Trinity, of God, and His Word, and His wisdom."[14] Though it appears Theophilus takes the basic narrative historically, he seems more interested in the spiritual, theological, and prophetic significance of the chapter.

A generation later, Origen of Alexandria (c. 184–253), argues that not all inspired Scriptures "contain throughout a pure history of events," to be taken literally. As an example, he uses the days of Genesis 1: "For who that has understanding will suppose that the first, and second, and third day, and the evening and the morning, existed without a sun, and moon, and stars? And that the first day was, as it were, also without a sky?"[15] It is important to note that in light of actual phenomena in the text itself, Origen was moved to seek an interpretation other than the strictly literal. He clarifies his approach this way: "Although it [Genesis 1] comprehends matters of profounder significance than the mere historical narrative appears to indicate, and contains very many things that are to be spiritually understood, and employs the letter, as a kind of veil, in treating of profound and mystical subjects; nevertheless the language of the narrator shows that all visible things were created at a certain time."[16]

The great and wildly influential theologian of the fifth century Augustine of Hippo (354–430) commented regarding the six days of Genesis 1, "What kind of days these were it is extremely difficult, or perhaps impossible for us to conceive, and how much more to say!"[17] Concerning the nature of the "days," Augustine argues:

> We see, indeed, that our ordinary days have no evening but by the setting, and no morning but by the rising, of the sun; but the first three days of all were passed without sun, since it is reported to have been made on the fourth day. And first of all, indeed, light was made by the word of God, and God, we read, separated it from

---

[13] Theophilus of Antioch, 2.13–14 (ANF 2:100).

[14] Theophilus of Antioch, 2.15 (ANF 2:100).

[15] Origen of Alexandria, *On First Principles* 4.16 (ANF 4:364–65).

[16] Origen, 3.5.1 (ANF 4:341).

[17] Augustine of Hippo, *City of God* 11.6 (NPNF 1.2:208).

the darkness, and called the light Day, and the darkness Night; but what kind of light that was, and by what periodic movement it made evening and morning, is beyond the reach of our senses; neither can we understand how it was, and yet must unhesitatingly believe it.[18]

It is even possible that some among the eminent fathers of the church would have been open to interpretations of the creation narrative that were compatible with something like theistic evolution—or at least the continued creation of living creatures from nature even after the flood. Augustine speculated concerning the repopulation of the earth with animals after the flood (which he took as a literal historical event), "If, however, they [the animals] were produced out of the Earth as at their first creation, when God said, 'Let the earth bring forth the living creature,' this makes it more evident that all kinds of animals were preserved in the ark, not so much for the sake of renewing the stock, as of prefiguring the various nations which were to be saved in the church; this, I say, is more evident, if the earth brought forth many animals in islands to which they could not cross over."[19] Again, Augustine is merely speculating here, but this demonstrates that the text was not universally regarded as "clear," nor was there a binding "traditional" interpretation of Genesis 1.

Even after the advent of Darwinism, very conservative Christian theologians thought it was possible to harmonize evolution and the creation narrative in Genesis 1 by reading the text in nonliteral ways. It might surprise some modern evangelicals to learn that fundamentalist champions of orthodox Protestant theology and particularly the inerrancy of Scripture B. B. Warfield (1851–1921) and James Orr (1844–1913) both suggested "that evolution should be regarded as the divinely ordained means of organizing the natural world."[20] Whether we would be persuaded by such interpretations of Genesis 1 designed to harmonize Scripture with evolution, of course, is another question.

---

[18]   Augustine of Hippo, 11.7 (NPNF 1.2:208).
[19]   Augustine of Hippo, 11.7 (NPNF 1.2:314).
[20]   Mark A. Noll, "Evangelicals, Creation, and Scripture: Legacies from a Long History," *Perspectives on Science and Christian Faith* 63, no. 3 (September 2011): 155.

MINI MYTHS

"The School of Antioch Interpreted the Bible Literally; the School of Alexandria Interpreted It Allegorically"

Rather than two radically different schools of interpretation in the early church—Antioch=literalists; Alexandria=allegorists—history reveals two groups more than willing to draw out "spiritual" lessons from the literal meanings of the text. A better distinction is that Antioch used typology while Alexandria used allegory. Both schools drew out spiritual propositions or lessons from the text, but where Antioch remained attentive to the narrative in deriving spiritual lessons, Alexandria sometimes saw words as a code to be cracked. Actually, the distance between Antioch and Alexandria's view of interpretation is much less than the distance between them and our own "literalism," which tends to focus only on the historical-grammatical meaning.[21]

Motivated by the Text

It is true that many church fathers, medieval theologians, and Protestant Reformers took a literal approach to Genesis 1, along with a rather conservative reckoning of the age of the earth, but together with this tradition we also see two other approaches, as illustrated by the quotations above. A few prominent figures took a purely allegorical or spiritual position on the meaning of Genesis 1. Many more combined these two approaches—accepting a straightforward "literal" historical meaning of the text as the foundation for additional spiritual, allegorical, moral, or prophetic interpretations of the creation event.

What were the motivations for these premodern interpretations of Genesis? Well, because the theory of evolution would not make its mark on biblical and theological studies until the nineteenth century, these nonliteral readings were not motivated by a desire to conform Scripture to the prevailing

---

[21] See Frances Young, *Biblical Exegesis and the Formation of Christian Culture* (Cambridge: Cambridge University Press, 1997).

evolutionary science or geological arguments on the age of the earth. Rather, readers such as Origen and Augustine were motivated by three factors. First, a close attention to details of the text surfaced verses that if interpreted literally, would lead to what they thought were absurd implications (e.g., day and night without a sun and moon, plants and trees without the sun, an apparent contradiction between the six days of creation [Genesis 1] and the single day of creation [2:4], etc.). Second, a desire to harmonize the reading of Genesis 1 with popular philosophical views about eternity, time, and creation led them to seek deeper significance than the straightforward interpretation (e.g., "heaven and Earth" referring to "spiritual and physical" realms). Third, the Fathers also understood the Bible as primarily a theological work that told the story not of an abstract concept like "cosmogony," but the trinitarian creation-fall-redemption narrative centered on the person and work of Christ in his first and second comings. Thus, they sought deeper theological and spiritual significance, often in addition to the literal reading of Genesis 1.

Application

Some Christians today insist on a literal reading of Genesis 1 that regards the six days as twenty-four-hour periods, rendering a world that is fewer than 10,000 years old, and utterly ruling out biological evolution. Often, they take this stance as a matter of orthodoxy—that is, any other reading of Genesis 1 is seen as deviant, deceptive, or downright heretical. However, in light of some of the perplexing aspects of Genesis 1 seen in the Hebrew text itself, as well as the diverse history of its interpretation, such hard stands on the details of Genesis 1 should be reined in.

The doctrine that all things were created by God, that nothing exists apart from him, and that he is thus Lord of heaven and earth—these things should never be surrendered. Nor should Christians give up on the authority of Genesis 1 in light of ever-changing scientific theories regarding the geological history of the earth and biological evolution. Too frequently Christians speak with an exclamation mark when Scripture itself speaks with a period, ellipsis, or even a question mark.

There are a number of exegetically defensible interpretations of Genesis 1 that take the grammar, syntax, genre, context, and theology of the text quite seriously, but stop short of denying the truthfulness of the text in order to capitulate to the theory of evolution. The range of views among evangelicals today in many ways reflects the diversity of views throughout history. We should let such differences of opinion spur us on to more careful and critical study of our own convictions and presuppositions, just as they have done for centuries.

Resources

Allert, Craig D. *Early Christian Readings of Genesis One: Patristic Exegesis and Literal Interpretation*. Downers Grove, IL: InterVarsity, Press, 2018.

Noll, Mark A. "Evangelicals, Creation, and Scripture: Legacies from a Long History." *Perspectives on Science and Christian Faith* 63, no. 3 (September 2011): 147–58.

CHAPTER 36

Atheism First Threatened the Church in the Modern Era

The Legendary Story

Human beings, created by God, have always held to some form of belief in God. The first people knew the true God, while later generations fell away and began to worship false gods. Indeed, humanity's worship has included not just an individual God, but many gods as well. Some have even seen god as equivalent to the universe. Though specific beliefs have varied, some divine being or power has been viewed as central to human life and worship throughout history.

Beginning around the seventeenth century, a new threat to religion developed in Europe: atheism. This startlingly new rejection of deity situated itself to attack the faith of God-fearing people. Atheism was rooted in an approach to knowledge based only in human reason—since people could not know God with certainty, many proposed that he did not exist. This movement has picked up steam in recent years with the development of the New Atheism.

Introduction: Unraveling the Legend

The myth of atheism as a modern invention has been embraced by both the religious and the atheist in contemporary times. As historian Tim Whitmarsh has written in his book *Battling the Gods*, this myth has been "nurtured by both sides of the 'new atheism' debate: adherents wish to present skepticism toward the supernatural as the result of science's progressive eclipse of religion, and the religious wish to see it as a pathological symptom of a decadent Western world consumed by capitalism."[1] In other words, contemporary atheists believe their way of thinking has finally overcome the backward ways of the ancients while the religious believe atheism an evidence of moral and spiritual decline in the Western world.

While the atheism of the Enlightenment and today strikes a number of different notes than what historians find in the ancient world, no one familiar with the ancient documents denies that atheistic ideas have existed in some form for millennia. This fact throws a wrench into the legendary story above, used to such striking effect by both atheistic and religious people. This chapter will highlight evidence for ancient atheism as well as draw out significant contrasts between early atheists and those of the Enlightenment era and today.

Old Atheists

The belief that no atheists existed in the ancient world was prevalent even among the ancients themselves. The Greek philosopher Plato (428–348 BC) placed this view in the mouth of Clinias in a dialogue Plato called *Laws*. Clinias said that "all Greeks and all foreigners are unanimous in recognizing the existence of gods."[2] While Plato didn't see this as a convincing argument for divine existence, neither did the dialogue argue for a mass of atheists either.

The ancient Greeks sought to encourage a society of universal belief in divine beings by punishing those who denied the existence of their deities. Most famously, Plato's teacher Socrates was charged with impiety (disbelief in the gods) and sentenced to death. While Socrates made a powerful argument against this charge in Plato's *Apology*, the fact that this charge even existed offers a general perspective on atheism in the ancient Greek world. Indeed, moving forward a few centuries, Christians defended themselves against charges of atheism—to disbelieve in the Greek and Roman gods was essentially to believe in no god/gods at all![3]

And yet, there were individuals who advocated views that look a lot like atheism—if not in name, then in substance. Carneades of Cyrene (213–129 BC) is one Greek often cited as an ancient example of atheism. Carneades doubted the notion of a universal belief in divine beings. In addition, he surmised that even if all people believed in a deity or deities, divine existence would

---

[1] Tim Whitmarsh, *Battling the Gods: Atheism in the Ancient World* (New York: Knopf, 2015), 4.
[2] Plato, "Laws 886a," in *Complete Works*, ed. John M. Cooper (Indianapolis: Hackett, 1997), 1543.
[3] Justin Martyr, *1 Apology* 5–6.

still not be proven. Rather, such universality of belief only proved that all people believed, but nothing about the actual existence of divine beings.[4] With this skeptical attitude, Carneades "denied that the universe was the product of a divine plan," and thought that belief in gods resulted from human fear of natural phenomena.[5] However, Carneades appears to have lived a long life in the academy, suggesting that his arguments against the existence of gods were seen as skeptical rather than as positively atheist.

Other ancients also presented atheistic ideas. Epicurus suggested that all knowledge comes through the senses and that the gods are not accessible via our senses. With the divine outside the realm of our senses, Epicurus advised that human beings "aim for tranquility and happiness in this life, because there is and will be nothing more."[6] Another ancient, the Roman poet Lucretius, followed an Epicurean model, arguing that all things were material. He warned people away from the fables of religion, hoping that people "would somehow find strength to defy irrational beliefs and the threats of the fable-mongers."[7]

Occasionally, ancient atheists were mentioned by Christians, indicating that they were at times a force to the reckoned with. One student of Origen of Alexandria (c. 184–253), Gregory the Wonderworker (c. 213–270), recalled that Origen had warned his students to avoid the writings of "the atheists, who, in their conceits, lapse from the general intelligence of man, and deny that there is either a God or a providence."[8]

While little evidence points to an organized movement of atheists in the ancient world, there were clearly individuals that seem to fit the label—even if they never took that label for themselves. It seems deniers and doubters of the existence of God are as ancient as humanity itself.

"Enlightened" Atheists

As the ancient world passed away and Christianity made its ascent, the Western (and Catholic) world saw no overt expression of atheism for well over 1,000 years. The philosopher Francis Bacon (1561–1626) wrote an essay in 1597 called "Of Atheism" in which he acknowledged the reality of skeptics. However, Bacon remained a theist, opening his essay with an affirmation of belief in some

---

[4]   William Thrower, *Western Atheism: A Short History* (Amherst, NY: Prometheus Books, 2000), 39.

[5]   Kerry Walters, *Atheism: A Guide for the Perplexed* (New York: Continuum, 2010), 25–26.

[6]   Michael Ruse, *Atheism: What Everyone Needs to Know* (Oxford: Oxford University Press, 2015), 10.

[7]   Lucretius, *On the Nature of Things*, bk. 1, 109–10 (Indianapolis: Hackett, 2001), 6.

[8]   Gregory Thaumaturgus, *Oration and Panegyric to Origen* 13 (ANF 6:34).

divine power: "I had rather believe all the fables in the Legend, the Talmud, and the Alcoran [Koran], than that this universal frame is without a Mind."[9]

The first true atheist of the Enlightenment period, Jean Meslier (1664–1729), was, believe it or not, a French priest! He wrote his posthumously published *Testament* during his life, though he kept it hidden while alive for obvious reasons. Meslier offered a host of arguments against the existence of God, from the idea that an infinite God would never enter the minds of finite humans to the notion that morality would be better off without God because God would be responsible for creating everything wrong with the world.[10]

Meslier became an inspiration to early French atheists such as Denis Diderot (1713–1784) and Baron d'Holbach (1723–1789). The latter inspired the work of English philosopher David Hume (1711–1776), whose essay *The Natural History of Religion* (1757) highlighted the many contradictions allegedly inherent in religion since it is rooted in individual psychology and collective society. If the roots of religion are in people, Hume said, there are bound to be contradictions. He concluded concerning religious belief that "the whole is a riddle, an enigma, an inexplicable mystery. Doubt, uncertainty, suspense of judgment, appear the only result of our most accurate scrutiny concerning this subject."[11] By asserting a lack of firm ground upon which to base religious belief, Hume created space in the English-speaking world for atheism to flourish in small but notable numbers throughout the nineteenth and twentieth centuries.

New Atheists

In the early twenty-first century, a new group of atheists took center stage in the debate. These so-called New Atheists offered many old arguments repackaged for a contemporary audience. Writing popular-level books—many of which have risen to bestseller status—these authors have gained a considerable following and brought atheism into the religious conversation in striking ways compared to the academics of the Enlightenment era. Key authors in this movement include Daniel Dennett, author of *Darwin's Dangerous Idea*, and Christopher Hitchens, author of *God Is Not Great*.

One of the foremost of these New Atheists, Richard Dawkins, wrote a

---

[9]   Francis Bacon, "Of Atheism," in *Complete Essays* (Mineola, NY: Dover Publications, 2008), 49

[10]   Jean Meslier, *Testament: A Priest's Dying Confession* (Mountain View, CA: Creative Commons, 2013), 36–37, 207–8.

[11]   David Hume, "General Corollary," sec. 15 in *The Natural History of Religion* (Stanford, CA: Stanford University Press, 1957).

book called *The God Delusion* (2006) in which he hoped that religious readers who open his book "will be atheists when they put it down."[12] Replacing what had been a largely academic and philosophical exercise, Dawkins and the New Atheists have embarked on an evangelistic tour, hoping to gain adherents to their "faith."[13]

After Sam Harris published his atheist work *The End of Faith* (2004), where he articulated a vision of the world without religion, he wrote what is from the Christian perspective an even more important book, *Letter to a Christian Nation* (2006). In this work, Harris claimed that religion, and Christianity specifically, is dangerous and tribal and should therefore be kept out of public policy debates. Rather than simply advocating for atheism, Harris set his sights on deconstructing the rational ground for Christianity. And that is exactly the modus operandi of the New Atheists—not simply to create the ground upon which atheism can thrive, but to tear away the ground upon which religion resides.

Application

This chapter has taken pains to show the existence of atheistic thought at multiple points in history. If Christians are to grapple with the realities of atheism today, understanding the distinction between ancient and modern atheism is essential. As essayist David Bentley Hart has written, "Ancient 'atheism' was a private skepticism toward certain received religious and mythic narratives; modern 'atheism' is the cultural embrace of an unprecedented metaphysical, anthropological, and social vision."[14]

Modern atheists are working within a Western culture that is, in important ways, different from the ancient world. Much of Western culture views the world as a fundamentally secular space, a reality that the church of the medieval era (and beyond) helped bring about with its emphasis on rational arguments for Christian doctrine. The Christian church in the West exists within this secular space, and even as the church attempts to bring the gospel to the world, it does so in contrast to the vast, mechanistic, and meaningless secular space around it.

---

[12]   Richard Dawkins, *The God Delusion* (New York: Houghton Mifflin, 2006), 28.
[13]   Interestingly, Dawkins titles the section in which he argues there is no God, "Why There Almost Certainly Is No God." Even he recognizes a bit of faith-oriented wiggle room in the atheist position.
[14]   David Bentley Hart, "Our Atheism Is Different," *Commonweal* (June 17, 2016), 27. I (John) am indebted to this essay of Hart's for providing many of the ideas in this application section.

Given this set of realities, Christians need to think more broadly about answering this atheistic onslaught. Our response should be less oriented toward responding to specific arguments or charges, and more about offering an alternative vision of the world—one that sees the whole world as sacred, the whole world as having the potential to encounter God. Consequently, Christians require a much sharper vision of their own beliefs—one that appreciates the fundamental reality of the triune God in the universe, and can therefore interact with ideas of all kinds from a truly Christian perspective.

Resources

Hart, David Bentley. "Our Atheism Is Different." *Commonweal* (June 17, 2016): 25–27.
McGrath, Alister. *The Twilight of Atheism*. New York: Doubleday, 2004.

———

CHAPTER 37

The Church Has Never Been as Divided as It Is in the Modern Era

The Legendary Story

When Jesus commanded that the church remain unified (John 17:11), his apostles applied that message to their work. Spirit-indwelled believers from the first and into the second century set a pattern of Christian unity that largely succeeded. That is, until the Protestant Reformation. Once Christians broke en masse from the Catholic Church, the floodwaters of rationalism and individualism drowned the church. The result has been akin to a rock splintering glass—fractures spreading outward in every direction, separating Christians from one another, and from the ideal that Jesus established just before his passion. The modern era has seen a proliferation of denominations and independent churches never seen before—rending the body of Christ into countless tiny pieces and utterly destroying the unity of the church.

Introduction: Unraveling the Legend

Perspective changes everything. The human tendency is to focus on the things in our immediate vision, to see only the close up and miss the broader context. When we feed ourselves a steady diet of social media and popular news, both of which thrive on negative content, our vision of the world—and the church in it—can become distorted. As novelist and essayist Fyodor

Dostoevsky (1821–1881) once wrote, "To see only the bad is worse than seeing nothing."[1]

When it comes to the unity of the church, too often we see only the bad. Our nearsightedness requires corrective lenses so we can better see the distant facts that bring context to what's near. Does the church struggle with unity today? Undeniably, yes. Is this different from the church's experience throughout the ages? Undeniably, no. While Christians of all stripes have struggled to preserve the unity of the Spirit (Eph 4:3), especially in areas of organization and practice, strong evidence exists of doctrinal continuity from the apostles down to today.

Christian Schisms

The Christian church has always struggled with division. The history of schisms goes back into the first century, during the apostolic era itself. The apostle Paul wrote a letter to the church at Corinth lamenting their fall into factionalism. Indeed, this was such a significant issue that Paul dove right into it from the very beginning of his letter: "It has been reported to me about you, my brothers and sisters, by members of Chloe's people, that there is rivalry among you" (1 Cor 1:11). Paul noted that such behavior conflicted with their confession of Christ as Savior as the Corinthian Christians ordered themselves around the leadership of their favorite celebrities: Paul, Apollos, Peter, or (for the truly "pious") Jesus. Unfortunately, many Christians have imitated the schismatic spirit of the Corinthian church for 2,000 years.

In the time between the first century and today, Christians have struggled to stay together—at the broad organizational level, interpersonally, and in local communities as well. In the late first century, Clement (c. 35–99), the bishop of Rome, continued Paul's exhortation to the Corinthian church. Those believers had continued to struggle with division even after they received Paul's letter. Clement rebuked them, writing: "Your schism has perverted many; it has brought many to despair, plunged many into doubt, and caused all of us to sorrow. And yet your rebellion still continues!"[2]

In the third century, under the emperor Decius, and again beginning in the fourth century under the emperor Diocletian, Christians were persecuted, leading in both cases to schisms within the Christian community. The source

---

[1]   Fyodor Dostoevsky, "The Latest Literary Controversies," in *Dostoevsky's Occasional Writings* (Evanston, IL: Northwestern University Press, 1997), 214.

[2]   *1 Clement* 46.9 (Holmes, 109)

of the schisms involved the Christian response to their persecutors. While some bore up and endured suffering and martyrdom, others offered sacrifices to appease the authorities or simply went into hiding. Splits occurred in the years afterward, as Christians disagreed on who should be considered a part of the community.

Doctrinal schisms occurred in the early church around the Council of Ephesus (431), as followers of Nestorius broke away and survive to this day as the Assyrian Church. And after the Council of Chalcedon (451), African bishops broke away and survive today as the Coptic Church. In 1054, the patriarch of Constantinople and the pope split, condemning each other over several divisive issues that had simmered for centuries and boiled over (see chapter 19). And numerous traditions developed separately within the Eastern Orthodox and Roman Catholic churches, leading to further fractures and schisms after the first millennium. And, of course, Protestants are well aware of similar debates over doctrine and practice—not just during the Reformation, but in every century since.

Today, counting independent and unaffiliated churches, there are thousands of what we might loosely define as denominations—independently run churches or associations of like-minded churches.[3] The numbers are striking and problematic. They also reflect the reality of many Christians in the world from diverse languages and cultures, thus more opportunities for fracture. While the church has certainly split many times over in both large- and small-scale fashions, the problem of Christians' separating themselves from one another has always been a struggle for the church.

One . . . Catholic Church

The Niceno-Constantinopolitan Creed (381), a statement that Christians the world over have returned to both explicitly and implicitly in articulating their core doctrines, described the church as "one, holy, catholic, and apostolic." In this discussion of division in the church, the terms "one" and "catholic" are especially pertinent.

What does it mean for the church to be "one" in light of the struggle with

---

[3] The *World Christian Encyclopedia* lists the number at more than 33,000—inflated, no doubt, by inclusion of groups such as the Mormons and Jehovah's Witnesses, as well as multiple Catholic "denominations." Even without the inflation, the number is still in the thousands. See David B. Barrett, George T. Kurian, and Todd M. Johnson, eds., *World Christian Encyclopedia* (Oxford: Oxford University Press, 2001), 1:16.

fracture and schism shown above? Certainly, Jesus desired that his followers would be one, praying for that very thing on the night Judas betrayed him (John 17:20–21). In that passage, Jesus also casts a vision of oneness that mirrors his own unity with the Father. The fact that this was Jesus's prayer suggests it would become a reality, even if not immediately in practice. Paul also speaks to the nature of the church's oneness when he describes the church as "God's temple" (Eph 2:19–22; 1 Cor 3:16–17). This speaks to the reality of a church that is one, even if, as was the case with the Corinthians Paul addressed, that reality has not yet been embodied in its fullness.

Many Protestants bristle at the term "catholic" as a descriptor of the church, given the term's association with the Roman Catholic Church. However, the lowercase "catholic" means "according to the whole"—that is, local churches are part of something bigger than just themselves. When Christians have applied the term to the church, the purpose has been to show the fullness of God's revealed message of redemption to the world. Indeed, virtually every theologically conservative church on the planet sees itself as in possession of God's entire redemptive message. Any church that considers itself Christian should have little problem acknowledging its catholicity in this broad sense.

An Evangelical Consensus

Theologians J. I. Packer (1926–) and Thomas Oden (1931–2016) have urged evangelicals to think in terms of consensus—those things they hold in common—in order to see more clearly our fundamental unity that keeps us connected in spite of our fragmented denominational structures. Too often, evangelicals (and others) have locked horns over secondary issues. Our overvaluing of those issues has led us to split from one another, doing greater damage to our sense of "catholicity" than if we had stayed together and worked through our differences in worship and prayer with one another. The idea of an evangelical consensus suggests we can all grasp "a comprehensive foundational design for the broad-based and lofty reality of the historic Christian life of faith, as expressed on paper in theologies, liturgies and hymns, and in life by repentance, trust, thanksgiving, hope, holiness, love and fellowship with the Father and his Son, Jesus Christ, through the agency of the Holy Spirit."[4] In other words, Packer and Oden believe there is a core set of doctrines and central practices

---

[4] J. I. Packer and Thomas C. Oden, *One Faith: The Evangelical Consensus* (Downers Grove, IL: InterVarsity Press, 2004), 16.

that unite believers everywhere, across denominational, national, racial, and gender lines. These core doctrines and practices we identify as "Christian." We should consider other discussions and debates as secondary.

Packer and Oden go on to identify the core set of doctrines using the methodology of consensus. Their book is largely a collection of quotations from throughout the recent history of the evangelical church—brought together to forge evangelical consensus by showing the doctrinal connections that have been made in many different corners of evangelicalism. In seeking to articulate such consensus, Packer and Oden drew from evangelical statements of faith (1) *composed* in community with other believers and in light of what Christians have always believed; (2) *embraced* by large numbers of people; and (3) *arranged* to highlight continuity rather than discontinuity.[5]

On the surface orthodox, Protestant, evangelical Christians appear more divided than ever. But just below the surface—if we look past those less-central beliefs and practices that have separated us organizationally—we see a common core of basic doctrines that keep us together. Things like the doctrine of the triunity of God; the fallenness of humanity; the deity and humanity of Christ; his virgin birth, sinless life, atoning death, resurrection, ascension, and future return; salvation by grace through faith; and church practices such as baptism and the Lord's Supper. If we were to focus on the most important elements in each of our traditions, we would see stunning unity. Only when we focus on less vital idiosyncrasies of our own individual churches do we see disunity.

Application

Christians have much to reflect upon when it concerns the unity of God's family. Too often, believers have allowed their unity to be compromised by doctrinal debates over secondary matters. Rather than holding the line on key matters, Christians have thrown rocks that fracture the delicate unity wrought by God's Spirit.

A better approach, informed by Christian history, prompts us to turn our attention toward affirming unity in the family through consensus. We should treat as secondary non-gospel issues where no consensus exists. One key passage that makes a great deal of sense in this context appears in Eph 4:3: "Keep the unity of the Spirit through the bond of peace." The only way for believers to embrace and live out Christ's command for the church to be

---

[5]   Packer and Oden, 13–15.

one is to pursue peaceable relationships with our brothers and sisters. The hard work of peace—including a great deal of humility and willingness to forgive—will yield a community marked by Jesus's ideals of love for God and neighbor (Matt 22:36–39).

A second point of application concerns the ability of Christian consensus to enhance the work of Christ in the world. Jesus told his disciples that "by this everyone will know that you are my disciples, if you love one another" (John 13:35). When Christians snipe at one another and seek out new ground upon which to build our separate kingdoms, we do a disservice to our mission, a disservice to love. Indeed, a striving for consensus that is rooted in the history of the church can help us recover "authentic Christian unity" and further "concerted Christian action."[6]

Resources

Holsteen, Nathan D., and Michael J. Svigel. *Exploring Christian Theology.* 3 vols. Minneapolis: Bethany House, 2014–15. (This series focuses attention on the broad orthodox, Protestant, evangelical faith that unites diverse Christian traditions rather than presenting the views of a single theologian or denomination.)

Packer, J. I., and Thomas C. Oden. *One Faith: The Evangelical Consensus.* Downers Grove, IL: InterVarsity Press, 2004.

---

[6]   Packer and Oden, *One Faith*, 25.

___

CHAPTER 38

The Swiss Theologian Karl Barth Was a Liberal

The Legendary Story

The twentieth-century theologian Karl Barth (1886–1968) was actually a liberal. He denied the inspiration and inerrancy of Scripture and rejected the historical fact of the resurrection of Jesus. He also taught modalism and universalism and believed that Jesus had a sin nature. Even though he wasn't as bad as some of the other liberals of his day, we should avoid him because of his heretical ideas about vital Christian truths. Too many evangelicals today are reading Barth and starting to go down the wrong path toward his brand of liberalism.

Introduction: Unraveling the Legend

Karl Barth *was* a liberal (emphasis on *was*). That is to say, he was educated in the bastions of German liberal theology and studied under the most influential liberal theologians of the time. However, during World War I, as he labored in a small parish church in Switzerland, he had a personal awakening and realized just how bankrupt his liberal theological training had been. In the following decades, Barth utterly rejected the philosophical foundations of liberal theology, returning to a firm commitment to the grace of God and embracing the historic doctrines of the classic Christian faith.

What Is Liberalism?

To understand where we should position Karl Barth in relationship to liberal theology, we first need to understand what is meant by "liberal theology." One historian notes, "The essential idea of liberal theology is that all claims to truth, in theology as in other disciplines, must be made on the basis of reason and experience, not by appeal to external authority."[1] In the premodern era (before the eighteenth century), theology rested on God's revelation, primarily his revelation in Scripture. Conservative theology maintained not only a high view of Scripture as the final authority in all matters of faith and practice but also fundamental doctrines of the faith, such as the triunity of God, the deity and humanity of Christ, the fallenness of humanity, salvation by grace through faith, and similar essential truths believed everywhere, always, and by all.

Yet the philosophical shift from reliance on God's revelation to reliance on reason and experience brought with it a rejection of long-held doctrines and a revision of the classic Christian faith. Jaroslav Pelikan notes, "The modern period in the history of Christian doctrine may be defined as the time when doctrines that had been assumed more than debated for most of Christian history were themselves called into question: the idea of revelation, the uniqueness of Christ, the authority of Scripture, the expectation of life after death, even the very transcendence of God."[2]

The father of German liberal theology, Friedrich Schleiermacher (1768–1834), surrendered to the scholarly criticisms of the Bible and rejected its inspiration and authority. Rather, he sought to "save" the Christian religion by reinterpreting it in modern, relevant, culturally acceptable categories. Appealing to the "cultured despisers" of the Christian religion in the sophisticated circles of German society in his day, he urged them to "turn from everything usually reckoned religion, and fix your regard on the inward emotions and dispositions" rather than on the classic foundations of Christianity.[3] The essence of religion, Schleiermacher said, which Jesus himself exhibited most fully, was a subjective God-consciousness—a feeling of absolute dependence. The dogmas of classic Christianity were jettisoned, including the Trinity, the deity of Christ, his resurrection, and thus his saving work.

---

[1]   Gary Dorrien, *The Making of American Liberal Theology: Idealism, Realism, and Modernity 1900–1950* (Louisville: WJK, 2003), 1.

[2]   Jaroslav Pelikan, *The Christian Tradition: A History of the Development of Doctrine*, vol. 5, *Christian Doctrine and Modern Culture (since 1700)* (Chicago: University of Chicago Press, 1989), viii.

[3]   Friedrich Schleiermacher, *On Religion: Speeches to Its Cultured Despisers*, trans. John Oman (London: Paul, Trench, Trubner, 1893), 18.

Following in Schleiermacher's footsteps, a long parade of liberal biblical scholars, theologians, historians, and pastors transformed the German universities, seminaries, and churches. They left behind true Christianity and pushed to the margins of the church those who really believed the Bible and embraced the classic Christian faith. It was at the climax of this dominance of liberal theology that Karl Barth was educated in the first decades of the twentieth century.

Barth's Conversion

The son of a seminary teacher in the Swiss Reformed Church, Karl Barth was born in Basel, Switzerland, in 1886. Eager to understand better the meaning of the confession of faith in which he had been raised, Barth began studying theology at the University of Bern, Switzerland, before moving to the center of modern theology at the time, Berlin, Germany. There, he studied under the "godfather" of liberal theology and historical studies at the time, Adolf von Harnack (1851–1930). He also studied under another liberal superstar, Wilhelm Herrmann (1846–1922), in Marburg. He fully imbibed the liberal theology of the day, including its human-centered beliefs and rejection of all the classic doctrines of the faith.

After his studies, Barth served as an assistant minister at Calvin's Church in Geneva, Switzerland (1910), then became pastor of a church in the small village of Safenwil. A few years into that pastorate, World War I broke out. To his utter shock, his liberal German professors who had proclaimed a "gospel" of the universal fatherhood of God and the universal brotherhood of humanity supported the German war effort. One historian describes Barth's response this way: "Barth had to witness the suicide of the European bourgeois culture for which liberal theology had provided an ideology. From neutral Switzerland he watched with horror as the liberally cultivated European nations slaughtered one another, with little reason and with a barbarity unknown for centuries. He read the "Declaration of German Intellectuals," including his revered teachers, calling for loyalty above all to *Kaiser* and *Vaterland*."[4]

From that point on, Barth took significant steps away from what he perceived as the rotten foundation of the German liberal theology in which he had been trained. Later he would reflect that Protestant theology "had become *religionist, anthropocentric,* and in this sense *humanistic* . . . For this

---

[4] Robert W. Jenson, "Karl Barth" in *The Modern Theologians: An Introduction to Christian Theology in the Twentieth Century*, 2nd ed., ed. David F. Ford (Oxford: Blackwell, 1997), 22.

theology, to think about God meant to think in a scarcely veiled fashion about man. There is no question about it: here man was made great at the cost of God."[5] In his rejection of liberal theology, Barth came to embrace the classic doctrines of the Christian faith articulated in the classic creeds and definitions of the first four ecumenical councils. He became a harsh critic of liberal theology in its roots and branches, sparking a kind of reformation that toppled the modernist empire of intellectual elites that had dominated mainstream theological thought in Europe for generations.

Barth's Theology

If we judge Barth's theology by the narrow standards of twentieth-century American fundamentalist theology, he will appear to be left of center. He never articulated the authority of Scripture in terms of "complete inerrancy."[6] Nor did he embrace the kind of revivalism and conversionism typical of many American evangelicals in the twentieth century. However, if we judge Barth's theology by the standards of the German liberal theology, he was clearly not a liberal. Consider some of the following statements from Barth's own writings:

ON THE AUTHORITY OF SCRIPTURE
Dogmatics measures the Church's proclamation by the standard of the Holy Scriptures, of the Old and New Testaments . . . We have no other document for this living basis of the Church; and where the Church is alive, it will always be having to re-assess itself by this standard . . . We must always be putting the question, "What is the evidence?" Not the evidence of my thoughts, or my heart, but the evidence of the apostles and prophets, as the evidence of God's self-evidence.[7]

ON GOD'S REVELATION AS TRINITY
Christian faith has to do with the object, with God the Father, the Son, and the Holy Spirit, of which the Creed speaks. Of course it is of

---

[5]   Karl Barth, "The Humanity of God," in *The Humanity of God*, trans. John Newton Thomas (Louisville: WJK, 1960), 39.

[6]   David Guretzki notes, however, "Perhaps with few peers in the history of the church, [Barth] is both *committed to* and practically *uses* the Bible as the basis for his theology more than any theologian I know. . . . Barth stands as one of the best exemplars of seeking to construct his theology under and submit his theology to the authority of Scripture." David Guretzki, *An Explorer's Guide to Karl Barth* (Downers Grove, IL: IVP Academic, 2016), 9, 10.

[7]   Karl Barth, *Dogmatics in Outline*, trans. G. T. Thomson, Harper Torchbook ed. (London: Student Christian Movement Press, 1949; repr., New York: Harper, 1959), 13.

the nature and being of this object, of God the Father, the Son, and the Holy Spirit, that He cannot be known by the powers of human knowledge . . . God is always the One who has made Himself known to man in His own revelation, and not the one man thinks out for himself and describes as God.[8]

On the Person of Jesus Christ

We understand this statement as the answer to the question: Who is Jesus Christ? and we understand it as a description of the central New Testament statement, Jn. I [14]: 'The Word was made flesh.' Therefore this New Testament verse must guide us in our discussion of the dogmatic statement that Jesus Christ is very God and very man.[9]

On the Atoning Work of Christ

At this point we can and must make the decisive statement: What took place is that the Son of God fulfilled the righteous judgment on us men by Himself taking our place as man and in our place undergoing the judgment under which we had passed. That is why He came and was amongst us . . . That is what happened when the divine condemnation had, as it were, visibly to fall on this our fellow-man.[10]

On the Resurrection and Return of Christ

The resurrection of Jesus Christ from the dead . . . has in fact happened. It has happened in the same sense as His crucifixion and His death, in the human sphere and human time, as an actual event within the world with an objective content. The same will be true of His return to the extent that as the last moment of time and history it will still belong to time and history.[11]

Barth also taught the virgin birth of Christ,[12] the doctrine of justification by faith alone,[13] and, in fact, the whole of the classic Christian Creed.[14] True,

---

[8]   Barth, 23.

[9]   Karl Barth, *Church Dogmatics*, vol. 1, *The Doctrine of the Word of God*, pt. 2, trans. G. T. Thomson and Harold Knight, ed. G. W. Bromiley and T. F. Torrance (Edinburgh: T&T Clark, 1956), 132.

[10]   Karl Barth, *Church Dogmatics*, vol. 4, *The Doctrine of Reconciliation*, pt. 1, trans. G. W. Bromiley, ed. G.W. Bromiley and T. F. Torrance (Edinburgh: T&T Clark, 1956), 222.

[11]   Barth, *Church Dogmatics*, 4.1, 333.

[12]   Barth, 207.

[13]   Barth, 608–42.

[14]   See his exposition of the Apostles' Creed in Barth, *Dogmatics in Outline*.

he had a unique approach to election that differed from the classic Calvinist understanding.[15] And though he explicitly denied being a universalist, several of his critics still insist that this is the logical outcome of his theology of reconciliation and election.[16] Also, Barth never subscribed to the doctrine of the complete inerrancy of Scripture as expressed by twentieth-century fundamentalists, though "Barth treats Scripture as if it were an absolute authority in theology."[17]

In the end, to call Barth a "liberal" is utterly false. On a scale from conservative evangelical to liberal Protestant, Barth must be regarded as overlapping significantly with the classic Christian faith, and thus he was, for the most part, conservative. To call him a liberal would be to misunderstand and misrepresent his theology and to slander his theological legacy.

The Blighted Barth

So, if Barth wasn't a liberal, how did he get that label? Why the deep distrust of Karl Barth in evangelical theology? *Christianity Today* editor Mark Galli points to an early misrepresentation and criticism of Barth's theology by Reformed theologian and Westminster Seminary professor Cornelius Van Til (1895–1987). In a number of published critiques that had a tremendous influence on evangelical theology, Van Til judged Barth by the standards of a strict fundamentalist Reformed confessionalism. Barth fell short, and thus he was deemed a liberal. Galli notes, "The damage had been done, and a generation of conservative theologians who looked to Van Til—because he was, in fact, an otherwise creative and thoughtful philosopher and theologian—continued to hold Barth at arm's length."[18]

In the wake of some of Barth's unique, obscure, and controversial views—and in light of the negative spin on his theology—Barth has sometimes been described as advocating "just a softer form of liberalism."[19] (Perhaps "softer form of conservatism" would be more accurate.) Other more radical and mili-

---

[15] See Bruce McCormack, "Grace and Being: The Role of God's Gracious Election in Karl Barth's Theological Ontology," in *The Cambridge Companion to Karl Barth*, ed. John Webster (Cambridge: Cambridge University Press, 2000), 92–110.

[16] See discussion in Mark Galli, *Karl Barth: An Introductory Biography for Evangelicals* (Grand Rapids: Eerdmans, 2017), 119–26.

[17] Stanley J. Grenz and Roger E. Olson, *20th Century Theology: God and the World in a Transitional Age* (Downers Grove, IL: IVP Academic, 1992), 76.

[18] Galli, *Karl Barth*, 6.

[19] Ken Temple, "Karl Barth and Carl Henry," blog post available at https://apologeticsandagape.wordpress.com/2017/08/26/karl-barth-and-carl-henry/, accessed March 6, 2019.

tant fundamentalist voices are less gentle. One extreme example characterizes Barth this way: "Although he uses many Christian words and phrases, Barth's theology is not Christianity. It is, just as modernism itself is, another religion. Barth is a wolf bleating."[20] Only a prejudicial, superficial, or selective reading of Barth's massive corpus would lead to such a conclusion. The fact is, Karl Barth was not a theological liberal in the normal sense of that word.

Application

Karl Barth was labeled a "liberal" not because he actually was a liberal, but because he failed to measure up to a very narrow definition of "conservative." He was also criticized by influential evangelical leaders who forever doused Barth and his theology with a bitter sauce, making it difficult for many evangelicals to read him charitably and interpret him outside the distorted lens of those initial criticisms. His fate and damaged reputation through misrepresentation and slander should be a warning to us. As Christians, we should not be eager to believe a bad report. Rather, we should give people the benefit of the doubt, treat them with charity, and do the hard work of checking for ourselves whether a negative characterization is accurate.

We must also appreciate the positive contributions of fellow Christians while treating their inaccuracies or errors with mercy and grace. Was Karl Barth perfect? Absolutely not.[21] Did his theology have problems? Yes. But for the most part, he must be regarded as a champion of orthodox trinitarianism, sound Christology, and a restoration of the historic Christian faith in a time and place where radical liberalism reigned. Someday we may want others to do the same for us.

Resources

Barth, Karl. *Dogmatics in Outline*. Translated by G. T. Thomson. Harper Torchbook ed. London: Student Christian Movement Press, 1949. Reprint, New York: Harper, 1959.

Galli, Mark. *Karl Barth: An Introductory Biography for Evangelicals*. Grand Rapids: Eerdmans, 2017.

Guretzki, David. *An Explorer's Guide to Karl Barth*. Downers Grove, IL: IVP Academic, 2016.

---

[20]　John W. Robbins, "Karl Barth," *Trinity Review* (February 1998): 3.

[21]　Though beyond the scope of this chapter, it must be acknowledged that Barth's reputation is understandably marred by personal moral failures in his marriage, though the details of this scandal are sometimes unclear. See Mark Galli, "What to Make of Karl Barth's Steadfast Adultery," *Christianity Today*, October 20, 2017, https://www.christianitytoday.com/ct/2017/october-web-only/what-to-make -of-karl-barths-steadfast-adultery.html.

CHAPTER 39

Calvinists Nearly Killed Evangelism and Missions: Non-Calvinists Revived Them

The Legendary Story

As the initial wave of the Protestant Reformation swept across Europe, some who were dissatisfied with the Roman Catholic Church found solace in the ideas of John Calvin (1509–1564). This reformer—based in Geneva, Switzerland—and the tradition that developed as a result of his ministry, placed a great deal of emphasis on God's sovereignty. This led Calvinist teaching on salvation to begin with a strong defense of predestination—the idea that God, before the creation of the world and based only on his love, chose those who would be saved.

As a result of this predestination doctrine, Calvinists pointed the Protestant movement as a whole away from evangelism and missions. In essence, the Calvinists simply trusted that God would handle evangelism without them. Thankfully, not all Christians were Calvinists, holding instead to a doctrine of salvation that emphasized spreading the message of the gospel around the world to give all people an opportunity to hear and respond individually to Jesus's message of salvation. Non-Calvinists have spearheaded the world missions movement and have had a huge hand in seeing the gospel spread to nations all over the world.

Introduction: Unraveling the Legend

Many non-Calvinists tell this legendary story as part of a centuries-old rivalry with Calvinists.[1] William Richey Hogg, a Methodist professor of missions, wrote of Reformers in general (and Calvinists specifically) that "the overwhelming and well-nigh unanimous evidence points in the Reformers to no recognition of the missionary dimension of the church."[2] But even some Calvinists push the story as well. For example, Ruth Tucker, in her classic work on world missions, noted that Calvinists affirmed that the Great Commission was only for the apostles, while "the doctrine of election . . . made missions appear extraneous if God had already chosen those he would save."[3]

However, this legendary story has one significant problem: while focusing on the way Calvinist theology supposedly limits missions, the legend has to ignore or minimize the actual mission efforts of Calvinists from the very beginning of the tradition, beginning with John Calvin himself.

Early Calvinist Mission Efforts

By the time of the Reformation, the Roman Catholic Church had begun to send missionaries to far-flung places. Travel had grown increasingly easy, with trade routes developing over land and by sea to ever further locations. Did the Calvinist movement, at the heart of the Reformation, continue this emphasis on missions? Or did missions die until non-Calvinists could gain enough strength to get it going again?

Even while John Calvin was still alive and leading the church in Geneva, he met regularly with the other pastors in the city. One topic of their conversations involved the reform movement in other regions, particularly in Calvin's native France.[4] Indeed, in the period from 1555 to 1570, more than 200 missionaries were sent out from Geneva.[5] Richard Gamble notes that

---

[1]   While this isn't the topic of the chapter, we should note the propensity of Calvinists to tell similar legendary tales about Arminians.

[2]   William Richey Hogg, "The Rise of Protestant Missionary Concern, 1517–1914," in *The Theology of the Christian Mission*, ed. Gerald H. Anderson (New York: McGraw Hill, 1961), 99.

[3]   Ruth Tucker, *From Jerusalem to Irian Jaya: A Biographical History of Christian Missions*, 2nd ed. (Grand Rapids: Zondervan, 2004), 97.

[4]   Jeannine E. Olson, "Calvin and Social-Ethical Issues," in *The Cambridge Companion to John Calvin*, ed. Donald McKim (Cambridge: Cambridge University Press, 2004), 157.

[5]   Kenneth J. Stewart, "Calvinism and Missions: The Contested Relationship Revisited," *Themelios* 34, no. 1 (2009): 68.

Geneva "sent out a host of well-trained missionaries, especially to France but even as far away as Brazil."[6]

Outside of Geneva, over the next century and a half, Calvinist missions flourished in many places, both in Europe and in North America. As Hungarians were educated in western Europe and returned to their home country, Hungary saw a Calvinist-themed Reformation in the 1540s and '50s. Later in the sixteenth century, Dutch theologian and pastor Adrian Saravia (1532–1612), also a Calvinist, wrote about the importance of spreading the gospel beyond Europe.

In the English-speaking world, Calvinist ministers zealous for getting out the message of the gospel (e.g., George Whitefield [1714–1770]) evangelized among the British on both sides of the Atlantic, not to mention among the Native Americans in North America. Missionaries John Eliot (1605–1690) and David Brainerd (1718–1747) devoted their evangelistic efforts to the Native Americans. While Eliot was the first of his kind, Brainerd's influence on later missionaries is undeniable. Brainerd's contemporary Jonathan Edwards (1703–1758), a preacher of the First Great Awakening (1730s–1740s) and himself a missionary to the Native Americans in western Massachusetts, reworked Brainerd's diary into a biography on his friend and co-laborer after Brainerd's death. This work, written by the Calvinist Edwards about the Calvinist Brainerd, became the single most influential missionary work in the coming centuries. Calvinists such as William Carey (1761–1834) and non-Calvinists such as John Wesley (1703–1791) read of Brainerd's life and were encouraged in their own missionary efforts.

Missions clearly didn't die with the early Calvinists. But missions would take on a new form in the late eighteenth century, thanks especially to even more Calvinists.

The Modern Missions Movement

The missions movement for Protestants began in the 1790s when a Baptist pastor named William Carey began to devote himself to the cause of taking Christ around the world. Having grown up Anglican and then become part of the dissenting church in England, Carey eventually received baptism in a Particular Baptist church in 1783. Particular Baptists—active in England

---

[6]   Richard C. Gamble, "Switzerland: Triumph and Decline," in *John Calvin: His Influence in the Western World* (Grand Rapids: Zondervan, 1982), 59.

from the 1630s—were those who followed the basic Baptist distinctives of believer's baptism by immersion and church organization, but were in other respects five-point Calvinists (see chapter 27).

Some have suggested that Carey moved away from "false Calvinism" toward "strict Calvinism," implying that "false Calvinism" was at the root of a failure to evangelize.[7] In reality, both "false" and "strict" Calvinists held to a common Reformed (Calvinist) soteriology, emphasizing that all salvation has occurred by grace through faith. Carey's Calvinist soteriology was at the heart of his mission work in India.

One distinguishing factor of Carey's ministry was establishment of the Particular Baptist Society for the Propagation of the Gospel Amongst the Heathen, later to be renamed the Baptist Missionary Society.[8] This ushered in an entirely new era of missions, where numerous churches and individuals could join together in support of missions work around the world. This model for missions, which earned Carey the nickname "the father of modern missions," continues to function, supporting missionaries all over the world.

Similar mission work proceeded in the centuries to come—Calvinist missionaries among those sent out by missions societies to the ends of the earth. David Livingstone (1813–1873), who had been raised in the Calvinism of the Church of Scotland, took the gospel into East and Central Africa. Robert Morrison (1782–1834), a Presbyterian (and therefore, Calvinist) preacher, became the first British missionary to China. Morrison translated the Bible into Chinese in 1819, and had about ten converts over the course of his twenty-plus years in China.

In more recent years, other Calvinists have contributed to the cause of evangelism and missions. John Stott (1921–2011), a noted writer and theologian, led a 1974 meeting of evangelicals to produce the Lausanne Covenant, a document designed to encourage and support the notion of worldwide evangelism. Another prominent Calvinist and Presbyterian pastor, D. James Kennedy (1930–2007), was a driving force behind an evangelism movement beginning in the 1970s (and continuing today) called Evangelism Explosion.

---

[7] See especially page 7 of Dan Lanning's paper, "Calvinism and Missions," at https://bit.ly/2YVc2P4, accessed April 5, 2019.

[8] Interestingly, this organization still exists: www.bmsworldmission.org.

Missions from a Calvinist Perspective

Clearly, the history of the Protestant missions movement would look a lot different without Calvinists. When people argue that Calvinism kills missions, they often do so from the perspective of a misunderstood Calvinist theology—that due to its emphasis on God's work in salvation, Calvinism discourages evangelism. However, many Calvinists would draw the opposite conclusion, believing that their Calvinism actually stands at the heart of their enthusiasm for missions.

Key to the Calvinist conception of humanity is the notion of total depravity, that because of our sin in Adam, we have a moral inability to choose God. Lost in our rebellion and dead in our sins, all human beings require God to pour out his grace in order for us to be saved. Without God's act of grace on our behalf, humans will forever be lost. Popularly, some have taken this to mean that Calvinists must believe evangelism is pointless, since no amount of sharing one's faith will bring about salvation. However, from a Calvinist perspective, sharing one's faith is God's chosen means by which he brings his grace into a nonbeliever's life. In other words, God does the work of salvation, but he uses individual human beings to accomplish his purposes on earth.

Other elements of Calvinism also speak to the importance of missions. Unconditional election is the idea that God, because of his love for his creation, chooses some to be saved. God has also given us a vision of his eternal family, people from every tribe, tongue, and nation (Rev 7:9). With God behind the choice of those who will worship him for eternity, the Calvinist evangelist or missionary will orient her work toward what God would choose (evangelizing people of all kinds), rather than what we would choose (sticking close to people most like us).

Limited atonement highlights the effectiveness of Christ's work on the cross for those who receive salvation. When the Calvinist evangelizes, he affirms that salvation comes only because Christ died for sins—all people need to hear this message so that they have a chance to respond.

A fourth point of Calvinism, irresistible grace, points to the notion that when God decides to save, he will not be thwarted. A Calvinist missionary would trust the work of God in salvation, knowing that God will always accomplish his purpose.

Perseverance of the saints suggests that God's people will persevere not just in their faith, but in good works as well. With God at the root of all salvation, drawing people to him, Calvinists have good reason to affirm that God will continue his work in transforming his people, conforming believers to the image of the Son (Rom 8:29).

Application

A commitment to missions and evangelism has captivated the Christian church throughout its history. The notion that Jesus brought a message to share with the world has united orthodox Christians for nearly 2,000 years. Over that time, different groups have practiced missions in different ways. Unfortunately, these differences have caused tensions over who evangelizes the most or the best.

When it comes to evangelism, the Calvinist emphasis on predestination and election leads them most often to focus on simple proclamation of the gospel, while a non-Calvinist or Arminian emphasis on human choice can lead them to focus on persuading someone of the truth of the gospel. Sometimes to an Arminian, a Calvinist proclaiming but not really persuading can look like a person to whom evangelism isn't important.

Given this reality and the discussion in this chapter, Christians of all stripes should take two action steps: (1) Instead of clinging to mutual suspicion, believers should look to affirm mutual commitments to the important things, such as evangelism, and in that context talk through implications of the specific ways we seek to evangelize. (2) Avoid reading another's theological positions and assuming certain actions (or non-actions) from that reading. When non-Calvinists repeat the idea that Calvinist emphases on predestination and election limit evangelism, they ignore the realities of Calvinist missionaries over hundreds of years. Christians should treat one another in these matters with all fairness and unanimity, rather than out of a competitive, one-upmanship mentality.

Resources

Carey, William. *An Enquiry into the Obligations of Christians to Use Means for the Conversion of the Heathens*. Dallas: Criswell, 1988.

Packer, J. I. *Evangelism and the Sovereignty of God*. Chicago: InterVarsity Press, 1961.

Stewart, Kenneth J. "Calvinism and Missions: The Contested Relationship Revisited." *Themelios* 34, no. 1 (2009): 63–78.

CHAPTER 40

Date Setters and Sign Seekers Are a Uniquely Modern Phenomenon

The Legendary Story

With the rise of end-times fanaticism in the modern era, people began seeking signs and setting dates for Christ's return. Before that, people held a more reasonable view of eschatology (the doctrine of last things). They believed the kingdom was a heavenly kingdom, that Christ would come back at an unknown time in the future, and that the world would end with judgment and a general resurrection. But popular movements like premillennialism and dispensationalism, which deviated from the historical view of eschatology held by all churches for centuries, brought with them a host of end-times enthusiasts who are constantly writing books matching biblical prophecies with current events and sometimes calculating the date of Christ's return. If we just went back to the traditional views of eschatology, we could avoid all this nonsense.

Introduction: Unraveling the Legend

The sad fact is that overeager Christians, earnestly longing for the return of Christ, have been interpreting end-times prophecies in light of current events for most of church history. From the early church, through the medieval period, into the Reformation, and down to our own day, even solid, mainline pastors, teachers, and theologians have been seeing signs of the nearness of Christ's coming and believed they were almost certainly living in the last generation.

Though actual date setting has always been a deviation by a minority fringe, even that uncouth practice has plagued the church from the earliest generations. This problem has infected every major tradition and every eschatological perspective, and it's one we need to avoid.

The Modern Date-Setting Trend

From flat-earth "science" to conspiracy theories, from fringe political movements to offbeat spirituality, anybody with an internet connection can promote harebrained ideas about anything. People living in the twenty-first century have more direct access to audiences than ever before. This means that any point of view—good or bad—can have an advocate and a worldwide audience. With the maelstrom of both information and misinformation swirling around us, it's easy to think that certain bad ideas have just lately begun to flood the free market of deception. This is the case with what we might call "date setters" and "sign seekers."

It seems that every few years somebody promotes a newly calculated date for the rapture or return of Christ. Or a new bestselling book with a black, orange, and red cover sets forth an "air-tight" argument for why ours is the last decade before the end of the world. More often than not, they point to biblical prophecies interpreted in light of current events. The way some have characterized this kind of date setting and sign seeking, we might be led to believe it's a distinctly modern phenomenon.

Some have closely tied date setting and sign seeking to the nineteenth-century development of futurist premillennialism and the closely associated approach to theology known as "dispensationalism." In 2014, one blog noted, "Date-setting has long plagued premillennialism, especially dispensationalism. The last twenty years are particularly rife with cries of the approaching end."[1] Fair enough. However, linking date setting with dispensationalism and modern premillennialism may cause some readers to conclude that the error is basically a recent development.

In light of the sensationalism surrounding recent rashes of date setting and sign seeking, it's easy to think they're modern developments. But the truth is, people have been setting dates and seeking signs from the first-century church straight through to modern times. In some cases, even today's end-times hacks

---

[1]   Kenneth L. Gentry, Jr., "Why Christ's Return Is Not 'Imminent,'" Postmillennialworldview.com, March 12, 2014, at https://postmillennialworldview.com/2014/03/12/why-christs-return-is-not-imminent.

and quacks, with their cheap-looking websites and self-published books written in ALL CAPS, are actually mild compared to some of the radical (and even deadly) apocalyptic movements throughout history. Let's examine a few snapshots from the photo album of church history.

MINI MYTHS

"The Councils of Constantinople and Ephesus Condemned Premillennialism"

Though touted both online and in books by respectable scholars, the claim that either the ecumenical Council of Constantinople (381) or Ephesus (431)—or both—condemned premillennialism as heresy are simply false. Both claims were debunked years ago in peer-reviewed journals by patristic scholars. Though the earliest church's premillennial views gradually fell out of favor with the majority of church leaders by the fifth century, no ecumenical council ever condemned premillennialism. To do so would have condemned early orthodox church fathers such as Papias of Hierapolis, Justin Martyr, and Irenaeus of Lyons.[2]

Dates That Will Live in Infamy

A scholar of patristic and medieval history, Frank Gummerlock, wrote a book that chronicles numerous examples of "misguided predictions" and false interpretations that led to date setting and sign seeking. He writes, "The more Christian history I read, the more I realized that this sort of thing was not new. Christians have been doing this in every generation for the last two thousand years."[3]

Already in the late first or early second century, a very popular Christian

---

[2]   See Francis X. Gummerlock, "Millennialism and the Early Church Councils: Was Chiliasm Condemned at Constantinople?" *Fides et Historia* 36 (Summer/Fall 2004): 83–95 and Michael J. Svigel, "The Phantom Heresy: Did the Council of Ephesus (431) Condemn Chiliasm?" *Trinity Journal* 24, no. 1 (Spring 2003): 105–12.

[3]   Francis X. Gummerlock, *The Day and the Hour: Christianity's Perennial Fascination with Predicting the End of the World* (Atlanta: American Vision, 2000), 2.

writing known as the *Epistle of Barnabas* (c. 75–135) strongly suggested they were living in the last days: "For the Master has made known to us through the prophets things past and things present, and has given us a foretaste of things to come. Consequently, when we see these things come to pass, one thing after the other just as he predicted, we ought to make a richer and loftier offering out of reverence for him."[4] This mild (and mostly positive) sense of urgency calls for renewed devotion to Christ. Had the early church stopped there, it would have been safe. However, it didn't. The church historian Eusebius of Caesarea (c. 263–339) recalled, "At this time another writer, Judas, discoursing about the seventy weeks in Daniel, brings down the chronology to the tenth year of the reign of Severus [c. AD 203]. He thought that the coming of Antichrist, which was much talked about, was then near. So greatly did the agitation caused by the persecution of our people at this time disturb the minds of many."[5]

Even the esteemed champion of orthodox trinitarian theology Athanasius of Alexandria (c. 290–374) found himself caught up with sign seeking when he made the case that the Arian emperor Constantius II (Costyllius), was the Antichrist: "For what mark of Antichrist is yet wanting? How can he in any way fail to be regarded as that one? or how can the latter fail to be supposed such a one as he is?"[6]

These examples are only the tip of the iceberg. Numerous end-times speculations, including date setting, accompanied the transition from the patristic to early medieval periods.[7] The expectation of the coming of the Antichrist led many to identify individuals and events as fulfillments of biblical prophecy and signs of the imminent end of days. With the rise of Islam in the seventh century, end-times enthusiasts had a new target to label as the antichrist and new events to point to and say, "This is it!" One historian notes, "From 800 on the coming of the antichrist was . . . linked to the presence of Islam. Elsewhere, other major calamities led to study of the apocalyptic writings."[8]

In the late medieval period, apocalyptic fervor heated up. Often it led to violence and bloodshed as radicals took it upon themselves to take up arms and overthrow the kingdom of the antichrist and usher in the kingdom of God through their own power. One profoundly troubling example is Fra Dolcino (1250–1307). One historian notes, "Fra Dolcino developed a new

---

4   *Epistle of Barnabas* 1.7–8 (Holmes, *Apostolic Fathers*, 383).

5   Eusebius, *Church History* 6.7 (NPNF 2.1.254).

6   Athanasius, *History of the Arians* 8.74 (NPNF 2.4:298).

7   See Gummerlock, *The Day and the Hour*, 5–54.

8   Adriaan H. Bredero, *Christendom and Christianity in the Middle Ages: The Relations between Religion, Church, and Society*, trans. Reinder Bruinsma (Grand Rapids: Eerdmans, 1994), 97–98.

theology of history and foretold the destruction of the established ecclesiastical order and the establishment of a new kingdom of peace under his own direction and that of his followers."[9] They identified the Roman Catholic Church as the whore of Babylon (Rev 17:3–5), believed St. Francis of Assisi (c. 1182–1226) was the angel of the sixth seal (Rev 6:12), and insisted that their movement represented the true church who would restore the world to a pure condition—going so far as to set a specific deadline for this overthrow of wickedness and commencement of righteousness.[10]

Of course, Fra Dolcino's predicted events never came to pass. In the wake of the disappointment, he doubled down on his extravagant claims and launched his own mini-kingdom characterized by wickedness and bloodshed, the brutality of which is unfitting to mention here.[11] Eventually their armed revolt and violent rampage was put down by a crusade called by Pope Clement V in 1306, in which Dolcino and his followers received no mercy. As they had done to others, so it was done to them.

In the centuries leading up to the Reformation, the sense that the end times were upon them rattled many Christians. Pelikan notes, "What made late medieval apocalypticism important doctrinally was the growing belief in this period that . . . the Antichrist whose coming was to be the principal sign of the end, was not some emperor (Nero or Frederick II) nor some false prophet (Arius or Mohammed), but the visible head of Christendom himself."[12] During the time of the Protestant Reformation, both mainline Reformers like Luther (1483–1546) and radical Reformers like the head of the Peasant Revolt, Thomas Müntzer (1489–1525), identified the Antichrist and believed they were living in the last days.[13]

Date setting and sign seeking were particularly prominent among some (though not all) Anabaptist communities. Historian C. Arnold Snyder notes, "Many of the early South German Anabaptists believed that they were living in the End Times, and that by reading the prophetic books of Scripture, they could figure out exactly when Jesus was coming back."[14] This fervor eventually led some radicals to pick up the sword and attempt to establish

---

[9]   Michael Frassetto, *The Great Medieval Heretics: Five Centuries of Religious Dissent* (New York: BlueBridge, 2008), 122.

[10]   Frassetto, 123–28.

[11]   Frassetto, 131–32.

[12]   Jaroslav Pelikan, *The Christian Tradition: A History of the Development of Doctrine*, vol. 4, *Reformation of Church and Dogma (1300–1700)* (Chicago: University of Chicago Press, 1984), 38.

[13]   Gummerlock, *The Day and the Hour*, 111–26.

[14]   C. Arnold Snyder, *Anabaptist History and Theology*, rev. student ed. (Kitchener, ON: Pandora, 1997), 6.

God's end-times kingdom on Earth. For example, a radical group led by self-proclaimed prophet Jan Matthijs (c. 1500–1534) managed to take over the German city of Münster in 1534 and establish it as the "New Jerusalem" by force. They "held the city against a military siege until June, 1535. The city finally fell, and most of the inhabitants were slaughtered."[15]

As the period of Reformation passed into history and the modern era dawned, eschatological fervor continued to influence theology and culture in the New World. Paul Boyer notes, "From the early seventeenth century through the late eighteenth, the entire span of American colonial history was marked by speculation about America's role in God's plan . . . American Puritans increasingly found prophetic meaning in their own history."[16] As one example of sign seeking, the Puritan religious and political leader Cotton Mather (1663–1728) explained the rash of witchcraft in New England (and defended the infamous Salem witch trials of 1692–1693) by connecting the events to the casting-down of Satan in Revelation 12:12.[17] Of course, not all date setting and sign seeking were wrapped up with armed revolts and witch trials, but it seems that fringe tends to give birth to fringe, and radicals always rise up to take bad teaching to its extreme.

Countless examples from every generation of Christian history could be added to this handful of instances of sign seeking and date setting. It isn't true that the fanatical interest in setting dates, seeing signs in the stars, and pointing to current events as fulfillments of prophecy are unique to the modern church. It's just that the rise of electronic media outlets today makes it look that way.

Application

As the old saying goes, "misery loves company." But the fact that modern-day date setters and sign seekers are not alone in their error shouldn't comfort anybody, nor should it absolve those who may get caught up in the "dating game" or succumb to a bad case of "this-is-that" syndrome. False teachers who calculate the day, year, season, or generation of the return of Christ are not in good company but in bad company. And the apostle Paul reminds us that "bad company corrupts good morals" (1 Cor 15:33).

---

[15]   Snyder, 7.
[16]   Paul Boyer, *When Time Shall Be No More: Prophecy Belief in Modern American Culture* (Cambridge, MA: Belknap/Harvard University Press, 1992), 68.
[17]   Cotton Mather, *The Wonders of the Invisible World: Being an Account of the Tryals of Several Witches, Lately Executed in New-England* (Boston: n.p., 1693).

The fact that so many people from so many backgrounds throughout church history have been guilty of these misguided ventures should not legitimize the practice. Rather it should serve as a warning to us: don't do it! Date setting and sign seeking are perennial diseases that occasionally afflict the body of Christ; but they should never be allowed to become chronic conditions that characterize it. If any teacher on television, online, onstage, in writing, or in the pulpit suggests some event is the fulfillment of a prophecy or tries to calculate a date for the return of Christ or the rapture, simply tune that person out and avoid him. And stay away from churches or denominations that were founded on such falsehoods or promote those wrongheaded ideas.

Resources

Boyer, Paul. *When Time Shall Be No More: Prophecy Belief in Modern American Culture.* Cambridge, MA: Belknap/Harvard University Press, 1992.

Gummerlock, Francis X. *The Day and the Hour: Christianity's Perennial Fascination with Predicting the End of the World.* Atlanta: American Vision, 2000.

Name and Subject Index